Machine Translation Summit 2025

Volume 2

Geneva, Switzerland
23 - 27 June 2025

ISBN: 979-8-3313-2677-7

Printed from e-media with permission by:

Curran Associates, Inc.
57 Morehouse Lane
Red Hook, NY 12571

Some format issues inherent in the e-media version may also appear in this print version.

Printed with permission by Curran Associates, Inc. (2026)

For permission requests, please contact the Association for Computational Linguistics at the address below.

Association for Computational Linguistics
209 N. Eighth Street
Stroudsburg, Pennsylvania 18360

Phone: 1-570-476-8006
Fax: 1-570-476-0860

acl@aclweb.org

Additional copies of this publication are available from:

Curran Associates, Inc.
57 Morehouse Lane
Red Hook, NY 12571 USA
Phone: 845-758-0400
Fax: 845-758-2633
Email: curran@proceedings.com
Web: www.proceedings.com

MTSummit 2025

MT SUMMIT
Geneva 2025

Machine Translation Summit XX

Volume 2

Edited by:
Pierrette Bouillon, Johanna Gerlach, Sabrina Girletti, Lise Volkart, Raphael Rubino, Rico Sennrich, Samuel Läubli, Martin Volk, Miquel Esplà-Gomis, Vincent Vandeghinste, Helena Moniz, Sara Szoc

UNIVERSITÉ DE GENÈVE
FACULTÉ DE TRADUCTION ET D'INTERPRÉTATION

EUROPEAN ASSOCIATION FOR MACHINE TRANSLATION

June 23-27, 2025

Geneva, Switzerland

Foreword from the General Chair

As president of the International Association for Machine Translation (IAMT) and General Chair of the 20th Machine Translation Summit, it is my utmost pleasure to write these opening words. Be most welcome to our MT Summit 2025!

The European Association for Machine Translation (EAMT) Executive Committee (EC) has been very busy. Mikel Forcada (treasurer) and Sara Szoc (secretary) have been tirelessly supporting all initiatives. Carolina Scarton and Sara Szoc took great care of our bursaries. Patrick Cadwell, André Martins, and Manuel Lardelli were our chairs for the Research Projects. Manuel Lardelli was also our policies chair, revisiting all our policies and contributing to inclusivity strategies. Our very own Mary Nurminen, chair of the bid proposals for our next events, has been busy selecting our next venue! EAMT 2026 venue will be disclosed in our closing ceremony in Geneva!

One of our core initiatives, the best thesis award – Rachel Badwen and Barry Haddow, chairs of the Best Thesis Award, had a very difficult time selecting a candidate, since the submissions were of very high quality. Our congratulations to Ricardo Rei's thesis "Robust, Interpretable and Efficient MT Evaluation with Fine-tuned Metrics" (Unbabel, INESC-ID, Instituto Superior Técnico, Portugal), supervised by Maria Luísa Torres Ribeiro Marques da Silva Coheur and Alon Lavie. We would also like to congratulate for the highly commended thesis of Sara Papi (University of Trento & Fondazione Bruno Kessler), entitled "Direct Speech Translation in Constrained Contexts: the Simultaneous and Subtitling Scenarios" and supervised by Marco Turchi and Matteo Negri.

EAMT, as full sponsor of the MT Marathon, would also like to thank the Institute of Formal and Applied Linguistics (ÚFAL), Charles University for organizing the 17th MT Marathon. The event included MT lectures and labs, covering the basics and tutorials; keynote talks from experienced researchers and practitioners; presentations of research and open source tools related to MT; and hacking projects to advance tools or research in one week or start new collaborations. A special thank you to Jindřich Helcl his commitment and passion for this event!

MT Summit 2025 will be a moment to celebrate our IAMT Award of Honour![1] We celebrate Professor Mikel Forcada, unanimously supported by all sister organizations (EAMT, AAMT, and AMTA), in recognition of his long-standing distinguished contribution to the EAMT and IAMT communities and for his impactful research on Machine Translation. Thank you for being an inspiration to us all!

Geneva, Switzerland, MT Summit 2025! Our conference will have a three-day, four-track programme put together by our chairs: Catarina Farinha and Marco Gaido (research: technical track chairs); Dorothy Kenny and Joke Adaems (research: translators & users track chairs); Samuel Läubli and Martin Volk (implementations & case studies track chairs); Miguel Esplà and Vincent Vandeghinste (products & projects track chairs) and François Yvon and Sheila Castilho (workshop and tutorial chairs). Our filters of quality and alignment! We really appreciate your work. We will continue with our tradition and also have a two-day workshops and tutorials event.

Our gratitude to all our keynotes speakers. Sarah Ebling, Full Professor of Language, Technology and Accessibility at the University of Zurich. Joss Moorkens, Associate Professor at the School of Applied Language and Intercultural Studies in Dublin City University (DCU). Eva Vanmassenhove, Assistant professor in the Department of Cognitive Science and Artificial Intelligence at Tilburg University (TiU). Our outstanding keynote speakers will demonstrate their extensive and global impactful work in translation studies and translation technologies, in a multidisciplinary motto which is the core of our community.

[1] https://eamt.org/iamt-award-of-honour/

MT Summit 2025 is the result of a very aligned, sharp, engaged, and hard working local organising team! What a diligent team! Our local co-chairs, Pierrette Bouillon, Johanna Gerlach, Sabrina Girletti and Lise Volkart (all from the University of Geneva, Switzerland) have put a lot of work in giving us a Geneva unforgettable event. To Sevita Caseres, Bastien David, Céline De Graaf, Julie Humbert-Droz, Rebeka Mali, Lucía Morado, Jonathan Mutal, Lucía Ormaechea, Aurélie Picton, Donatella Pulitano, Silvia Rodríguez, Raphael Rubino, Valentin Scourneau, Marianne Starlander, Irene Strasly, Nikolaos Tsourakis, Florine Voisard (all from the University of Geneva, Switzerland) and Rico Sennrich (University of Zurich, Switzerland), our deepest appreciation.

EAMT has been supported by generous sponsors in its initiatives along the years.[2] This year is no exception in a summit year! In fact, it is a very exceptional year in terms of sponsoring activities. Our gratitude to our Platinum sponsors who will also be giving a research oral presentation, BIG Language Solution, STAR, WIPO. Our Gold sponsor Systran by ChapsVision. Our Silver sponsors: Translated, Reverso, and Unbabel. To our Bronze sponsors: AppTek, CrossLang, TransPerfect, and Zoo Digital. To all our Supporter sponsors: Apertium, iguanodon.ai, prompsit, Springer Nature (our Supporter sponsor for the Best Paper award) and Supertext. Finally, to our Media sponsors, MultiLingual and Slator. Your support is vital in our efforts to give back to our community through grants and other initiatives.

A note still to all our IAMT members and our participants! Without you no effort would make sense! Let us take this opportunity to create scientific collaboration and give constructive feedback. To fully enjoy the conference, please check our Code of Conduct.[3] I'm looking forward to seeing you all and celebrating our community gathering!

Our sister organizations have been renewed with new board of Directors. The best wishes to AMTA's new board, represented by the President, Jay Marciano, and to the AAMT's Directors, Hisahiro Adachi, SunFlare Co., Ltd. (President of AAMT) and Masao Utiyama, National Institute of Information and Communications Technology, Japan (Vice President of AAMT). MT Summit 2027 will be held by AMTA! More soon!

It is our organisation's greatest wish to continue giving back to our community and to drive and be driven by our community's energy and enthusiasm. Reach out to us if you have new ideas or suggestions you would like to implement. We will try hard to accomplish it with you. Learn more about us.

Helena Moniz

President of the IAMT
General Chair of MT Summit 2025
University of Lisbon, Portugal

[2] https://mtsummit2025.unige.ch/sponsors.html
[3] https://mtsummit2025.unige.ch/about.html#codeOfConduct

Message from the Local Organising Committee

It is our great pleasure to welcome you to the Faculty of Translation and Interpreting (FTI) for this 20th edition of the MT Summit. We are particularly proud that for the first time in its history, the Summit is being hosted by a translation faculty, highlighting the importance of the human factor in today's technology. This is also a sign that technology has become an imperative in professional translation. Our faculty has long embraced this evolution, as illustrated by its translation technology department, first established back in the 1970s (first under the name of ISSCO, and then TIM). It was long spearheaded by Prof Maghi King, who, as some of you may recall, received the prestigious IAMT Award of Honour in 2005.

Our department has always been committed to building bridges between research in MT and professional translators. The conference taking place here today is further proof that this bridge is now well established and solid! The structure of the conference itself also reflects this dual focus, with two dedicated research tracks, one Technical, and the other for Translators and Users.

This year also brings an important new initiative: authors of papers involving computational experiments are encouraged to include sustainability reports. Most authors engaged with the initiative, reflecting the willingness of our community to embrace more transparent and thoughtful research practices.

We hope you will enjoy the rich and carefully curated program put together by our dedicated track chairs and made possible by the thorough work of our reviewers. We are also deeply grateful to our keynote speakers, as well as the organizers of the workshops and tutorials, whose contributions are crucial to the success of this conference.

We also want to thank our sponsors, more generous than ever before! Their presence is a strong indicator of the fruitful and trustworthy collaboration that exists between academia and industry in our field.

When we signed up to organise this conference, we had no idea of the summit that we would have to climb, nor how much determination, patience and endurance it would require of us. But thanks to our experience of the mountains, a dedicated team, and the valuable support of EAMT Executive Committee and previous organisers, we reached the (MT) Summit (almost) without problems. As in every climb, it is the strength of the team that gets you to the top!

We wish you an excellent MT Summit!

On behalf of the MT Summit 2025 Organising Committee:
Pierrette Bouillon
Johanna Gerlach
Sabrina Girletti
Lise Volkart

Department of Translation Technology (TIM)
Faculty of Translation and Interpreting
University of Geneva, Switzerland

Preface by the Programme Chairs

The **Research Technical track** received 57 submissions, out of which 28 were accepted, for an acceptance rate of 49%. 14 papers will be presented orally and the other 14 will be part of two poster sessions. The topics covered by the submitted papers include named entity aware translation, context-aware machine translation, domain-specific translation, multilingual and low-resource translation, and translation evaluation. We express our most heartfelt thanks to the 83 reviewers, who made this track possible, with a particular gratitude for the emergency reviewers who promptly accomplished their duties, enabling us to respect the timeline for author notification.

Catarina Farinha (Unbabel)
Marco Gaido (Fondazione Bruno Kessler, Italy)

The **Translators and Users track** initially received 28 submissions, of which 21 could be considered for this track, the other 7 covered more technical aspects of machine translation and were therefore considered for the Technical track instead. Of these 21, 19 were accepted (an acceptance rate of 90%, showing the overall high quality of submission to the track). As track chairs, we noticed a few trends in these accepted papers, and we tried to group the submissions in sessions accordingly. The large language model trend, established in earlier EAMT conferences, clearly continues. Large language models are used for literary translation (post-editing) and emergency response text translation, and there is a clear interest in how these technologies are currently being used by students as well as perceived by professionals. From the text types that are being studied, it is obvious that 'literary translation' is most strongly represented in this track, with 5 submissions covering the topic. This is particularly striking, given that this MT Summit is also hosting a dedicated workshop on Creative-text Translation and Technology. The intersection of creativity, literature and automatic translation has clearly arrived as a field of inquiry. We thank all PC members for their time and dedication in delivering insightful feedback, ensuring the quality of the submissions to this track. Special thanks to the emergency reviewers who helped us avoid any delays. You all made this conference possible.

Joke Daems (Ghent University, Belgium)
Dorothy Kenny (Dublin City University, Ireland)

The **Implementation and Case Studies track** received 12 submissions out of which 9 were accepted for presentation at the MT summit (6 talks and 3 posters). The papers cover a broad range of topics, e.g. speech translation, LLM-based translation, low-resource settings, productivity evaluation and translator satisfaction. We would like to express our gratitude and appreciation to our reviewers from academia and industry for their time and effort in commenting and grading the submissions.

Samuel Läubli (Textshuttle/Supertext, Switzerland)
Martin Volk (University of Zurich, Switzerland)

The **Products and Projects track** received 22 submissions, of which 20 have been accepted for a short, two-page description and a poster presentation at the conference. Our selection highlights a diverse range of products and projects created by our community, covering research projects and cutting-edge services and innovations from distinguished industry and research leaders. Expect a lively session filled with poster boasters and engaging poster presentations. We wish to thank the 26 members of the program committee for this track for their timely and thorough reviews.

Miquel Esplà-Gomis (University of Alicante, Spain)
Vincent Vandeghinste (KU Leuven, Belgium)

The **Workshop and Tutorials** received seven workshop proposals, five of which were finally selected: four are reiterations of workshops that have already been collocated with MT conferences in the past: these are the "2nd Workshop on Creative-text Translation and Technology" (CTT 2025), the 3rd "International Workshop on Gender-Inclusive Translation Technologies" (GITT 2025), the 3rd "International Workshop on Automatic Translation for Signed and Spoken Languages" (AT4SSL), and the 11th "Workshop on Patent and Scientific Literature Translation" (PSLT 2025). We are also happy to see the start of a hopefully equally successful new series, with the 1st "Workshop on Artificial Intelligence and Easy and Plain Language in Institutional Contexts" (AI & EL/PL). With the exception of PSLT, they will all run for a full day, on the 23rd or on the 24th of June. Five half-day tutorials were also submitted, and three will be offered to the participants: "Understanding Large Language Model-Generated Translations", "Leveraging Examples in Machine Translation", and "Best practices for data quality in human annotation of translation datasets". Our hope is that the choice between such diverse and exciting proposals will be a difficult one, and that these two pre-conference days will be as enjoyable and rewarding as possible, sparking new ideas, collaborations, and conversations in Geneva and beyond.

Sheila Castilho (Dublin City University, Ireland)
François Yvon (Sorbonne University, France)

EAMT 2024 Best Thesis Award (Anthony C. Clarke Award)

Six PhD theses defended in 2024 were received as candidates for the 2024 year edition of the EAMT Best Thesis Award, all of which were eligible. Eight external reviewers were recruited to examine and score the theses alongside five EAMT executive committee members. Each thesis was evaluated according to predefined criteria: how challenging the topic was, how relevant the results were to the MT field and the strength of its impact in terms of scientific publications. As in previous years, 2024 was another strong year for PhD theses in machine translation.

All PhD theses were of good quality, focused on interesting topics and were all highly appreciated by reviewers. A panel of two EAMT Executive Committee members (Barry Haddow and Rachel Bawden) was assembled to process the reviews and select a winner that was later ratified by the EAMT executive committee.

We are pleased to announce that the **winner of the 2024 edition of the EAMT Best Thesis Award is Ricardo Rei's thesis "Robust, Interpretable and Efficient MT Evaluation with Fine-tuned Metrics"** (Unbabel, INESC-ID, Instituto Superior Técnico, Portugal), supervised by Maria Luísa Torres Ribeiro Marques da Silva Coheur and Alon Lavie.

In addition, the committee judged that the thesis of **Sara Papi** (University of Trento & Fondazione Bruno Kessler) entitled "Direct Speech Translation in Constrained Contexts: the Simultaneous and Subtitling Scenarios" and supervised by Marco Turchi and Matteo Negri was **"highly commended"**.

The awardee will receive a prize of €500, together with an inscribed certificate. In addition, Dr. Rei will present a summary of their thesis at the 20th Machine Translation Summit in Geneva, Switzerland, receive complimentary membership to the EAMT in 2026 and will receive a travel bursary of €200.

Chairs of the EAMT Best Thesis Award 2024
Rachel Bawden, Inria, Paris, France
Barry Haddow, University of Edinburgh, UK

Organising Committee

General Chair

Helena Moniz, Universidade de Lisboa / INESC-ID, Portugal

Local Organising Committee

Pierrette Bouillon, University of Geneva, Switzerland
Johanna Gerlach, University of Geneva, Switzerland
Sabrina Girletti, University of Geneva, Switzerland
Lise Volkart, University of Geneva, Switzerland

Local Support Team

Sevita Caseres, University of Geneva, Switzerland
Bastien David, University of Geneva, Switzerland
Céline De Graaf, University of Geneva, Switzerland
Julie Humbert-Droz, University of Geneva, Switzerland
Rebeka Mali, University of Geneva, Switzerland
Lucía Morado Vázquez, University of Geneva, Switzerland
Jonathan Mutal, University of Geneva, Switzerland
Lucía Ormaechea Grijalba, University of Geneva, Switzerland
Aurélie Picton, University of Geneva, Switzerland
Donatella Pulitano, University of Geneva, Switzerland
Silvia Rodríguez Vázquez, University of Geneva, Switzerland
Valentin Scourneau, Université de Mons
Marianne Starlander, University of Geneva, Switzerland
Irene Strasly, University of Geneva, Switzerland
Nikolaos Tsourakis, University of Geneva, Switzerland
Florine Voisard, University of Geneva, Switzerland

Publications Chair

Raphael Rubino, University of Geneva, Switzerland
Rico Sennrich, University of Zurich, Switzerland

Track Chair: Research Technical

Catarina Farinha, Unbabel, Portugal
Marco Gaido, Fondazione Bruno Kessler, Italy

Track Chair: Research Translators and Users

Joke Daems, Ghent University, Belgium
Dorothy Kenny, Dublin City University, Ireland

Track Chair: Implementations and Case Studies

Samuel Läubli, Textshuttle/Supertext, Switzerland
Martin Volk, University of Zurich, Switzerland

Track Chair: Products and Projects

Miquel Esplà-Gomis, University of Alicante, Spain
Vincent Vandeghinste, KU Leuven, Belgium

Workshops and Tutorials Chair

Sheila Castilho, Dublin City University, Ireland
François Yvon, Sorbonne University, France

Programme Committee

Track: Research Technical

Benyamin Ahmadnia	UC Davis
Dr Khetam Al Sharou	Imperial College London
Àlex R. Atrio	HEIG-VD / HES-SO & EPFL
Vicent Briva-Iglesias	SFI CRT D-REAL, Dublin City University
José G. C. de Souza	Unbabel
Vera Cabarrão	Unbabel Lda.; INESC-ID
Michael Carl	Kent State University
Luisa Coheur	INESC-ID
Mattia Antonino Di Gangi	AppTek
Siddharth Divi	SSN College of Engineering
Konstantin Dranch	Custom.MT
Kevin Duh	Johns Hopkins University
Hiroshi Echizenya	Hokkai-Gakuen University
Carlos Escolano	UPC - BSC
Miquel Esplà-Gomis	Universitat d'Alacant
Mikel Forcada	Universitat d'Alacant
Javier García Gilabert	Barcelona Super Computing Center (BSC)
Cyril Goutte	National Research Council Canada
Barry Haddow	University of Edinburgh
Rejwanul Haque	South East Technological University
Iikka Hauhio	University of Helsinki, Kielikone Oy
Javier Iranzo-Sánchez	Universitat Politecnica de Valencia
Josef Jon	Charles University
Swarang Joshi	IIIT Hyderabad
Alina Karakanta	Leiden University
Maria Kunilovskaya	University of Saarland
Natalie Kübler	University of Paris
Gorka Labaka	University of the Basque Country
Tsz Kin Lam	University of Edinburgh
Ekaterina Lapshinova-Koltunski	University of Hildesheim
Yves Lepage	Waseda University
Qun Liu	Huawei Noah's Ark Lab
John Mendonca	INESC-iD
Miguel Menezes	Lisboa, Inesc-ID, Unbabel
Thomas Moerman	Ghent University
Kenton Murray	Johns Hopkins University
Jonathan Mutal	UNIGE
Masaaki Nagata	NTT
Artur Nowakowski	Laniqo / Adam Mickiewicz University
Constantin Orasan	University of Surrey
David Orrego-Carmona	University of Warwick
Antonio Pareja-Lora	ATLAS (UNED) / FITISPos (UAH) / DMEG (UdG, México) / DSIC, ILSA (UCM)
Seong-Bae Park	Kyung Hee University
Patrícia Pereira	Instituto Superior Técnico
Andrea Piergentili	University of Trento
Esther Ploeger	Aalborg University

David Ponce	Vicomtech
Andrei Popescu-Belis	HEIG-VD / HES-SO
Maja Popovic	ADAPT Centre @ DCU
Bo Ren	Microsoft
Fatiha Sadat	UQAM
Beatrice Savoldi	Fondazione Bruno Kessler
Yves Scherrer	University of Oslo
Dimitar Shterionov	Tilburg University
Michel Simard	National Research Council Canada (NRC)
Patrick Simianer	Lilt, Inc.
Sokratis Sofianopoulos	ILSP / Athena R.C.
Rubén Solera-Ureña	INESC-ID Lisboa
Rui Sousa-Silva	University of Porto
Felix Stahlberg	Google Research
Katsuhito Sudoh	Nara Women's University
Marek Suppa	Comenius University in Bratislava
Felipe Sánchez-Martínez	Universitat d'Alacant
Marina Sánchez-Torrón	Smartling
Aleš Tamchyna	Phrase a.s.
Antonio Toral	Universitat d'Alacant
Marco Turchi	Zoom
Jannis Vamvas	University of Zurich
Vincent Vandeghinste	Instituut voor de Nederlandse Taal, Leiden // Centre for Computational Linguistics, KU Leuven
David Vilar	Google
Taro Watanabe	Nara Institute of Science and Technology
Guillaume Wisniewski	LLF - Université de Paris
Tong Xiao	Northeastern University (CN)
Jinan Xu	Beijing Jiaotong University
Rik van Noord	University of Groningen

Track: Research Translators and Users

Sergi Alvarez-Vidal	UPF
Fabio Alves	UFMG
Nora Aranberri	University of the Basque Country
Lynne Bowker	Université Laval
Vicent Briva-Iglesias	SFI CRT D-REAL, Dublin City University
Patrick Cadwell	Dublin City University
Dragos Ciobanu	University of Vienna
Helle Dam Jensen	Aarhus University
Christophe Declercq	Utrecht University
Silvana Deilen	University of Hildesheim
Félix Do Carmo	CTS - University of Surrey
Aletta G. Dorst	Leiden University
Maria Fernandez-Parra	Swansea University
Federico Gaspari	ADAPT Centre, Dublin City University
Ana Guerberof Arenas	University of Groningen
Sari Hokkanen	Tampere University
Maarit Koponen	University of Eastern Finland
Ekaterina Lapshinova-Koltunski	University of Hildesheim
Manuel Lardelli	University of Graz

Rudy Loock	Université de Lille, France, & CNRS "Savoirs, Textes, Langage" research unit
Lieve Macken	Ghent University
Joss Moorkens	Dublin City University
Lucas N Vieira	University of Bristol
Masaaki Nagata	NTT
Mary Nurminen	University of Eastern Finland and Tampere University
Antoni Oliver	Universitat Oberta de Catalunya
Constantin Orasan	University of Surrey
David Orrego-Carmona	University of Warwick
John Ortega	Columbia and New York Universities
Jun Pan	Hong Kong Baptist University
Celia Rico	Universidad Complutense de Madrid
Akiko Sakamoto	Kansai University
Vilelmini Sosoni	Ionian University
Sanjun Sun	Beijing Foreign Studies University
María Del Mar Sánchez Ramos	Universidad de Alcala
Susana Valdez	Leiden University Centre for Linguistics
Kirti Vashee	Translated Srl
Mihaela Vela	Universität des Saarlandes
Callum Walker	University of Leeds

Track: Implementations and Case Studies

Chantal Amrhein	Supertext
Thomas Brovelli	Google
Oliver Czulo	Universität Leipzig
Marcello Federico	AWS AI Labs
Mark Fishel	University of Tartu
Tim Graf	Supertext
Ana Guerberof Arenas	University of Groningen
Silvia Hansen-Schirra	Johannes Gutenberg-Universität Mainz
Martin Kappus	Zürcher Hochschule für Angewandte Wissenschaften
Judith Klein	STAR Group
Maarit Koponen	University of Eastern Finland
Alon Lavie	Phrase
Christian Lieske	SAP
Helena Moniz	University of Lisbon
Mary Nurminen	University of Eastern Finland and Tampere University
Carla Parra Escartín	RWS Language Weaver
Matiss Rikters	Tilde
Florian Schottmann	Supertext
Sara Szoc	CrossLang
Carlos Teixeira	Universitat Rovira i Virgili
Jannis Vamvas	University of Zurich
Masaru Yamada	Rikkyo University
Maike Züfle	Karlsruher Institut für Technologie

Track: Products and Projects

Sergi Alvarez-Vidal	UPF
Eleftherios Avramidis	German Research Center for Artificial Intelligence (DFKI)
Romane Bodart	Université catholique de Louvain

Pedro Luis Díez-Orzas	Linguaserve I.S. S.A.
Judith Klein	STAR Group
Rebecca Knowles	National Research Council Canada
Ekaterina Lapshinova-Koltunski	University of Hildesheim
Manuel Lardelli	University of Graz
Marie-Aude Lefer	Université catholique de Louvain
Lieve Macken	Ghent University
Maite Melero	UPF
Yasmin Moslem	ADAPT Centre, Dublin City University
Vlad Niculae	Instituto de Telecomunicacoes, Lisboa
Mary Nurminen	University of Eastern Finland and Tampere University
Antoni Oliver	Universitat Oberta de Catalunya
Juan Antonio Pérez-Ortiz	Universitat d'Alacant, Departament de Llenguatges i Sistemes Informàtics
Shenbin Qian	University of Surrey
Felipe Sánchez-Martínez	Universitat d'Alacant
Arda Tezcan	Ghent University
Antonio Toral	Universitat d'Alacant
Daniel Torregrosa	WIPO
Tom Vanallemeersch	CrossLang NV
Bram Vanroy	Instituut voor de Nederlandse Taal
Rik van Noord	University of Groningen

Keynote Talk
Sign Language Machine Translation

Sarah Ebling
University of Zurich (UZH)

Abstract: In this talk, I will highlight the challenges of automatic translation between spoken languages and sign languages, touching on the topics of representation, data, and ethics. Additionally, I will introduce preprocessing tasks and discuss their state of the art. I will present research conducted in our group in the different areas.

Bio: Sarah Ebling is Full Professor of Language, Technology and Accessibility at the University of Zurich. Based in the field of computational linguistics, her research focuses on language-based assistive technologies in the context of persons with disabilities. Specifically, Sarah Ebling's research takes place in the context of deafness and hearing impairment, blindness and visual impairment, cognitive impairment, and language disorders. She is conducting research on sign language technologies, automatic text simplification, technologies for the audio description process, and computer-aided language sample analysis. Sarah Ebling is involved in international and national projects and is the PI of a large-scale Swiss innovation project entitled Inclusive Information and Communication Technologies"(2022-2026; `https://www.iict.uzh.ch/`).

Keynote Talk

Losing Our Tail – Again: Unnatural Selection and Translation Technologies

Eva Vanmassenhove
Tilburg University (TiU)

Abstract: Language is humanity's primary tool to preserve and transmit knowledge, evolving alongside and with cultural technologies. Today, multilingual large language models (LLMs) represent the latest leap. Emerging evidence, however, suggests that LLMs might subtly (or not so subtly) distort language over time, amplifying frequent patterns while eroding linguistic richness, a phenomenon linked to *model collapse* which had already been observed in Neural Machine Translation (NMT) systems even before it was formally named. Unlike the visible artefacts that have already been observed in the AI-generated images created by computer vision models, linguistic shifts, such as the loss of the long tails of language, risk going unnoticed. Yet, they mayhave profound implications for language, translation, diversity, and the integrity of communication across different languages. This keynote will explore these ideas and connect them to specific translation issues, asking: What is (or will be) at stake when our world of words becomes increasingly shaped by multilingual LLMs.

Bio: Eva Vanmassenhove is a researcher specializing in Machine Translation and Language Technology, with a strong focus on tackling gender and algorithmic biases in translation systems. She earned her PhD from Dublin City University and now serves as an assistant professor in the Department of Cognitive Science and Artificial Intelligence at Tilburg University (TiU). At TiU, she contributes to the Computation and Psycholinguistics Research unit and the Inclusive and Sustainable Machine Translation Research Line. Her work aims to enhance machine translation by addressing biases, especially in gender representation, while preserving linguistic richness.

Keynote Talk

Ethics and MT Evaluation: An Exploded View

Joss Moorkens
Dublin City University (DCU)

Abstract: This talk reflects on ethical issues with MT using LLMs, looking particularly at a recent evaluation study in the medical domain. This study, and the potential for its findings to be used as a basis for action, bring abstract ethical issues into focus. More broadly, the heightened attention and potential for impact of MT and LLM research brings an added sense of responsibility for researchers, although this might be balanced with opportunities to contribute to the common good.

Bio: Joss Moorkens is an Associate Professor at the School of Applied Language and Intercultural Studies in Dublin City University (DCU), Science Lead at the ADAPT Centre, and member of DCU's Institute of Ethics and Centre for Translation and Textual Studies. He has published over 60 articles and papers on the topics of translation technology interaction and evaluation, translator precarity, and translation ethics. He is General Co-Editor of the journal Translation Spaces with Prof. Dorothy Kenny, co-editor of a number of books and journal special issues, and co-author of the textbooks Translation Tools and Technologies (Routledge 2023) and Automating Translation (Routledge 2024). He sits on the board of the European Masters in Translation Network.

Tutorial

Understanding Large Language Model-Generated Translations: How Can They Adapt to Different Translation Specifications and Pass the Translation Turing Test?

Longhui Zou[1], **Michael Carl**[2], **Alan Melby**[3], **Brandon Torruella**[4], **Masaru Yamada**[5]
[1]University of Montana, [2]Kent State University - CRITT, [3]International Federation of Translators,
[4]Brigham Young University, [5]Rikkyo University

Abstract: This tutorial explores the practical application of the Translation Turing Test (TTT) within today's evolving generative AI landscape, addressing the growing need for human-centered approaches to translation project management and machine translation evaluation. While substantial research has examined large language models (LLMs)' translation quality, little attention has been paid to their potential in managing the complex human interactions that characterize real-world translation project negotiations.

The TTT is a translation-specific adaptation of the classic Turing Test, evaluating whether a machine-managed translation project can successfully imitate a professional human project manager. In the TTT, a requester interacts with both human and computer systems to negotiate translation specifications and conduct a complete translation project. The machine passes if the requester cannot distinguish between the two managers more than 30% of the time.

This half-day tutorial guides participants through current language industry practices and the three major TTT components: specification negotiation, target text quality assessment, and complaint negotiation. By comparing three translation project cycles (managed by a human professional, a trained amateur, and a generative AI agent), we evaluate whether LLM-powered agents can handle complex coordination tasks characteristic of language service providers.

The program includes four sessions: introduction to the TTT, demonstration of requester-provider negotiations, translation quality evaluation including MQM customization and syntactic complexity analysis, and complaint negotiations. Participants gain both theoretical understanding and practical experience assessing the feasibility of integrating LLMs into real-world translation projects that support or enhance human project managers' roles.

Tutorial

Leveraging Examples in Machine Translation: A Guide to Retrieval and Integration Strategies

Maxime Bouthors[1], **Josep Maria Crego**[2]
[1]ISIR - Sorbonne Université - CNRS, [2]SYSTRAN by ChapsVision

Abstract: Retrieval-Augmented Generation (RAG) systems are growing popular in the era of Large Language Models (LLM). Nonetheless, retrieval augmentation has a long time story tied to Machine Translation (MT). This tutorial aims to put in perspective the various techniques used to (1) retrieve relevant examples for databases; (2) integrate them into MT models. We will uncover how the selection of examples can be performed (fuzzy matching, cross-lingual retrieval), some of the model architectures (edit-based models, augmented encoder-decoder generation models, LLMs), as well as how the augmentation affects the output. The target audience are academics and industry professionals wishing to incorporate examples to improve their translation quality.

Tutorial

Best Practices for Data Quality in Human Annotation of Translation Datasets

Marina Sánchez Torrón[1], **Jennifer Wong**[1]
[1]Smartling

Abstract: High-quality human annotations are essential for developing and evaluating machine learning (ML) models. However, annotation is a complex task, and creating reliable annotation datasets requires addressing multiple challenges. This tutorial provides comprehensive guidance on best practices for managing data quality in human annotation of translation datasets using the Multidimensional Quality Metrics (MQM) framework. Drawing from both academic research and industry experience, we cover the complete annotation lifecycle: from initial setup and annotator management to quality evaluation and improvement strategies. Through theoretical foundations and a practical demonstration, participants will learn concrete guidelines they can apply to create more reliable and consistent annotation datasets.

Table of Contents

Using AI Tools in Multimedia Localization Workflows: a Productivity Evaluation

Ashley Mondello[1], Romina Cini[1], Sahil Rasane[1], Alina Karakanta[2], Laura Casanellas[3],
[1]Language Scientific, Boston, MA, USA
[2]Leiden University Centre for Linguistics, Leiden University
[3]LCTM Solutions, Dublin, Ireland

Abstract

Multimedia localization workflows are inherently complex, and the demand for localized content continues to grow. This demand has attracted Language Service Providers (LSPs) to expand their activities into multimedia localization, offering subtitling and voice-over services. While a wide array of AI tools is available for these tasks, their value in increasing productivity in multimedia workflows for LSPs remains uncertain. This study evaluates the productivity, quality, cost, and time efficiency of three multimedia localization workflows, each incorporating varying levels of AI automation. Our findings indicate that workflows merely replacing human vendors with AI tools may result in quality degradation without justifying the productivity gains. In contrast, integrated workflows using specialized tools enhance productivity while maintaining quality, despite requiring additional training and adjustments to established practices.

1 Introduction

The demand to provide culturally and linguistically relevant content to global markets is at an all-time high. To remain competitive, businesses are pressured to produce broad-scale localized multimedia content faster and cheaper than ever before. As a result, Language Service Providers (LSPs) must find more efficient ways to provide multimedia localization services to meet these evolving client expectations. The evolution of artificial intelligence (AI) has introduced a plethora of tools designed to solve efficiency challenges for complex multimedia workflows. Existing research on AI tools in multimedia workflows has focused mainly on subtitling productivity, with studies investigating post-editing of machine-translated subtitles (Matusov et al., 2019; Koponen et al., 2020; Karakanta et al., 2022) or AI-enhanced subtitling workflows (Massidda and Sandrelli, 2023; Tardel, 2023). Research on AI-enhanced voice-over (VO) workflows is even scarcer, mainly focusing on quality assessment models (Spiteri Miggiani, 2024). In a recent survey, Mondello et al. (2024) evaluated several categories of multimedia AI tools for their suitability in LSP business operations. The categories evaluated were transcription, translation, subtitling, and VO, with tools ranging from modular task-specific applications, which proved to be most suitable for LSPs with low workloads, to fully integrated multimedia platforms, which demonstrated suitability for LSPs with high-volume workloads. However, the effectiveness of AI tools in enhancing productivity in real world multimedia workflows and the impact to end product quality have been largely unexplored.

Moreover, productivity gains must be weighed against the costs of leveraging AI. Incorporating AI in traditional workflows often requires additional computational power, specialized technical skills, training project managers and linguists in using new tools, and restructuring well-tested existing workflows. Thus, the questions for LSPs become: Are the productivity gains of leveraging AI worth the upfront cost and effort? Is the potential risk to end product quality worth the productivity gains?

In this paper, we address these questions by conducting a productivity study, comparing quality, time and cost gains in different AI localization workflows. This study focused on localizing two videos for subtitling and voice-over into Spanish-US and Simplified Chinese. To evaluate the gains and quality impact of AI tools on multimedia localization, we compared three different workflows: *i)* manual, where subtitling and VO were performed without the support of any AI tools, *ii)* cascaded, where the existing manual workflow was enhanced using automatic transcription, machine translation, and voice synthesis, and *iii)* integrated, where dedicated subtitling and VO platforms incorporating

Proceedings of Machine Translation Summit XX Volume 2, pages 1–7, June 23-27, 2025

AI were used to execute the workflow end-to-end. Our findings compare total time and cost, end product quality, and challenges associated with each workflow. Through the comparison of the traditional workflow against AI-augmented workflows for impact on quality, cost and time savings, our goal is to provide guidance to LSPs and other stakeholders on the implementation of AI automation in multimedia workflows.

2 Multimedia workflows and LSPs

Localizing multimedia content, such as videos, consists of projects focused on adapting audiovisual materials into different languages, in order to make them applicable and accessible to different linguistic and cultural audiences. These projects have traditionally been complex, time-consuming, and costly for LSPs, due to the fact that they require the involvement of a myriad of different specialized human resources to complete several different tasks, such as transcription, translation, subtitling, voice-over recording, and others. Some of the resources involved include: desktop publishing specialists, native-speaking and subject-matter expert linguists, video editors, subtitlers, voice-over artists, localization engineers, and Quality Assurance (QA) resources.

The nature of these workflows poses further challenges for LSPs. The fact that each step requires specialized and highly-trained resources not only increases the operational cost and execution time, but it also requires dedicated, proficient, and meticulous planning and resource allocation. Meeting tight deadlines becomes challenging, especially when handling large volumes of content or multiple language pairs simultaneously. Additionally, quality control entails ensuring consistency and quality across all stages and, since each step involves human intervention, this can introduce variability in the output quality. Maintaining high standards requires rigorous QA processes, further adding to the time and cost. The challenge of sourcing specialized subtitlers and voice-over artists to cover the diverse range of languages required by LSPs serves as a key motivation for this article. Unlike dedicated multimedia providers or streaming services whose main revenue comes from multimedia projects, LSPs have distinct needs and workflows that may differ from those in the audiovisual industry. This distinction underpins our decision to test these workflows in this context.

3 Methodology

3.1 Data

This study involved subtitling and voice-over of two brief videos[1] (approximately 11 minutes in total) with two speakers (male, female). The videos are an interview between two doctors and contain specialised terminology, spontaneous speech, on-screen text and no background noise or music.

3.2 Workflows

We compare quality, time and cost savings in localizing the videos through three separate workflows: manual, cascaded, and integrated. The tools selected for the cascaded and integrated workflows are the ones found to be most efficient for LSPs and providing high quality for life science content based on Mondello et al. (2024).

Manual workflow The manual workflow is the workflow traditionally followed by LSPs for subtitling and VO of videos. For subtitling, we started with a transcription of the videos, followed by a transcription QA step, and then prepared the scripts to be uploaded to our CAT Tool. The benefit of a CAT tool is that linguists can leverage translation memories (TM), glossaries and other resources, necessary to support the translation process in specialized domains. We proceeded with human translation and editing, which were handled by two different linguistic resources. The translated and edited script was sent to a subtitler who formatted the subtitle lengths and lines and burned them to the video. We sent the subtitled video to a linguist, who performed a video QA and identified issues to be resolved by a second round of subtitle editing. Once these updates were applied by the subtitler, the linguistic QA resource reviewed the videos again to ensure they were properly implemented and the subtitled video was final.

For voice-over, the workflow is equally, if not more, time-consuming and rigorous as for subtitling. We began with transcription, timecoding, and transcription QA to produce the final original scripts, which were then prepared by a different resource for CAT Tool upload. Then, two separate but equally qualified linguists handled the translation and editing of the scripts. Once these steps were completed, we sent the translated and edited scripts to voice-over talents, broken into different

[1] https://www.youtube.com/watch?v=9xla1ZccFno
https://www.youtube.com/watch?v=ibw6-qKQMSY

segments which needed to be delivered as separate recordings. The recorded audio clips were sent to a linguist, who reviewed them for accuracy, appropriate pronunciation and intonation, and faithfulness to the script. The segments that needed updates were sent back to the voice-over talents, along with the description of the issues, who re-recorded them and provided updated audio clips. The final audio clips were sent to a video engineer, who applied them to the original video, making sure the audio and video were appropriately aligned. The video engineer delivered a video that was sent to a linguist to perform a final and comprehensive video QA. The findings from this step were sent back to the video engineer for implementation. Finally, a linguist reviewed the updated video to verify that all updates were properly applied and to confirm the video was final.

Cascaded workflow The cascaded workflow followed the manual workflow but replaced the manual steps of transcription, translation and voice synthesis with AI tools followed by post-editing and/or review. The advantage of this strategy lies in maintaining the familiar workflow and processes for project managers and linguists, with the sole modification being the introduction of AI tools.

In the cascaded workflow, the transcription was done using Amazon Transcribe, which offers transcription with timestamp prediction. This can be done through the graphic user interface and requires uploading and downloading various files. For MT, we evaluated Amazon Translate, ChatGPT (OpenAI, 2023) and Google Translate. The outputs were similar in quality but we used Amazon Machine Translation in XTM since that is the main CAT tool in terms of familiarity for the linguists and the project managers. Once the translation has been generated, the subtitling and VO workflows separate. For subtitling, the scripts were converted to subtitle format (*.srt*), using a python script and the srt library[2]. The subtitles were then burned onto the video using ffmpeg[3]. For VO, the translated scripts were used for synthetic voice generation. Synthetic voices were generated through Amazon Polly for Spanish and Google Text-to-Speech for Chinese. This choice was motivated by the lack of availability of Chinese voices in Amazon. Applying the synthetic voices obtained to the video is performed by a sound engineer as in the manual workflow.

Integrated workflow The integrated workflow substituted the manual workflow, by moving the entire localization process under a dedicated platform. This process not only integrates AI tools, but also transforms the workflow by automating some of the project management tasks, avoiding the need for file conversions, importing and exporting documents and sharing them per email. We selected Matesub[4] for subtitling and Speechify Studio[5] for voice-over.

For subtitling, we uploaded the videos to Matesub and ran automatic transcription. Then, we had a linguist conduct a transcription QA step directly on the tool and apply any necessary corrections. Then, the source language subtitles were automatically translated into the target languages and linguists conducted post-editing. During the post-editing step, the linguists were also tasked with conducting a subtitle QA, which focused on correcting any issues related to length, synchronization and reading speed, legibility, positioning, and appropriate line breaks, among other issues.

For voice-over, we uploaded the videos to Speechify and ran automatic transcription. A linguist conducted a transcription QA step, directly on the tool and updated the script as needed. Then, we applied machine translation to the script and selected the synthetic voices that would be used to create the audio in the target languages. A separate group of linguists was asked to perform two simultaneous tasks: post-editing and audio QA. The post-editing portion focused on reviewing the translations and making any necessary updates in order to correct any translation issues and ensure accuracy to the source material. The audio QA task involved playing the audio and performing *live* updates in the translation (such as reducing, incrementing, or eliminating pauses, condensing the text, paraphrasing sections or switching terminology choices whenever necessary) in order to aid the synthetic voice generation tool in producing the most appropriate audio renditions of the written script, in terms of pronunciation, timing, and intonation.

3.3 Evaluation criteria

The evaluation focused on productivity gains and final quality. For productivity, the criteria included

[2]https://pypi.org/project/srt/
[3]https://ffmpeg.org/
[4]https://matesub.com/
[5]https://speechify.com/

time (hs) and cost ($) savings, reported both per task and as total. For quality, an evaluation of the final videos of the three workflows was conducted by a separate set of four expert linguists (one per language per task). To obtain unbiased quality results, each linguist assessed all three videos using an error annotation scheme, without knowing which video corresponded to which workflow. For the subtitled videos, professional subtitlers annotated errors related to translation quality, length, reading speed, synchronization, line segmentation and visual aspects (font, color, positioning). For voice-over, translators with experience as voice artists were recruited. They annotated errors related to fluency of speech (natural, fluent pronunciation), pace (too fast, too slow), synchronization to the speaker, background noise, room echo or distortion or robotic sound (audio that sounds flat, or does not convey emotion).[6]

The evaluation followed a penalty system. Critical errors (-1) are errors that impact comprehension completely or render outputs that are offensive or inappropriate for the target locale. Major errors (-0.5) are highly visible, could potentially impact comprehension, produce a mismatch between the speaker on screen or their gender and audio/subtitles, or result in a subtitle not being comfortable to read, for example, due to high reading speed, excessive length, lack of synchronization of about one second, or segmentation on linguistic units. Minor errors (-0.25) are errors that would be noticed, e.g. unnatural or artificial, and could decrease stylistic quality or fluency, but do not impact comprehension, or result in non-conforming but still readable subtitles, for example, subtitles that are max 3 characters above the length/reading speed limit, that appear fractions of a second before or after the corresponding dialogue, or that split linguistic units without impacting readability.

Finally, we report qualitative findings related to the efficiency in integration and usability of the tools in each workflow based on the feedback from the parties involved in the workflows (project managers, engineers, linguists).

4 Results

4.1 Productivity

The productivity gains in terms of time cost savings for subtitling and VO are shown in Tables 1 and 2 respectively. Both time and cost savings were very similar for both language pairs, therefore we only report them once. We found significant time and cost savings between the manual workflow and the cascaded and integrated workflows. The cascaded workflow for subtitling needed 10 working hours instead of 22 and the VO workflow needed 13.5 hours instead of 27 per language, resulting in a 41% cost reduction for the subtitling workflow and a 73% cost reduction for the VO workflow compared to the manual workflow. Finally, the integrated workflow showed the biggest time and cost reductions. Both subtitling and VO integrated workflows needed 7 working hours per language to complete the project and showed a 71% cost reduction for subtitling and 86% for VO when compared to the manual workflows.

While the cascaded workflow rendered quite considerable cost and time savings when compared to the manual workflow, we found that it was significantly more labor-intensive and complex than the integrated workflow. This was mostly due to the fact that the AI-assisted steps included in the cascade workflow had to be handled by a dedicated resource (engineer), since the selected tools needed a high level of technology expertise and were too complex for the project management and linguistic teams to be trained on during a feasible timeline. For this reason, even though the cascaded workflow showed considerable benefits, it may not be the most time- and cost-effective workflow, especially when considering its final quality results, which are explained in detail in the next section.

4.2 Quality

The quality assessment scores for the three workflows are shown in Table 3. In general, the manual workflow has the highest scores, closely followed by the integrated workflow, except for the Spanish subtitling where the integrated workflow remarkably resulted in an error-free output.

Comparing the scores among the workflows, for subtitling into Chinese, most minor errors in the manual workflow are related to synchronization and line segmentation, while in the cascaded and integrated workflows to positioning. In Spanish, the manual workflow showed a few stylistic issues, such as formality and acronyms. The cascaded workflow demonstrated severe quality issues, as shown by the negative score (-0.25). While the translation was of sufficient quality, the technical aspects showed several major synchronization

[6]The scorecards can be found at: `https://tinyurl.com/3y2c6cby`

	Manual		Cascaded		Integrated	
Task	Step	hs	Step	hs	Step	hs
Transcription	Transcription Transcription QA	3 1	Auto Transcription Transcription QA	0 2	Auto Transcription Transcription QA	0 2
Translation	Translation Editing	8 2	Machine Translation Post-editing Editing	0 3 2	Machine Translation Post-editing & Subtitle QA	0 3
Subtitling	Subtitle engineering Video QA	7 1	Subtitle engineering 1 Video QA Subtitle engineering 2	1 1 1	Final QA	2
Total		22		10		7
Cost reduction				41%		71%

Table 1: Productivity gains for subtitling in terms of time (hs) for each task and in total, as well as cost reduction (in percentage) of the total workflow.

	Manual		Cascaded		Integrated	
Task	Step	hs	Step	hs	Step	hs
Transcription	Transcription Transcription QA	3 1	Auto Transcription Transcription QA	0 2	Auto Transcription Transcription QA	0 2
Translation	Translation Editing	8 2	Machine Translation Post-editing Editing	0 3 3	Machine Translation Post-editing & VO QA	0 3
voice-over	VO Recording 1 Audio QA 1 VO Recording 2 Audio QA 2 Video Engineering 1 Video QA 1 Video Engineering 2 Video QA 2	4 1 1 0.5 4 1 1 0.5	Voice generation Engineering 1 Video QA Engineering 2 Video QA	2 1 1 0.5 1	Final QA	2
Total		27		13.5		7
Cost reduction				73%		86%

Table 2: Productivity gains for VO in terms of time (hs) for each task and in total, as well as cost reduction (in percentage) of the total workflow.

	En→Zh		En→Es	
	Sub	VO	Sub	VO
Manual	9.67	9.5	9.38	8.375
Cascaded	9.58	9.25	-0.25	2.625
Integrated	9.58	9.375	10.00	7.375

Table 3: Quality assessment of the final videos in the three workflows based on the error annotation. 10 equals to an error-free output.

and line break issues, as well as overlapping text. Specifically, "since most subtitles appear in one long line instead of two, the viewer must direct their eyes from end to end of the screen to read it". The integrated workflow was assessed as error-free, with the evaluator reporting that the translation quality is the best of all three conditions and having correct terminology, great grammar and syntax and good readability. Specifically for the technical aspects, the subtitles were found "centered and distributed in two lines, concise yet accurate, readable in full within the time they remain on screen and in synchrony with the sound. Font, colour and position are appropriate at all times, making sure that they never get on top of other on-screen text or important visual information".

For VO, in Chinese the manual workflow has the highest scores with only a few minor synchronization errors and cases where the voices sound unnatural. The cascaded workflow obtained lower scores, mainly due to synchronization and fluency issues. The evaluator reported that "the synchronization issue exists, but a bigger problem is that both male and female voices sound quite robotic, making me believe that they were read by AI instead of humans". For the integrated workflow, a few minor synchronization issues were spotted. In Spanish, the output of the manual workflow was found fluent, with some minor synchronization and overmodulation issues in some of the sections. As in subtitling, the cascaded workflow scored low due to several major and minor fluency issues, with voice sometimes sounding robotic and distorted. The audio "sounds like reading a list of non-related sentences with no natural intonation, chopped at random points that do not follow the original syntax". The scores for the integrated workflow are higher. A few synchronization issues were reported, for example lip movements at the end of sentences. "Male VO has good fluency, pace and intonation in most sections and is easy on the ears. Female VO is more robotic sounding with exaggerated intonation, particularly in questions or exclamations".

We found that the integrated workflow performed remarkably well, especially for subtitling. Additionally, when considering how extensive the time and cost savings were for this workflow, our assessment is that this can be an extremely beneficial option for clients who need fast and cost-effective localization services for multimedia assets of this nature. The subtitled videos were found to be of very high quality by our linguistic reviewers and, while there were a few existing issues in the VO final videos, none of them were related to comprehension, ambiguity, or readability.

5 Recommendations

The goal of this experiment was to identify potential strategies of making the process of localization of multimedia products leaner and more cost effective. We think we have achieved that. Here are some recommendations to LSPs who want to test AI for such workflows:

- If you are going to apply AI in one task only, you might want to choose a standalone technology, rather than a platform.
- It is important to test the quality of the output in order to assess the human effort that will be required afterwards.
- Check the format of the output, as some formats are more user friendly than others: can you work with it directly?
- Make sure the languages required are fully covered by the provider, as there is variability in that regard.
- Visualize the workflow and add quality checks after AI.
- Bear in mind that most subtitling/VO AI tools do not have basic functionalities such as spell and QA checks, glossary or TM support.
- Decide who within your team is going to be the owner when it comes to applying the technology: will it be a developer, a technically competent project manager?
- If you are going to use integrated platforms, you will need to train your team; you might want to add that to your cost.

6 Conclusion

Our productivity and quality analysis showed that AI technologies can be used successfully in the localization of multimedia products. Amongst all the tasks analysed (transcription, translation, subtitle generation and voice-over), the one that is still lacking finesse and human quality is artificial voice generation. Having said that, there are a large range of voice generation providers that were not tested during this exercise. A key observation from this experiment is that most AI tools, especially those offering AI dubbing/VO, are not designed with post-editing in mind, as they lack fundamental functionalities commonly found in CAT tools. At the end of the day, companies need to strike a balance between quality of the end AI product, cost, learning curve and experience. The human element is still important in the form of post-editing (the transcribed source and the translation) and QA (subtitles and voice-over). The integrated workflow, with the use of platforms designed for the specific tasks, is the real winner in terms of quality and productivity, especially for subtitle generation. But it implies a steep learning curve, as language workers need to learn how to work in an alien environment. One of the clear conclusions of this experiment is that there is a need for training language providers workforce on the use of AI technologies; not only on the physical use of the various interfaces, but on the fundamentals of AI. By doing that, production teams will understand the possibilities of AI on their day to day tasks.

References

Alina Karakanta, Luisa Bentivogli, Mauro Cettolo, Matteo Negri, and Marco Turchi. 2022. Post-editing in automatic subtitling: A subtitlers' perspective. In *Proceedings of the 23rd Annual Conference of the European Association for Machine Translation*, pages 261–270, Ghent, Belgium. European Association for Machine Translation.

Maarit Koponen, Umut Sulubacak, Kaisa Vitikainen, and Jörg Tiedemann. 2020. MT for subtitling: User evaluation of post-editing productivity. In *Proceedings of the 22nd Annual Conference of the European Association for Machine Translation*, pages 115–124, Lisboa, Portugal. European Association for Machine Translation.

Serenella Massidda and Annalisa Sandrelli. 2023. ¡ sub! localisation workflows (th) at work. *Translation and Translanguaging in Multilingual Contexts*, 9(3):298–315.

Evgeny Matusov, Patrick Wilken, and Yota Georgakopoulou. 2019. Customizing neural machine translation for subtitling. In *Proceedings of the Fourth Conference on Machine Translation (Volume 1: Research Papers)*, pages 82–93, Florence, Italy. Association for Computational Linguistics.

Ashley Mondello, Sahil Rasane, Alina Karakanta, and Laura Casanellas. 2024. Leveraging AI technologies for enhanced multimedia localization. In *Proceedings of the 16th Conference of the Association for Machine Translation in the Americas (Volume 2: Presentations)*, pages 145–151, Chicago, USA. Association for Machine Translation in the Americas.

Giselle Spiteri Miggiani. 2024. Quality assessment tools for studio and ai-generated dubs and voice-overs. *Parallèles*, 2.

Anke Tardel. 2023. A proposed workflow model for researching production processes in subtitling. *Trans-Kom*, 16(1):140–173.

Replacing the Irreplaceable: A Case Study on the Limitations of MT and AI Translation during the 2023 Gaza-Israel Conflict

Abeer Alfaify
King Abdulaziz University
Department of Modern Languages and Literatures
Jeddah, Saudi Arabia
abeer.alfaify@gmail.com

Abstract

Despite the remarkable development of artificial intelligence (AI) and machine translation (MT) in recent years, which has made them more efficient, less costly and easier to navigate, they still struggle to match the abilities of human translators. The limitations shown by AI and MT, which have been detected in various domain-specific texts and contexts, sustain the debate over whether they can fully replace human translators. Nevertheless, very few studies have examined the translation abilities of AI and MT during conflicts and high-stakes contexts. This paper explores some of these limitations that were detected during the 2023 Gaza-Israel conflict, illustrating significant examples from X (formerly Twitter). These examples showcase limitations in 1) translating cultural references, 2) avoiding critical errors in high-stakes context, 3) preventing bias and intervention, and 4) translating cursive handwriting. This is done through a combination of descriptive, comparative and experimental analysis methods, highlighting risks and implications associated with using these tools in such sensitive contexts, while contributing to the broader discussion on whether advances in AI and MT will diminish the need for human translators.

Keywords: translation, artificial intelligence, machine translation, Google translate, Gaza, Israel, conflict, High-stakes context, translation technology

1 Introduction

Advances in translation technologies have made it easier, quicker and cheaper to translate different types of text for a wide range of users. However, despite all the significant developments in recent years, artificial intelligence (AI) and machine translation (MT) still face challenges in replicating human abilities. These challenges continue to fuel the debate over whether they can take the place of human translators in the near future.

Although limitations of AI and MT have been explored across various domain-specific texts and contexts, very little research has been done on their limitations in the political domain, specifically during conflicts. This paper explores some of the limitations that were encountered during the 2023 Gaza-Israel conflict, illustrating significant examples from X (formerly Twitter) in four different key areas. The study employs a combination of descriptive, comparative, and experimental analysis methods to provide a comprehensive investigation into the limitations of text, image and audiovisual translation.

Since this study focuses on a single conflict, the examples provided are not intended to be exhaustive. Nonetheless, they effectively illustrate the limitations of AI and MT and merit further discussion for several reasons: (1) they highlight the risks associated with relying on such tools in conflicts and high-stakes contexts; (2) they help pinpoint specific areas where AI and MT require further refinement; and (3) they contribute to the ongoing debate about whether advancements in AI and MT will reduce the demand for human translators.

2 Literature Review

2.1 Translation in Conflict Contexts

Translation plays a crucial role in shaping how conflicts are perceived globally, particularly in today's interconnected world, where disputes are no longer confined to local audiences. According to Newmark (1989), translators facilitate communication between nations, mediate between conflicting sides, and uphold both moral integrity and factual accuracy. Similarly, Baker (2010) emphasizes the crucial, yet often unrecognized role translators play in how wars are represented and understood. However, conflicts often arise from ideological differences and opposing political stances (Tang, 2007), which can inevitably affect translators working on either side. Despite this, their influence in shaping war narratives remains largely overlooked. Venuti (1998) argues that translation is influenced by political and ideological conflicts, as it is shaped by the social institutions that produce it, often serving particular cultural and political agendas. Similarly, Lefevere and Bassnett (2001) assert that translation is never truly neutral; rather, it is a form of rewriting that reflects the ideologies and values of the society from which it originates. With the rise of global conflicts, translation studies have increasingly focused on ideological struggles, where competing sides attempt to discredit each other due to conflicting interests, values, and objectives. Baker (2006) notes that each party aims to validate its own narrative of events. In such contexts, true neutrality becomes highly challenging, as Palmer (2007) suggests that achieving complete impartiality is nearly impossible. Tymoczko and Gentzler (2002) highlight the intricate nature of translation, describing it as an intentional and thoughtful process of choosing, organizing, and reconstructing information, which may lead to distortion, omission, deception, or the development of concealed meanings.

2.2 AI and MT Translation across Domains

Despite the advances of machine translation and AI, the debate over their limitations and inability to replace human translators has been a reoccurring topic in the literature. Many agree that although such tools are improving tremendously, they still do not measure up to human translators across the various domains and contexts, particularly in fields of literature, religion, law, medicine and media.

In literature for instance, despite the semantic abilities and narrative skills displayed by translation technologies, they still have obvious limitations in capturing the complexity of a poem. In a study conducted on the translation of poems from Arabic into English, Alowedi and Al-Ahdal compared the abilities of machine and human translations and reached the conclusion that 'the limitations of machine translation are stark in capturing the socio-cultural context of poetry' (2023). These results resemble the findings of another study that used Chinese literary texts to compare human and AI translations. The results showed that AI lacks the ability to capture cultural aspects, narrative perspectives and human-like subjectivity (Qi, 2024), an evaluation that aligns with the findings of Bernhart and Richter (2021). Additionally, AI does not measure up to human translators because literary translation requires a good imagination (Škobo and Petričević 2023), artistic sense (Qi 2024), creativity and personal interpretation (Tomasello 2019), as well as the ability to capture the original creator's intentions (Makridakis 2017; Edmond 2019).

Religious documents have also pushed the limitations of translation technologies. One example is a study conducted by Zaid and Bennoudi on Arabic religious texts, which found that AI tools were not efficient enough to accurately translate the grammatical structure or the cultural and religious aspects of the text (2023). This conclusion was supported by Alharazi, who stated that such difficulties arise from variations of terminology, cultural elements and idiomatic expressions (2024).

In the legal field, texts often have a complex structure and specialised terminology that require precision and accuracy in translation, given that errors carry a high risk and bear severe consequences. Additionally, legal terms have various meanings across different types of documents, requiring human proficiency to produce accurate translations (Moneus and Sahari, 2024). AI has been found to lack the ability to understand legal specialised terminology, as well as the capacity to capture the contextual aspects of a legal text (Al-Romany and Kadhim, 2024). Machine systems in general base their translations on the most probable meaning, which may not be the accurate meaning, especially when dealing with specialized terminology and contexts, such as legal texts (Moorkens, 2018).

Errors are even more critical in the medical field and could lead to catastrophic results. This is because 'MT technology can in its current state exacerbate social inequalities and put certain communities of users at greater risk' (Vieira et al., 2021). A study that investigated the translation of medical reports found that, without human assistance, translation systems were not able to construe many abbreviations created by doctors (Uličná 2023). Another study looked into translations from English into seven other languages including Basque, French, German, Portuguese, Russian and Spanish, using different machine systems. The results showed that such tools are 'still not good enough in such a domain where 100% of accuracy is required' (Costa-Jussà et al., 2012). But the study also suggested that machine translation systems can be an excellent complementary tool to human translators, as long as post-editing and human revision are implemented.

Aside from written texts, examinations of oral translations have shown that AI is still limited in not being able to process multimodal aspects such as gestures and facial expressions that contribute to the understanding of the overall meaning of the source text—something that human translators can achieve effortlessly (Qian & Qian, 2020).

Ultimately, AI and MT, while remarkable, often fall short of human translation standards across most domain-specific texts and contexts, especially in situations where errors have critical consequences (Brynjolfsson et al., 2018).

3 Methodologies

During the 2023 Gaza-Israel conflict, users on X utilized AI tools to translate videos shared by other users from both sides of the conflict. These tools included EzDubs, an AI-powered tool designed to dub videos effortlessly from and into various languages, and TranslateMom, an AI-powered tool designed to caption videos from and into various languages. Both tools operate through bots specifically designed to translate videos on multiple platforms, including X. In addition, users relied on the translation tool integrated into X and powered by Google Translate[1], to translate texts posted on X during this conflict. Google Translate is a well-known online service that can translate text in over 100 languages, and is listed in G2.com as the top machine translation system[2].

In this study, the performance of the AI tools EzDubs and TranslateMom is examined, as well as the abilities of Google translate. These include the ability to translate text via the integrated feature on X, which allows users to instantly translate posts and comments within the platform, and the ability to translate text embedded in images by using the "Camera Translation" feature, which enables users to capture a photo of text and translate it instantly.

The dataset was selected after examining hundreds of MT and AI translations shared by X users during the conflict. Particular emphasis was placed on translations that met the following criteria: (1) they generated controversy or public outrage; (2) they were widely circulated or featured in prominent hashtags; or (3) they were actively contested through user comments or critically addressed by news outlets. With the assistance of two bilingual Arabic-English translators and two bilingual Hebrew-English translators with no less than five years of experience, the accuracy of these translations was examined, and only materials that were conclusively identified as inaccurate and containing errors were explored in this study. The concept of accuracy in this context refers to the degree of correctness and fidelity to the source text (Molina and Albir 2002).

The study integrates descriptive, comparative and experimental analyses, showcasing four different limitations of AI and MT. The term 'limitation' is used in this study to encompass not only the failures of MT and AI, but also their inherent constraints, including instances of human intervention and text manipulation, as can be seen in Section 4.3. The descriptive analysis includes highlighting errors in the translations, analysing the nature of these errors and explaining the circumstances of their delivery. The comparative analysis compares AI and MT performance in translating some of these encounters against reference translations provided by professional Arabic and Hebrew translators, in order to highlight errors and differences in accuracy. Lastly, due to instances where translation technologies were evidently used and resulted in errors, but the specific tools employed were not identified, a systematic experimental analysis was conducted to investigate these issues rigorously using a well-

[1] https://help.x.com/en/using-x/translate-posts

[2] https://www.g2.com/categories/machine-translation?utf8=%E2%9C%93&order=g2_score

documented tool, namely Google Translate, as can be seen in Section 4.4.

4 Findings and Discussion

4.1 Translating cultural references

After reviewing the English translations of hundreds of Arabic videos, as generated by EzDubs and TranslateMom, it was observed that they often struggle to accurately convey cultural references (CRs). An example of this can be seen in the translations of a video that was posted by Arabic Post (2023), of a released Palestinian prisoner chanting in Arabic.

EzDubs and TranslateMom were both used to translate this video and, as can be seen in Table 1, both tools failed to accurately translate the name Mohammad Deif, who was a Palestinian militant and the head of the Izz al-Din al-Qassam Brigades, the military wing Hamas. They both truncated the full name to 'Muhammad', a common name across the Arab world, thereby diminishing the contextual significance and individuality conveyed by the complete form.

Table 1: Comparison of EzDubs and TranslateMom in Translating CRs from Arabic to English #1

Reference Translation	EzDubs translation	TranslateMom translation
We are *Mohammad Deif*'s men	And we returned to *Muhammad*	And we will return to *Muhammad*

Another example is observed in a video that was posted by Mohammad Zubair (2023), of a released Palestinian woman speaking in Arabic. EzDubs and TranslateMom were both used to translate this video and, as can be seen in Table 2, both tools failed to accurately translate the CR 'Netzarim Corridor', which is a zone set up by Israel in the Gaza Strip. The CR was deleted all together by EzDubs, whereas TranslateMom falsely rendered it as 'AL-Tarim', at least recognizing it as a proper name by adding 'Al', a common prefix for Arabic proper names.

These observations align with previous research showing that machine-generated translations often miss the cultural aspects of a text (Ahrenberg 2017), resulting in a literal and awkward translation that often confuses and misleads the target audience.

Table 2: Comparison of EzDubs and TranslateMom in Translating CRs from Arabic to English #2

Reference Translation	EzDubs Translation	TranslateMom Translation
Every day I go to *Netzarim Corridor*	And everyday I went to this bed	And everyday I go to AL-Tarim

4.2 Avoiding critical errors

One of the biggest limitations of AI and MT is the risk of relying on them during high-stakes contexts when there is so much on the line. An example of this is a pattern that was detected in the translation of some Arabic posts that were posted on X during the conflict. The integrated tool powered by Google Translate was observed minimising the intensity of some ongoing events, as can be seen in Figure 1.

Figure 1: An Arabic post and its translation, as produced by Google Translate on X (Barbar, M., 2024)

In this post from the account, ManalBarbar (2024), a reference is made to a recording of a 15-year-old Palestinian girl saying 'عمو بطخوا علينا'. The standard translation for this should be 'Uncle, they are shooting at us'. However, Google Translate translated this as 'Uncle, they beat us up', which is not accurate to the source text, since it does not describe the same severity of what was happening.

Similar issues were detected when examining Hebrew posts. An example of this is a post by the prime minister of Israel, Benjamin Netanyahu, where Google Translate made an error in translating 'עוטף עזה' Otef Aza, a region boarding

Gaza from the south. This region is normally translated as 'Gaza Envelope', but was translated as 'Gaza Strip', as can be seen in Figure 2, which basically indicated the prime minister was calling for the colonising of Gaza in the middle of an ongoing conflict. The error gained widespread attention and triggered a wave of outrage that persisted for some time, even after Google Translate corrected it. This serves as a clear reminder of the risks associated with relying on translation technologies at the heights of conflicts.

Figure 2: The controversial post from the prime minister of Israel and its translation before and after (Netanyahu, B., 2023)

The amendment of the mistake also illustrates that translation tools are subject to human intervention, a topic that is explored further in the next section.

4.3 Preventing bias and intervention

Many assume that translation tools are more objective and free of bias.[3] However, these tools are still influenced by human decisions and are susceptible to human intervention. An example of this comes from a post on X by the Israeli Minister of National Security, Itamar Ben-Gvir (2023), as seen in Figure 3.

In his post, Itamar referred to an Israeli man who had just died as 'Kushi'. The original translation of this word was 'nigger', as produced by Google Translate that is integrated into X. This is because the word 'Cushi' or 'Kushi' (כּוּשִׁי) is a Hebrew colloquial used to refer to a dark-skinned person of African descent.[4] It was not until a few hours later that the translation was changed from 'nigger' to 'Kushi'. Some users were quick to defend the translation by claiming it was the man's actual name, and that it was just an unfortunate mistranslation. However, further research revealed that the man's name was in fact Shimon Rimon, and that he was given the nickname 'Kushi' for being a dark-skinned Mizrahi from Yemen.

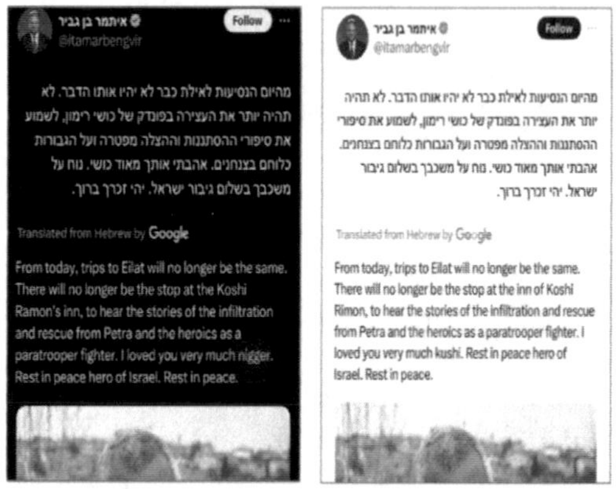

Figure 3: The post from Itamar Ben-Gvir and its translation before and after (Ben-Gvir, I., 2023)

Interestingly, when the actual Google Translate website was used to translate 'Kushi' (כּוּשִׁי), it produced the translation 'black person', 'negro', and 'nigger'. Furthermore, when looking up some other posts on X that used the same word, they were translated by Google Translate as 'negro', as can be seen in Figure 4.

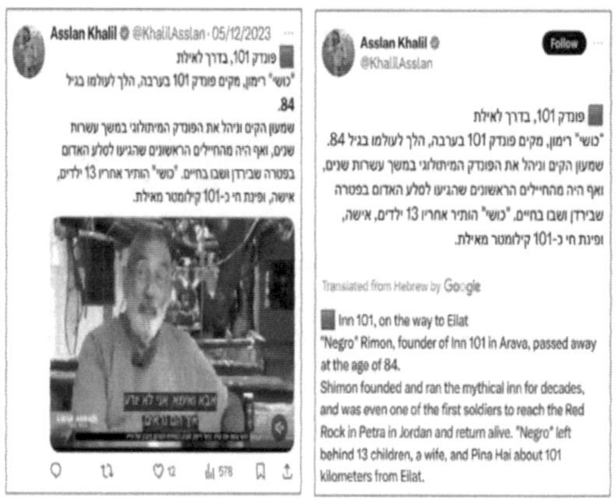

Figure 4: An example of a post on X that used the word 'כושי' but was translated differently (Khalil, A., 2023)

[3] https://www.aimyths.org/ai-can-be-objective-or-unbiased

[4] https://en.wikipedia.org/wiki/Cushi

This is a clear indication that such a change was limited to Ben-Gvir's post on X and was done by deliberate human intervention.

Another form of human intervention was observed in the censorship of some AI tools that demonstrated their significance during the conflict. An example of this can be seen in the suspension of the AI tool EzDubs from X for several months back in the early 2024 and during the heights of the Gaza-Israel conflict. The timing was suspicious given that the tool had been available since 2022. This occurred when the tool was utilized beyond its primary function as a translation tool during the conflict, serving as a means of verification to either corroborate or challenge human translations disseminated on platform X. In this capacity, it proved to be an effective instrument for countering propaganda, especially when precise, reliable, and prompt information is crucial during crisis (Fischer, 1998; Seeger, 2006; Altay and Labonte, 2014). Immediately after Hebrew was removed from the list of languages supported by EzDubs, the tool was reinstalled into the platform. Efforts were made to reach out to EzDubs concerning this issue, but no response was received.

4.4 Translating cursive handwriting

One of the most significant translation features introduced by AI is the ability to translate text from images. A photo or a screenshot with text is uploaded, then is translated into a seamless text like the original. However, this feature showed limitations during the conflict when used to translate images with cursive handwriting.

An example of this comes from the spokesman for the Israeli Defense Forces (IDF), Daniel Hagari, who claimed in a video that the IDF had found Hamas weapons in the Rantisi Children's Hospital in Gaza, as well as an Arabic 'guardian list where every terrorist writes his name, and every terrorist has his own shift guarding the people' (2023), referring to the Israeli hostages. However, Arabic speakers on social media and some news outlets were quick to point out that the only thing on that 'list' was the days of the week, as can be seen in Figure 5. The IDF later acknowledged their mistake, attributing it to a translation error in Hagari's statement.[5]

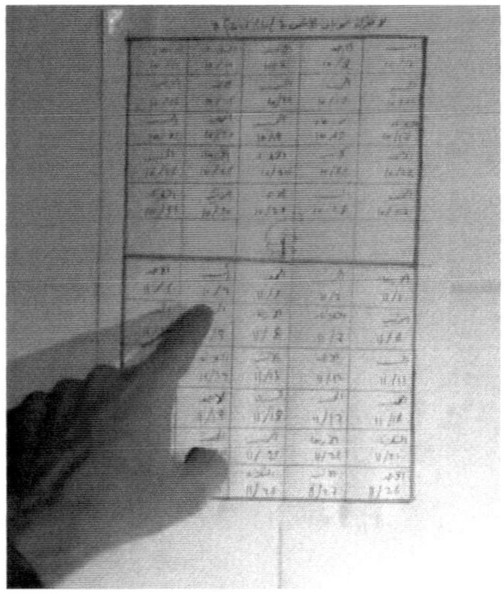

Figure 5: IDF spokesman points to an Arabic calendar in the Rantisi Children's Hospital in Gaza (Israel Defense Forces, 2023)

Since the IDF did not disclose the tool responsible for the error, an experimental analysis was conducted using the AI-powered feature in Google Translate, which enables text translation from images. As a result, out of the 55 Arabic words displayed on the calendar, 38 words were translated into their accurate English equivalents, indicating a high level of accuracy. However, 17 words were mistranslated into unrelated terms, as can be seen in Table 3.

Table 3: The Arabic words on the calendar and their English translation as generated by Google Translate

Source Text	Reference Translation	Google Translate	Arabic Back Translation
الأربعاء	Wednesday	Dimensions	أبعاد
الجمعة	Friday	Fever	حمه
الخميس	Thursday	Al-Hamid	الحامد
الجمعة	Friday	Association	منظمة/رابطة
الخميس	Thursday	praiseworthy	الجدير بالثناء
الأربعاء	Wednesday	Ijaa	-
الاثنين	Monday	The Ethneed	-
الثلاثاء	Tuesday	The three	الثلاثة
الاثنين	Monday	Al-Asheed	-
الأحد	Sunday	AL-Ahmad	الأحمد
الجمعة	Friday	Hummus	حمص
السبت	Saturday	The reason	السبب
الخميس	Thursday	praiseworthy	الجدير بالثناء
الاثنين	Monday	Ethanir	-
الخميس	Thursday	praiseworthy	الجدير بالثناء
الخميس	Thursday	Praise	مديح
الأربعاء	Wednesday	Dimensions	أبعاد

5 https://www.yahoo.com/news/cnn-quietly-cut-disputed-israeli-005939159.html

When examining the Arabic source text and the Arabic back translation closely, orthographic similarities can be established. For instance, a similarity can be observed between the source word ‘جمعة’ /ˈd͡ʒu.mʕa/ and its back translation ‘حمه’ /ˈhim.ma/, with the letters 'ج' (/d͡ʒ/) and 'ح' (/h/) sharing a similar structural form, differing only by the presence of a diacritical dot in the former. Another similarity can be seen between the source word ‘السبت’ /æs.sabt/ and its back translation ‘السبب’ /æs.sæ.bab/. More significantly, out of the 17 mistranslated words, three words had the Arabic definite article ‘Al’ added to them; ‘Al-Hamid’, ‘Al-Sheed’, and ‘Al-Ahmad’. This is significant because, as mentioned in section 4.1, ‘Al’ usually prefixes Arabic proper names, and when it prefixes a human name, it usually signifies belonging to an Arab tribe. This may have contributed to the IDF's misinterpretation of the text as a list of names rather than a calendar.

Unlike printed text, handwritten text, particularly in cursive, introduces significant variability in character shape, spacing, and connectivity, making it more difficult for AI to recognize characters reliably. This challenge is further compounded by the fact that certain AI models must encounter each individual token in isolation within the training images in order to effectively learn how to render it accurately (Ramesh et al., 2022). In the context of AI and machine learning, a token refers to a discrete unit of input, which may consist of a word, a part of a word, or an individual character.

Another example of AI’s limitation in translating cursive handwriting can be observed in the translation of a letter written by an Israeli hostage named Danielle Aloni, who wrote a thank you letter to Al-Qassam Brigades on behalf of herself and her daughter Emilia (Doam, 2023). The letter was widely circulated and has since been translated into multiple languages, including English, as can be seen in Figure 6.

However, users on X have expressed their frustration due to their inability to verify the accuracy of the human-translated letter, suggesting that existing translation tools have failed to generate an adequate rendition of the text.

As the specific tools used were not identified, an experimental analysis was undertaken utilizing the AI-powered feature of Google Translate. As can be seen in Figure 7, the failure to translate the source text was overwhelmingly higher than the previous example, which was also written in cursive handwriting. This leads us to believe the accuracy is affected by another factor here, which could be the language pair involved, an issue that Google Translate is known for (Taira et al. 2021). This is noteworthy because both Arabic and Hebrew are Semitic languages that share many similarities, yet the accuracy of the translation of their cursive handwriting varied significantly.

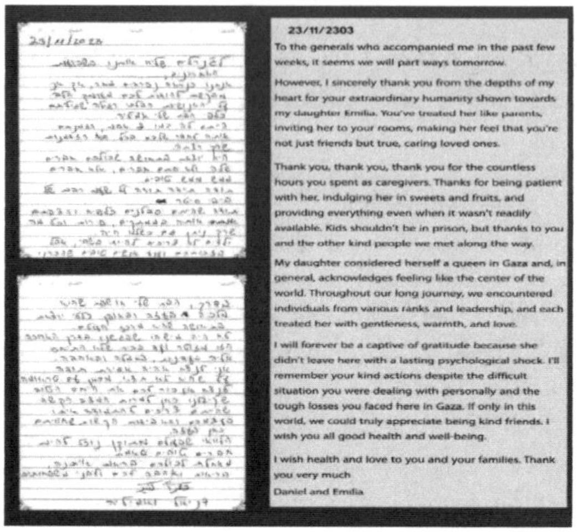

23/11/2303

To the generals who accompanied me in the past few weeks, it seems we will part ways tomorrow.

However, I sincerely thank you from the depths of my heart for your extraordinary humanity shown towards my daughter Emilia. You've treated her like parents, inviting her to your rooms, making her feel that you're not just friends but true, caring loved ones.

Thank you, thank you, thank you for the countless hours you spent as caregivers. Thanks for being patient with her, indulging her in sweets and fruits, and providing everything even when it wasn't readily available. Kids shouldn't be in prison, but thanks to you and the other kind people we met along the way.

My daughter considered herself a queen in Gaza and, in general, acknowledges feeling like the center of the world. Throughout our long journey, we encountered individuals from various ranks and leadership, and each treated her with gentleness, warmth, and love.

I will forever be a captive of gratitude because she didn't leave here with a lasting psychological shock. I'll remember your kind actions despite the difficult situation you were dealing with personally and the tough losses you faced here in Gaza. If only in this world, we could truly appreciate being kind friends. I wish you all good health and well-being.

I wish health and love to you and your families. Thank you very much

Daniel and Emdia

Figure 6: A letter written to Al-Qassam Brigades by the Israeli Hostage Danielle Aloni (Doam, 2023)

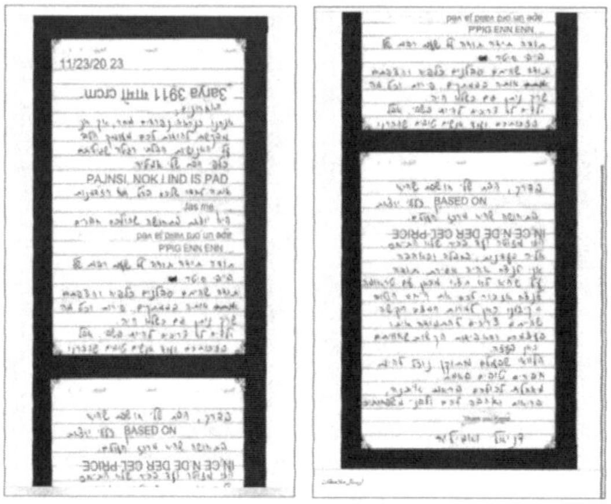

Figure 7: The controversial letter, as translated by Google Translate into English

Further evidence of this can be seen when the only Arabic phrase in the letter was the only part Google Translate was able to accurately translate, aside from the out-of-context phrase 'based on'. As can be seen in Figure 8, the Arabic phrase 'شكرا كثير' meaning 'thank you very much' was translated into 'thank you'.

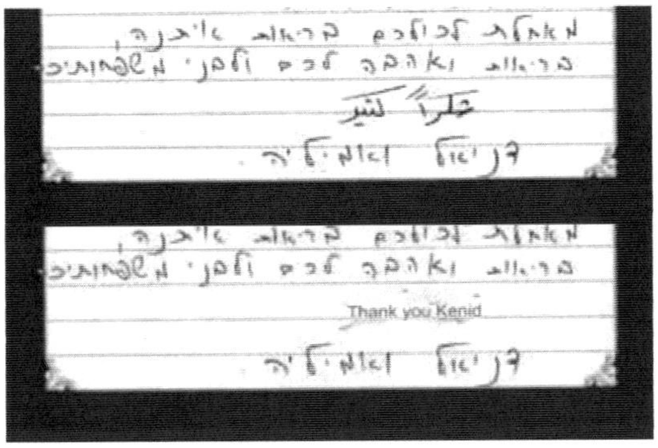

Figure 8: The Arabic phrase in the letter was the only accurate part translated into English by Google Translate

5 Conclusion

Although AI and MT are improving significantly, they still have limitations that make them unreliable, and even too risky to trust at times. This paper highlighted some of these limitations in the political field, specifically during conflicts and high-stakes contexts. Such limitations appeared in translating cultural references and cursive handwriting, as well as the inability to avoid errors at critical times and a susceptibility to bias and intervention. These limitations should serve as evidence that human translators are indispensable, especially in situations where translation tools are unable to fully and accurately translate the content, and that relying on translation tools is a risk that should not be taken in conflicts and high-stakes contexts. There is a reason such tools require post-editing carried out by humans, especially when errors in translation can cause unrepairable damage.

It would be best, moving forward, to balance the two; translation technologies with all their abilities to translate large amount of text at speed, and human translators with all their intelligence and comprehension abilities. Additionally, the limitations of such tools and best ways to use them need to be clarified for their users. It is essential to raise public awareness regarding their propensity for error and bias, especially in light of the evolving state of AI.

Continued research that builds upon the limitations outlined in this study is essential for advancing MT and AI. These technologies must draw on such findings to refine their performance and ensure more accurate and appropriate outputs. More research is also needed to understand the nature of the risks imposed when such tools are used during conflicts and high-stakes contexts. Lastly, further research is warranted not only on the limitations and failures of MT and AI, but also on issues related to fact-checking and the potential for data manipulation.

References

Lars Ahrenberg. 2017. Comparing machine translation and human translation: A case study. In RANLP 2017: The First Workshop on Human-Informed Translation and Interpreting Technology (HiT-IT) pages 21–28, Shoumen, Bulgaria, Association for Computational Linguistics.

M. Shalehuddin Al-Ayubi. 2017. "Utilization of Google Translation as a Learning Medium at Foreign News Text Translation." Jurnal Teknodik 21, no. 2: 155–66.

Noha Alowedi and Arif Ahmed Mohammed Hassan Al-Ahdal. 2023. Artificial intelligence based Arabic-to-English machine versus human translation of poetry: An analytical study of outcomes. Journal of Namibian Studies. 33:1523–1538. https://doi.org/10.59670/jns.v33i.800

Tahseen Ali Hussein Al-Romany and Maryam Jawad Kadhim. 2024. Artificial intelligence impact on human translation: Legal texts as a case study. International Journal of Linguistics, Literature and Translation, 7:89–95. http://dx.doi.org/10.32996/ijllt.2024.7.5.11.

عربي بوست (@arabic_post). 2023, November 25. [Tweet.] X, https://x.com/arabic_post/status/1728181053016400064?s=46&t=79GyHEQ-RfwCSZenFQJ7iQ. (Accessed January 6, 2025).

Nezih Altay and Melissa Labonte. 2014. "Challenges in Humanitarian Information Management and Exchange: Evidence from Haiti." Disasters 38 (1): 50–72.

Khalil Asslan (@KhalilAsslan). 2023, December 5. [Tweet.] X.

https://x.com/khalilasslan/status/1731960447518011457. (Accessed August 11, 2024).

Mona Baker. 2006. Translation and Conflict: A Narrative Account. 1st ed. London: Routledge. https://doi.org/10.4324/9780203099919.

Mona Baker. 2010. "Interpreters and Translators in the War Zone: Narrated and Narrators." The Translator 16, no. 2: 197–222.

Manal Barbar, (@ManalBarbar). 2024, November 18. [Tweet.] X. https://x.com/ManalBarbar/status/1752328854385897760. (Accessed August 11, 2024).

Itamar Ben-Gvir, (@itamarbengvir). 2023, December 5. [Tweet.] X. https://x.com/itamarbengvir/status/1731927825991581728. (Accessed August 11, 2024).

Toni Bernhart and Sandra Richter. 2021. Frühe digitale Poesie. Informatik Spektrum, 44:11–18. https://doi.org/10.1007/s00287-021-01329-z.

Erik Brynjolfsson, Tom Mitchell, and Daniel Rock. 2018. What can machines learn, and what does it mean for occupations and the economy? In AEA Papers and Proceedings 108: 43–47. http://dx.doi.org/10.1257/PANDP.20181019.

Marta Costa-jussà, Miriea Farrús, and Jordi Serrano Pons. 2012. Machine translation in medicine: A quality analysis of statistical machine translation in the medical domain. Paper presented at: Advanced Research in Scientific Areas; 2012 Dec 3–7; Slovakia.

Doam (@doamuslims). 2023, November 27. [Tweet.] X. https://x.com/doamuslims/status/1729209592352067974. (Accessed August 11, 2024).

Cameron Edmond. 2019. Poetics of the machine: Machine writing and the AI literature frontier [Doctoral Thesis, Macquarie University]. http://hdl.handle.net/1959.14/1270851.

Hadis Ghasemi and Mahmood Hashemian. 2016. "A Comparative Study of Google Translate Translations: An Error Analysis of English-to-Persian and Persian-to-English Translations." English Language Teaching 9, no. 3: 13–22. https://doi.org/10.5539/elt.v9n3p13.

Hassan Ali Hebresha and Mohd Jafre Ab Aziz. 2013. "Classical Arabic English Machine Translation Using Rule-based Approach." Journal of Applied Sciences 13, no. 1: 79–86. https://doi.org/10.3923/jas.2013.79.86.

Israel Defense Forces (@IDF). 2023, November 13. [Tweet.] X. https://x.com/idf/status/1724169252054188276. (Accessed August 11, 2024).

Henry W. Fischer. 1998. Response to Disaster: Fact Versus Fiction and Its Perpetuation. The Sociology of Disaster. New York, NY and Oxford: University Press of America.

Carol Kit and Timothy Wong. 2008. "Comparative Evaluation of Online Machine Translation Systems with Legal Texts." Law Library Journal 100, no. 2: 299–321.

André Lefevere and Susan Bassnett. 2001. "Introduction: Where Are We in Translation Studies?" In Constructing Cultures: Essays on Literary Translation, edited by Susan Bassnett and André Lefevere, 1–11. Shanghai: Shanghai Foreign Language Education Press.

Hong Li, Arthur C. Graesser, and Zhixiong Cai. 2014. "Comparison of Google Translation with Human Translation." Paper presented at the Twenty-Seventh International Florida Artificial Intelligence Research Society Conference, USA.

Qi Li. 2024. Bridging languages: The potential and limitations of AI in literary translation—a case study of the English translation of 'A Pair of Peacocks Southeast Fly'. Advances in Humanities Research, 8:1–7.

Spyros Makridakis. 2017. The forthcoming artificial intelligence (AI) revolution: Its impact on society and firms. Futures, 90:46–60. https://doi.org/10.1016/j.futures.2017.03.006.

Seeger, Matthew W. 2006. "Best Practices in Crisis Communication: An Expert Panel Process." Journal of Applied Communication Research 34 (3): 232–244.

Ahmed Moneus and Yousef Sahari. 2024. Artificial intelligence and human translation: A contrastive study based on legal texts. Heliyon. 10:e28106. 10.1016/j.heliyon.2024.e28106.

Joss Moorkens. 2018. Under the microscope: The translation industry and machine translation. Translation Spaces, 7:20–30.

Benjamin Netanyahu. (@netanyahu). 2023, November 23. [Tweet.] X. https://x.com/netanyahu/status/1729935192716980400. (Accessed August 11, 2024).

Peter Newmark. 1989. "Introductory Survey." In The Translator's Handbook, 2nd ed., edited by Catriona Picken, 1–26. London: ASLIB.

Jerry Palmer. 2007. "Interpreting and Translation for Western Media in Iraq." In Translating and Interpreting Conflict, edited by Myriam Salama-Carr, 13–28. Amsterdam and New York: Rodopi.

Ming Qian and Davis Qian. 2020. Defining a human-machine teaming model for AI-powered human-centered machine translation agent by learning from human-human group discussion: Dialog categories and dialog moves. In Artificial Intelligence in HCI, pages 70–81. https://doi.org/10.1007/978-3-030-50334-5_5.

Aditya Ramesh, Prafulla Dhariwal, Alex Nichol, Casey Chu and Mark Chen. (2022). Hierarchical Text-Conditional Image Generation with CLIP Latents. 10.48550/arXiv.2204.06125.

Milena Škobo and Vedran Petričević. 2023. Navigating the challenges and opportunities of literary translation in the age of AI: Striking a balance between human expertise and machine power. DHS, 2:317–336. https://doi.org/10.51558/2490-3647.2023.8.2.317

Breena Taira, Vanessa Kreger, Aristides Orue, and Lisa C. Diamond. 2021. A pragmatic assessment of Google Translate for emergency department instructions. Journal of General Internal Medicine 36:3361–65. https://doi.org/10.1007/s11606-021-06666-z.

Jun Tang. 2007. "Encounters with Cross-cultural Conflicts in Translation." In Translating and Interpreting Conflict, edited by Myriam Salama-Carr, 135–147. Amsterdam and New York: Rodopi.

Laura Tomasello. 2019. Neural machine translation and artificial intelligence: What is left for the human translator? [Doctoral Thesis, Universita degli Studi di Padova], http://tesi.cab.unipd.it/62159/1/Laura_Tomasello_2019.pd.

Maria Tymoczko and Edwin Gentzler, (eds.). 2002. Translation and Power. Boston: University of Massachusetts Press.

Dominika Uličná. 2023. Accuracy of machine translation of selected medical discourse: Expert to patient oriented discourse. [Bachelor's Thesis, University of Presov, Faculty of Arts.] doi:10.13140/RG.2.2.31011.84008.

Lawrence Venuti. 1998. The Scandals of Translation: Towards an Ethics of Difference. London and New York: Routledge, 1998.

Lucas Nunes Vieira, Minako O'Hagan, and Carol O'Sullivan. 2020. Understanding the societal impacts of machine translation: A critical review of the literature on medical and legal use cases. Information, Communication & Society, 24:1515–32. doi:10.1080/1369118X.2020.1776370.

Abdelali Zaid and Hanane Bennoudi. 2023. AI vs. human translators: Navigating the complex world of religious texts and cultural sensitivity. International Journal of Linguistics, Literature and Translation, 6:173–182.
https://doi.org/10.32996/ijllt.2023.6.11.21.

Mohammad Zubair, (@zoo_bear). 2023, November 12. [Tweet.] X. https://x.com/zoo_bear/status/172362034911420049 9?s=46&t=79GyHEQ-RfwCSZenFQJ7iQ. (Accessed January 6, 2025).

Speech-to-Speech Translation Pipelines for Conversations in Low-Resource Languages

Andrei Popescu-Belis[1,3], Alexis Allemann[1], Teo Ferrari[1], Gopal Krishnamani[2]

[1]HEIG-VD / HES-SO, 1401 Yverdon-les-Bains, Switzerland
[2]Bhaasha Sàrl, 1400 Yverdon-les-Bains, Switzerland
[3]EPFL, 1015 Lausanne, Switzerland
Correspondence: andrei.popescu-belis@heig-vd.ch

Abstract

The popularity of automatic speech-to-speech translation for human conversations is growing, but the quality varies significantly depending on the language pair. In a context of community interpreting for low-resource languages, namely Turkish and Pashto to/from French, we collected fine-tuning and testing data, and compared systems using several automatic metrics (BLEU, COMET, and BLASER) and human assessments. The pipelines included automatic speech recognition, machine translation, and speech synthesis, with local models and cloud-based commercial ones. Some components have been fine-tuned on our data. We evaluated over 60 pipelines and determined the best one for each direction. We also found that the ranks of components are generally independent of the rest of the pipeline.

1 Introduction

One of the most challenging applications of spoken language translation is real-time interpreting of human conversations. We consider the application to community interpreting, for ethnic minorities who need assistance to access services across a language barrier, e.g., for healthcare, asylum rights, or education. The case study presented here involves Bhaasha, a company that provides services for community interpreting, and the Data Science group of HEIG-VD, an academic partner. Due to a growing demand, the company aims to clarify whether a system for automated interpreting meets certain quality thresholds and can be offered when human interpreters are not available. While several online offers exist, these systems do not include the desired language pairs, or their quality is clearly insufficient, and privacy is not guaranteed.

We present the methods and the results of a joint project aimed at determining the best speech-to-speech translation pipeline made from off-the-shelf components, cloud-based services, or fine-tuned models, for two language pairs that are in high demand, but are insufficiently supported by existing systems: French-Turkish and French-Pashto. The paper is organized as follows. In Section 3, we present methods for collecting and annotating data representative of the intended context of use. In Section 4, we outline the design of translation pipelines, whose components can be smoothly interchanged. In Section 5, we evaluate all combinations of four ASR, three MT, and two TTS components, either local or cloud-based, also including two fine-tuned components and a speech-to-text translation one. We present evaluation scores from automatic metrics and determine the best combination of components per direction. We also show that the ranking of components is generally independent of the other modules in a pipeline. Finally, we present human scores over a subset of the data, showing that accuracy, fluency and intonation of the best pipelines are considered as 'good' or 'very good'.

2 State of the Art

Methods for speech-to-*text* translation (e.g. for subtitling) have been the subject of many recent publications, unlike methods for speech-to-*speech* translation, as the speech synthesis part is difficult to train. Moreover, spoken translation has been studied more often for monologues than for conversations. The three necessary components are automatic speech recognition (ASR, or speech-to-text, STT), machine translation (MT), and speech synthesis (or text-to-speech, TTS).

Research interests, however, have shifted from loosely coupled cascades of ASR and MT, to tighter coupling, and finally to recent end-to-end models

Proceedings of Machine Translation Summit XX Volume 2, pages 18–27, June 23-27, 2025

(Sperber and Paulik, 2020; Xu et al., 2023). For instance, an approach to multilingual speech-to-text translation through efficient transfer learning from a pretrained speech encoder (wav2vec) and text decoder (BERT), is proposed by Li et al. (2021). Dong et al. (2021) propose a Listen, Understand and Translate (LUT) approach to train end-to-end speech-to-text translation.

Bentivogli et al. (2021) compare the two paradigms – cascaded vs. end-to-end – and claim that the gap between them is almost closed. However, for low-resource languages, end-to-end systems are difficult to train due to the lack of data, while cascaded systems can use components trained with simpler tasks. Alternatively, massively multilingual systems such as Whisper (Radford et al., 2022) for ASR + MT claim that low-resource languages are improved thanks to higher-resource similar languages. For instance, cascaded approaches can take advantage of optimized low-resource MT components (Atrio and Popescu-Belis, 2022).

The IWSLT 2022, 2023 and 2024 evaluation campaigns (Anastasopoulos et al., 2022; Agarwal et al., 2023; Ahmad et al., 2024) featured various shared tasks, including speech-to-text and speech-to-speech translation for low-resource languages. A typical low-resource system presented at IWSLT 2023 is the Marathi to Hindi submission by Kesiraju et al. (2023a), including an end-to-end and a cascaded system. Various techniques for improving low-resource speech-to-text translation, in particular with initialization from a multilingual ASR system, have been proposed (Khosravani et al., 2021; Fu et al., 2023; Kesiraju et al., 2023b).

Large corpora exist for well-resourced language pairs, but not for the low-resource ones that we target. While datasets of recorded speech can be more easily found, datasets with transcriptions and translations are scarce or inexistent. The MuST-C (Di Gangi et al., 2019) and Multilingual TEDx corpora include speech and translation in English and 8 other European languages, but not Turkish or Pastho. CoVoST-2 (Wang et al., 2021) covers speech translation from several languages to/from English and includes Turkish. This resource was used to test the Whisper ASR + MT used here.

Recent developments of generative AI and large language models have enabled significant progress in speech translation and synthesis, but low-resource languages are still insufficiently supported. For instance, several companies advertise multilingual speech translation systems on the Web, as apps for smartphones, or as cloud-based services, mostly for for a few well-resourced languages. For instance, one of the major players, Google, offers the three components individually via APIs, but also bundles them into a pipeline that often appears in informal tests as one of the best translation apps for several language pairs. Other commercial offers include DeepL, Microsoft's Bing Translator, iTranslate, SayHi, Translate Now, Yandex, or Talking Translator. Many of the related apps have received reviews from their users, which provide a form of evaluation, although ratings for specific language pairs are rarely found. In our tests, we observed that these solutions are not ready for the low-resource languages studied here, nor for use in the setting of community interpreting.

3 Data Gathering and Formatting

To the best of our knowledge, there are no datasets with parallel conversational speech (i.e. interpreted in both directions) for Turkish-French and Pashto-French (tr-fr, ps-fr). Therefore, we collected new data which suits our project's needs.

The central idea of our parallel dataset is to include complete dialogues in situations encountered by Bhaasha's community interpreters. For each utterance, we have a reference transcript and an audio recording, in each of the three languages of the project: an excerpt is shown in Table 1. For each utterance, in each language, the dataset contains indexing information (dialogue codename, utterance number, and language), the transcript of the utterance, the name of the audio file with the utterance (similarly indexed), and whether it is used in the fine-tuning or the testing subsets. With this structure, the dataset can be used to fine-tune or to test speech translation pipelines in any translation direction.

3.1 Data Sources

Collecting such a dataset requires an abstraction over the complex reality of community interpreting, which involves three speakers: the two persons between whom the dialogue takes place, and the interpreter, who interprets consecutively the speech in both directions. However, it appeared early in the project that real dialogues mediated by interpreters *could not be recorded due to privacy reasons.*

Therefore, for most of our data, we settled on the following protocol. We gathered or wrote dialogues

dial.	utt.	lang	audio	transcription
B001	1	fr	B001-1-fr.wav	Bonjour Monsieur, qu’est-ce qui vous amène ?
B001	1	ps	B001-1-ps.wav	سلام ښاغلی، تاسو دلته څنګه راغلي یاست؟
B001	1	tr	B001-1-tr.wav	Merhabalar beyefendi, bugün neden buradasınız?
B001	2	fr	B001-2-fr.wav	J’ai mal à la tête, très mal depuis déjà plus de deux semaines.
B001	2	ps	B001-2-ps.wav	زه له دوو اونو راهیسې ډر بد سر درد لرم
B001	2	tr	B001-2-tr.wav	2 haftadan fazla başım ağrıyor.
B001	3	fr	B001-3-fr.wav	Qu’est-ce que vous prenez pour calmer ces douleurs ?
B001	3	ps	B001-3-ps.wav	تاسو د دې درد څخه د خلاصون لپاره څه اخلي؟
B001	3	tr	B001-3-tr.wav	Ağrılar geçsin diye ne alıyorsunuz?

Table 1: Three utterances from our dataset: each one is available in three languages and two modalities.

similar to those handled by Bhaasha interpreters, writing them in French, in some cases with the help of the GPT-4 LLM. Then, we asked interpreters from Bhaasha to write translations of the entire dialogues into Turkish or Pachto, by postediting automatic translations from the Google or Microsoft online systems. Finally, we recorded interpreters reading aloud these translations, and added French audios read by different native speakers, manually segmenting all audios into utterances.

This text-centric protocol appeared to be much more efficient than an audio-based one in which interpreters listen to a source sentence (or read a sentence) and then utter the spoken translation in the target language, which is recorded and then transcribed. This solution was very demanding for interpreters, and was not entirely natural as it required interpreting both dialogue participants in the same direction. Enacting original new spoken dialogues appeared also to have too high transcription and translation costs. The current dialogues, although more fluent than real ones, are the best substitute that could be found within the frame of our project.

The sources of the dialogues included in our project data are the following ones. Each dialogue is identified by a letter coding the generation method and an index number. Each separate sentence (utterance) appears on one line, and speaker turns can be made of one or more lines (as indicated in the metadata, see 3.2).

- ‘G’ series (G001–G013, 630 lines): dialogues generated with GPT-4.[1] This was the quickest technique and provided about half of our data. Given a precise prompt in French,[2] GPT-4 generated a realistic in-domain dialogue of the desired size and style, which was improved to satisfactory levels with minimal human edits from the experimenters.
- ‘C’ series (C001–C004, 498 lines): excerpts from the CoVoST-2 corpus (Wang et al., 2021), Turkish-English parallel subset, mostly with spoken news (admittedly, not dialogues). We translated the data into French by post-editing MT output, and added French audio from native speakers.
- ‘B’ series (B001–B006, 180 lines): dialogues created as French text by interpreters from Bhaasha, in the spirit of those that they encounter as community interpreters.
- ‘P’ series (P001–P004, 110 lines): four samples of learners’ material in French, corresponding to our style and topics.

	Utterances		**Durations**		
	train	**test**	**sec.**	**min.**	**words**
fr	722	723	4,138	69	11,986
tr	722	723	4,985	83	8,295
ps	0	400	1,741	29	3,717
total	3,290		10,864	181	23,998

Table 2: Data used for fine-tuning and testing.

As summarized in Table 2, our dataset includes 28 dialogues with 1,445 utterances (lines). All utterances are available in French and Turkish, with

[1]https://chat.openai.com

[2]Prompts describe in detail a situation, matching closely those encountered by interpreters, e.g., “Write a dialogue at the welfare office with this topic: a young man has found a part-time job (50%) and wants to know what impact this will have on his welfare. He will have a long and costly commute. Generate 30 to 40 turns.”

transcript and audio, but Pashto translation is partial, from lack of availability of Pashto interpreters. We randomly sampled 723 lines for testing and 722 for fine-tuning from the French side, and similarly from the Turkish side. We did not sample entire dialogues, to ensure better similarity between fine-tuning and testing data. For Pashto, all 400 lines were used for testing.

3.2 Exchange Format

The exchange format is kept simple, to ensure easy reuse. The dataset is contained in two text-based files and one folder with audio files:

- `dialogues.json` – metadata in JSON format, described below.
- `dataset.csv` – indexed transcripts and names of audio files, as shown in Table 1.
- `audios` – contains one audio file per utterance, named using indexes, from recordings on smartphones or laptops in silent environments (2 channels, 48 kHz, 32 bits).

As metadata, we include for each dialogue identified by its codename: long name or brief description, creation method (including prompt to GPT-4 for the G series), date of recording, and number of utterances. For each language, we indicate whether it is an original or translated version, how it was translated, and the total duration of audios. Finally, we indicate the grouping of utterances in speaker turns using their index numbers.

4 Speech-to-Speech Translation Pipelines

4.1 Components

We considered all possible combinations of the following ASR, MT and TTS components. Table 3 below provides the exact names and URLs of all of them. We evaluated ASR/MT/TTS cloud-based commercial components from Google and Microsoft, as well as the following open-weight models run locally. For ASR, we tested Whisper from OpenAI (Radford et al., 2022) in 'transcribe' mode, i.e. in the same language, and MMS from Meta (Pratap et al., 2023). For MT, we tested the multilingual NLLB-200 model with 3.3B parameters (NLLB Team et al., 2022). But for TTS, no competitive local model could be found for our languages. Moreover, we fine-tuned Whisper and NLLB-200 with 1.3B parameters on the training subset of the fr-tr data (see Table 2), resulting in the models prefixed with 'ft' below.

4.2 Architecture

We built a flexible application to support experimentation, but also real-time demonstration. Hence, the application includes a frontend and a backend, and is hosted on the Kubernetes infrastructure of the Swiss AI Center[3] with S3 MinIO storage. The dataset is managed using DVC.

The frontend of the application is developed using the React framework, while the backend is built in Python with FastAPI, providing several HTTP endpoints to enable the use of different versions of the ASR, MT, and ST modules. The frontend orchestrates the sequence of calls across the various stages of the speech-to-speech translation pipeline. These endpoints allow responses to be generated using either local models running on GPUs or remote models accessed via third-party APIs. Additionally, for every request, the backend stores copies of the audio and model outputs at each stage in a S3 bucket, which facilitates analysis and human evaluation.

A frontend interface allows human users to inspect or demonstrate the system. The interface enables on-the-fly change of components in the pipeline, depending on the desired source and target languages. A laptop with a regular microphone can be used for demos.

4.3 Evaluation Metrics

We use Word Error Rate (WER) to score ASR components, with the JiWER Python package.[4] We use four automatic metrics for MT: three of them, available from the Sacrebleu library (Post, 2018),[5] use various form of edit distance between candidate and reference translations: BLEU, ChrF, and Translation Error Rate (TER). The fourth metric, COMET (Rei et al., 2022)[6], compares source and target embeddings using a large language model (wmt22-comet-da), and is applicable to French-Turkish as well as French-Pashto. We found that there is a strong correlations between these metrics: using each system as a data point, average pairwise Pearson correlation is 0.89 for fr-tr and 0.97 for fr-ps, with four metrics. Therefore, we use below two representative and least correlated metrics, namely BLEU and COMET.

[3]https://swiss-ai-center.ch
[4]https://github.com/jitsi/jiwer
[5]https://github.com/mjpost/sacrebleu
[6]https://github.com/Unbabel/COMET

Stage	Type	Name	URL
ASR	cloud	Google STT	https://cloud.google.com/speech-to-text/v2
	cloud	Microsoft STT	https://speech.microsoft.com/portal
	local	OpenAI Whisper-large-v3	https://huggingface.co/openai/whisper-large-v3
	local	Fine-tuned Whisper	https://huggingface.co/openai/whisper-large-v3
	local	Meta MMS	https://huggingface.co/facebook/mms-1b-all
ASR+MT	*local*	*Whisper Translate*	https://huggingface.co/openai/whisper-large-v3
MT	cloud	Google MT	https://cloud.google.com/translate
	cloud	Microsoft MT	https://www.microsoft.com/en-us/translator
	local	NLLB-200 3.3B	https://huggingface.co/facebook/nllb-200-3.3B
	local	Fine-tuned NLLB (1.3B)	https://huggingface.co/facebook/nllb-200-1.3B
	local	*HelsinkiNLP*	https://huggingface.co/Helsinki-NLP
TTS	cloud	Google TTS	https://cloud.google.com/text-to-speech
	cloud	Microsoft TTS	https://speech.microsoft.com/portal
	local	*YourTTS*	https://github.com/Edresson/YourTTS

Table 3: Components used in our speech-to-speech translation pipelines (in italics, preliminary studies only).

5 Results

5.1 ASR Scores (WER)

The WER scores for the ASR components are given in Table 4 (lower is better). The rankings are consistent across French and Turkish, although the differences between systems are not. For Turkish, the fine-tuning of Whisper on our data brings a visible improvement (from 0.14 to 0.09), while the untuned Whisper performs on par with the Microsoft cloud-based service. The Google service and the Meta local model follow at some distance.

French ASR	WER
ft_whisper_transcribe	**0.04**
whisper_transcribe	0.06
microsoft_stt	0.08
google_stt	0.23
meta_mms	0.24
Turkish ASR	
ft_whisper_transcribe	**0.09**
whisper_transcribe	0.14
microsoft_stt	0.15
google_stt	0.31
meta_mms	0.40
Pashto ASR	
microsoft_stt	**0.45**
google_stt	0.89
whisper_transcribe	0.92

Table 4: WER for French, Turkish, and Pashto.

5.2 MT Scores (BLEU and COMET)

The scores of written MT for Turkish and French (both directions) for all combinations of modules, with four metrics, are shown in Table 8 in the Appendix. Similarly, the MT scores for Pashto and French are shown in Table 9. These tables indicate the best ASR+MT pipelines, with substantial agreement between metrics:

- **tr-fr:** fine-tuned Whisper (or not fine-tuned) with Google MT (or Microsoft MT).
- **fr-tr:** fine-tuned Whisper (or not fine-tuned) with Microsoft MT (or Google MT).
- **ps-fr:** Microsoft ASR with Microsft MT (or Microsoft MT).
- **fr-ps:** fine-tuned Whisper (or not fine-tuned) with Google MT.

To perform a systematic analysis of the intrinsic quality of each module and of the effects of their combinations, we propose the following approach, applied to each translation direction.

5.2.1 Turkish and French

We first present a detailed analysis of **Turkish $\rightarrow$ French** pipelines, and then summarize conclusions for the other direction, and then for Pashto and French. We organize the COMET scores in two ways. First, as shown in Table 5, pipelines are grouped by MT systems, and the groups are ranked by average COMET. Inside each group, ASR components are ranked too. We find that the ranking of ASR is the same inside the first and second best

ASR	MT	COMET	AVG
whisper	google_mt	**89.60**	87.47
ft_whisper	google_mt	89.40	
microsoft_stt	google_mt	87.87	
google_stt	google_mt	87.28	
meta_mms	google_mt	83.20	
whisper	microsoft_mt	88.42	86.04
ft_whisper	microsoft_mt	88.06	
microsoft_stt	microsoft_mt	86.64	
google_stt	microsoft_mt	86.49	
meta_mms	microsoft_mt	80.61	
whisper	ft_nllb-1.3B	86.14	83.86
ft_whisper	ft_nllb-1.3B	85.30	
microsoft_stt	ft_nllb-1.3B	84.21	
google_stt	ft_nllb-1.3B	84.21	
meta_mms	ft_nllb-1.3B	79.42	
whisper	nllb-3.3B	85.92	83.62
ft_whisper	nllb-3.3B	84.99	
microsoft_stt	nllb-3.3B	84.02	
google_stt	nllb-3.3B	83.81	
meta_mms	nllb-3.3B	79.38	

Table 5: COMET scores for Turkish-to-French speech-to-text translation, grouped by MT system, and ranked by average COMET over each group.

ASR	MT	COMET	AVG
whisper	google_mt	**89.60**	87.52
whisper	microsoft_mt	88.42	
whisper	ft_nllb-1.3B	86.14	
whisper	nllb-3.3B	85.92	
ft_whisper	google_mt	89.40	86.94
ft_whisper	microsoft_mt	88.06	
ft_whisper	ft_nllb-1.3B	85.30	
ft_whisper	nllb-3.3B	84.99	
microsoft_stt	google_mt	87.87	85.69
microsoft_stt	microsoft_mt	86.64	
microsoft_stt	ft_nllb-1.3B	84.21	
microsoft_stt	nllb-3.3B	84.02	
google_stt	google_mt	87.28	85.45
google_stt	ft_nllb-1.3B	86.49	
google_stt	microsoft_mt	84.21	
google_stt	nllb-3.3B	83.81	
meta_mms	google_mt	83.20	80.65
meta_mms	microsoft_mt	80.61	
meta_mms	ft_nllb-1.3B	79.42	
meta_mms	nllb-3.3B	79.38	

Table 6: COMET scores for Turkish-to-French speech-to-text translation, grouped by ASR system, and ranked by average BLEU over each group.

groups, which are those with Google MT and Microsoft MT (with a large difference between them). The ranking of the first two ASR systems is permuted when we move to the third and fourth groups. Therefore, the following stable ranking is found for Turkish ASR. Fine-tuning Whisper turns out to be beneficial to BLEU scores but not to COMET ones.

`Whisper` > `Fine-tuned Whisper` > `Microsoft ASR` > `Google ASR` > `Meta MMS ASR`

Second, as shown in Table 6, pipelines are grouped by ASR system, and the groups are ranked by average COMET; inside each group, MT components are ranked too. We find that the ranking of MT is almost always the following one (except in one group where the second and third ranks are permuted):

`Google MT` > `Microsoft MT` > `Fine-tuned NLLB 1.3B` > `NLLB 3.3B`

For the **French → Turkish pipelines**, a similar analysis shows that the stable ranking of ASR components in each grouping based on MT is the following one (the ranking of the last two components is reversed in half of the groups):

`Fine-tuned Whisper` > `Whisper` > `Microsoft ASR` > `Google ASR` ≈ `Meta MMS ASR`

Conversely, when grouping by ASR, fine-tuned Whisper ahead of the others in BLEU score, but the untuned Whisper is slightly ahead on COMET. They are followed by Microsoft ASR, and then at some distance by Meta MMS and Google ASR, which are quit close. When grouping by ASR, the stable ranking of MT components is the following one, with some uncertainty over the fine-tuned NLLB, and a reversal of the first two ranks with COMET:

`Microsoft MT` > `Google MT` > `Fine-tuned NLLB 1.3B` > `NLLB 3.3B`

5.2.2 Pashto and French

Similar to the above strategy, the scores for the **Pashto → French** pipelines are either grouped by MT systems to observe the rankings of ASR in each group, or grouped by ASR systems to observe the rankings of MT. The actual scores are shown in Table 9 in the Appendix. We make the following observations using COMET scores. When grouping by MT system (Google or Microsoft), the ranking of ASR is always the same: `Microsoft ASR` > `Whisper` > `Google ASR`. In terms of the actual average score per ASR, Microsoft ASR is much better than Whisper or Google ASR, which do not seem usable here. When grouping by ASR, the ranking of MT is the same for the first two ASR systems, but is reversed for the last one, likely due to the poor quality of input to MT: `Google MT` > `Microsoft MT`. In terms of average per MT, Google MT is also slightly ahead of Microsoft MT, as in the observations grouped per ASR.

Finally, for the **French → Pashto** pipelines, when grouping by MT, the rankings of ASR differ, although the best system is the Fine-tuned Whisper in both cases. For Google MT, Whisper is the second best, although it is ranked fourth when using Microsoft MT. However, given the poor quality of this last MT system, the rankings may not be reliable. In terms of average per ASR, the Fine-tuned Whisper is first, followed by Whisper and by Microsoft ASR, and then by Meta MMS and Google ASR. (As they concern French ASR, these rankings are similar to those for fr-tr.) When grouping per ASR, the ranking of MT is always the same: `Google MT` > `Microsoft MT`, with large differences between the two (8–9 COMET points).

5.3 End-to-end Scores (BLASER)

The BLASER 2.0 scores (Dale and Costa-jussà, 2024) of the speech-to-speech translation pipelines are given in Table 7. They were computed for Turkish and French, as no models are available for Pashto. We selected two representative ASR + MT pipelines: Whisper + NLLB is entirely local and not fine-tuned, while Google + Google is the commercial cloud-based offer from Google. We combined each of them with two cloud-based speech synthesis solutions, respectively from Google and Microsoft, as no local TTS was satisfactory. We computed BlaserQE and BlaserRef scores for each of the four pipelines. For each sentence, BlaserQE compares the embeddings of the *source* and of the *candidate* translation in the audio modality, while BlaserRef also considers the embedding of the *written reference* translation.

The BLASER 2.0 scores indicate that using Google TTS is *always* slightly better than Microsoft TTS. The difference between these systems for fr-tr is statistically significant at the 1% level (as measured by a t-test) with the BlaserRef metric, regardless of the ASR + MT part. As for tr-fr, the difference is significant at the 1% level (t-test) only when combined with Google ASR + MT. Moreover, the Google-only pipeline scores significantly better than both local ones.

ASR+MT	Whisper+NLLB		Google+Google	
TTS	Google	MS	Google	MS
	fr-tr systems			
WER	0.06		0.23	
BLEU	25.76		22.72	
COMET	89.37		87.49	
BlaserQE	3.07	3.02	3.06	3.01
BlaserRef	3.24	3.16	3.25	3.18
Meaning	4.43		4.27	
Correctness	4.55		4.69	
Intonation	4.55	4.55	4.50	4.57
	tr-fr systems			
WER	0.14		0.31	
BLEU	38.46		43.43	
COMET	85.92		87.26	
BlaserQE	3.18	3.16	3.28	3.26
BlaserRef	3.19	3.18	3.34	3.32

Table 7: Results of automatic evaluation with BLASER 2.0 and of human evaluation of speech-to-speech translation. For comparison purposes, we reproduce the WER, BLEU and COMET scores. MS stands for the Microsoft speech synthesis component.

5.4 Human Evaluation

As a pilot experiment, we showed 21 utterances to two human judges, native speakers of Turkish, one of them being an interpreter. We presented them with source audio and translations from French to Turkish by the same four pipelines as in the previous section. For each utterance, they were asked to grade three aspects: (1) how well the original meaning is communicated by the translation; (2) how correct is the wording of the translation; and (3) how good is the intonation of the translation. The first two aspects are akin to the traditional *adequacy* and *fluency* dimensions, but here no transcript is seen by evaluators. The third one is aimed specifically at speech synthesis. To speed up evaluation, when the ASR + MT pipeline is the same but the TTS is different, we ask evaluators to rate only once the meaning and correctness, and to rate separately the two different TTS outputs. At the top of the interface, which includes links to the audios and a drop-down menu for each rating, we briefly defined each aspect. The possible values for ratings are the following ones (originally in French):

- Meaning: (1) not at all; (2) the general idea; (3) some elements; (4) almost entirely; (5) entirely.
- Correctness: (1) very incorrect; (2) quite incorrect; (3) medium; (4) quite correct; (5) very correct.
- Intonation: (1) not understandable; (2) a little understandable; (3) medium; (4) well understandable; (5) perfectly understandable.

Average ratings for each aspect by the two judges are given in Table 7. The estimated quality by the human judge is overall between 4 and 5 for all aspects and systems. Communicated meaning is scored around 4, i.e. 'almost entirely', which is the lowest of the three scores, likely due to the combination of errors from ASR and MT. Grammatical correctness, depending almost exclusively on the ASR + MT pipeline, is also between 'quite correct' and 'very correct', here with a slight advantage to the Google components (4.9 vs. 4.5). This could be due to NLLB being a multilingual MT system, which has a lower fluency for Turkish than the Google's dedicated system. Intonation, either generated by Google TTS or by Microsoft TTS, scores close to 4.5, i.e. between 'well' and 'perfectly understandable'. There is no significant difference between the two systems, despite a slightly higher BLASER score for Google TTS. The human ratings give an idea of the calibration of automatic metrics, with BLEU scores of around 25 and COMET scores of nearly 90 being already perceived as good quality.

6 Conclusion

We have produced data and assembled numerous speech-to-speech translation pipelines, for interpreting Turkish ↔ French and Pashto ↔ French conversations. Specifically, we have produced three hours of data in settings compatible with community interpreting, and used half of it for fine-tuning two Turkish ↔ French ASR and MT systems, and the other half for evaluation. We scored over 60 pipelines of ASR, MT and TTS systems, either based on open-weight models run locally, or on commercial cloud-based services. We identified the best-performing pipeline in each direction, and found that the ranking of components was consistent, regardless of the other components of pipelines. We used four automatic evaluation metrics (WER, BLEU, COMET and BLASER), along with pilot human evaluations. The implementation of an online system with a push-to-talk interface, along with an offline version allowing batch processing, now paves the way towards usability testing of automatic interpretation solutions, which will also need to take into consideration factors such as privacy, cost, and deployment strategy.

Acknowledgments

We thank the HES-SO for support through the INTERCOM project (AGP n. 130496) and the Swiss AI Center (`https://swiss-ai-center.ch`) for support with the demonstrator in their Core Engine. We are grateful to Dr. Selin Ataç from HEIG-VD, Egeas Papadopoulos from EPFL and two interpreters from Bhaasha for their help with data collection and annotation, and to Prof. Bertil Chapuis from HEIG-VD for the initial project at the Swiss AI Center. We thank the three anonymous MT Summit reviewers for their valuable feedback.

References

Milind Agarwal et al. 2023. Findings of the IWSLT 2023 evaluation campaign. In *Proceedings of the 20th Int. Conf. on Spoken Language Translation (IWSLT 2023)*, pages 1–61, Toronto, Canada. Association for Computational Linguistics.

Ibrahim Said Ahmad et al. 2024. Findings of the IWSLT 2024 evaluation campaign. In *Proceedings of the 21st Int. Conf. on Spoken Language Translation (IWSLT 2024)*, pages 1–11, Bangkok, Thailand. Association for Computational Linguistics.

Antonios Anastasopoulos et al. 2022. Findings of the IWSLT 2022 evaluation campaign. In *Proceedings of the 19th Int. Conf. on Spoken Language Translation (IWSLT 2022)*, pages 98–157, Dublin, Ireland. Association for Computational Linguistics.

Àlex R. Atrio and Andrei Popescu-Belis. 2022. On the interaction of regularization factors in low-resource neural machine translation. In *Proceedings of the 23rd Annual Conference of the European Association for Machine Translation*, pages 111–120, Ghent, Belgium. European Association for Machine Translation.

Luisa Bentivogli, Mauro Cettolo, Marco Gaido, Alina Karakanta, Alberto Martinelli, Matteo Negri, and Marco Turchi. 2021. Cascade versus direct speech translation: Do the differences still make a difference? In *Proceedings of the 59th Annual Meeting of the Association for Computational Linguistics and the 11th International Joint Conference on Natural Language Processing (Volume 1: Long Papers)*, pages 2873–2887, Online. Association for Computational Linguistics.

David Dale and Marta R. Costa-jussà. 2024. BLASER 2.0: a metric for evaluation and quality estimation of massively multilingual speech and text translation. In *Findings of the Association for Computational Linguistics: EMNLP 2024*, pages 16075–16085, Miami, Florida, USA. Association for Computational Linguistics.

Mattia A. Di Gangi, Roldano Cattoni, Luisa Bentivogli, Matteo Negri, and Marco Turchi. 2019. MuST-C: a Multilingual Speech Translation Corpus. In *Proceedings of the 2019 Conference of the North American Chapter of the Association for Computational Linguistics: Human Language Technologies, Volume 1 (Long and Short Papers)*, pages 2012–2017, Minneapolis, Minnesota. Association for Computational Linguistics.

Qianqian Dong, Rong Ye, Mingxuan Wang, Hao Zhou, Shuang Xu, Bo Xu, and Lei Li. 2021. Listen, understand and translate: Triple supervision decouples end-to-end speech-to-text translation. In *Proceedings of the AAAI Conference on Artificial Intelligence*, pages 12749–12759.

Yu-Kuan Fu, Liang-Hsuan Tseng, Jiatong Shi, Chen-An Li, Tsu-Yuan Hsu, Shinji Watanabe, and Hung-yi Lee. 2023. Improving cascaded unsupervised speech translation with denoising back-translation. *arXiv:2305.07455*.

Santosh Kesiraju, Karel Beneš, Maksim Tikhonov, and Jan Černocký. 2023a. BUT systems for IWSLT 2023 Marathi - Hindi low resource speech translation task. In *Proceedings of the 20th International Conference on Spoken Language Translation (IWSLT 2023)*, pages 227–234, Toronto, Canada (in-person and online). Association for Computational Linguistics.

Santosh Kesiraju, Marek Sarvaš, Tomáš Pavlíček, Cécile Macaire, and Alejandro Ciuba. 2023b. Strategies for improving low resource speech to text translation relying on pre-trained ASR models. In *Proceedings of Interspeech 2023*, page 2148–2152. ISCA.

Abbas Khosravani, Philip N Garner, and Alexandros Lazaridis. 2021. Learning to translate low-resourced Swiss German dialectal speech into Standard German text. In *2021 IEEE Automatic Speech Recognition and Understanding Workshop (ASRU)*, pages 817–823. IEEE.

Xian Li, Changhan Wang, Yun Tang, Chau Tran, Yuqing Tang, Juan Pino, Alexei Baevski, Alexis Conneau, and Michael Auli. 2021. Multilingual speech translation from efficient finetuning of pretrained models. In *Proceedings of the 59th Annual Meeting of the Association for Computational Linguistics and the 11th International Joint Conference on Natural Language Processing (Volume 1: Long Papers)*, pages 827–838, Online. Association for Computational Linguistics.

NLLB Team, Marta R. Costa-jussà, et al. 2022. No language left behind: Scaling human-centered machine translation. *arXiv:2207.04672*.

Matt Post. 2018. A call for clarity in reporting BLEU scores. In *Proceedings of the Third Conference on Machine Translation: Research Papers*, pages 186–191, Brussels, Belgium. Association for Computational Linguistics.

Vineel Pratap, Andros Tjandra, Bowen Shi, Paden Tomasello, Arun Babu, Sayani Kundu, Ali Elkahky, Zhaoheng Ni, Apoorv Vyas, Maryam Fazel-Zarandi, Alexei Baevski, Yossi Adi, Xiaohui Zhang, Wei-Ning Hsu, Alexis Conneau, and Michael Auli. 2023. Scaling speech technology to 1,000+ languages. *arXiv:2305.13516*.

Alec Radford, Jong Wook Kim, Tao Xu, Greg Brockman, Christine McLeavey, and Ilya Sutskever. 2022. Robust speech recognition via large-scale weak supervision. *arXiv:2212.04356*.

Ricardo Rei, José G. C. de Souza, Duarte Alves, Chrysoula Zerva, Ana C Farinha, Taisiya Glushkova, Alon Lavie, Luisa Coheur, and André F. T. Martins. 2022. COMET-22: Unbabel-IST 2022 submission for the metrics shared task. In *Proceedings of the Seventh Conference on Machine Translation (WMT)*, pages 578–585, Abu Dhabi, United Arab Emirates (Hybrid). Association for Computational Linguistics.

Matthias Sperber and Matthias Paulik. 2020. Speech translation and the end-to-end promise: Taking stock of where we are. In *Proceedings of the 58th Annual Meeting of the Association for Computational Linguistics*, pages 7409–7421, Online. Association for Computational Linguistics.

Changhan Wang, Anne Wu, Jiatao Gu, and Juan Pino. 2021. CoVoST 2 and massively multilingual speech translation. *Proceedings of Interspeech 2021*, pages 2247–2251.

Chen Xu, Rong Ye, Qianqian Dong, Chengqi Zhao, Tom Ko, Mingxuan Wang, Tong Xiao, and Jingbo Zhu. 2023. Recent advances in direct speech-to-text translation. *arXiv 2306.11646*.

A Appendix

		tr-fr				fr-tr			
ASR	**MT**	**BLEU**	**ChrF**	**TER**	**COMET**	**BLEU**	**ChrF**	**TER**	**COMET**
ft_whisper	ft_nllb-1.3B	39.79	62.13	52.97	85.30	30.77	60.22	54.49	89.80
ft_whisper	google_mt	**55.78**	**72.88**	**37.05**	**89.40**	**36.93**	**65.19**	**50.31**	**90.95**
ft_whisper	microsoft_mt	*45.38*	*67.66*	*43.53*	*88.06*	**38.11**	**65.51**	**49.40**	*90.20*
ft_whisper	nllb-3.3B	38.06	58.95	54.54	84.99	26.99	57.63	59.98	89.24
google_stt	ft_nllb-1.3B	35.77	58.63	54.62	85.30	22.38	54.37	62.61	87.10
google_stt	google_mt	43.43	66.49	46.32	87.28	22.72	58.69	62.12	87.49
google_stt	microsoft_mt	37.14	63.37	51.04	86.49	26.24	60.55	60.98	88.26
google_stt	nllb-3.3B	34.65	55.96	57.39	83.81	20.06	53.33	65.61	87.24
microsoft_stt	ft_nllb-1.3B	38.46	59.88	54.82	84.21	27.45	57.65	57.95	88.79
microsoft_stt	google_mt	*51.19*	*69.31*	*40.74*	87.87	32.98	62.92	53.77	90.07
microsoft_stt	microsoft_mt	42.67	65.03	47.43	86.64	*34.47*	62.75	53.37	89.37
microsoft_stt	nllb-3.3B	36.48	57.72	55.78	84.02	24.81	55.71	62.66	88.62
meta_mms	ft_nllb-1.3B	32.70	55.93	59.08	79.42	24.88	56.14	59.86	86.81
meta_mms	google_mt	41.92	65.07	49.33	83.20	23.41	59.35	61.41	86.94
meta_mms	microsoft_mt	34.26	60.11	56.54	80.61	28.02	60.42	60.55	87.29
meta_mms	nllb-3.3B	31.15	53.55	61.14	79.38	20.00	53.53	65.78	86.40
whisper	ft_nllb-1.3B	40.16	62.15	52.36	86.14	28.64	58.95	56.03	89.62
whisper	google_mt	**54.27**	**71.57**	**37.52**	**89.60**	34.27	*63.96*	*52.46*	**90.93**
whisper	microsoft_mt	44.97	67.07	44.67	*88.42*	*36.02*	*64.02*	*51.43*	*90.48*
whisper	nllb-3.3B	38.46	59.54	53.69	85.92	25.76	56.65	61.41	89.37

Table 8: MT scores of all tested combinations of modules for Turkish and French (both directions). The two best scores in each column are in **bold** and the next two in *italics*. The pipelines are ordered alphabetically by name of ASR and then of MT.

		ps-fr				fr-ps			
ASR	**MT**	**BLEU**	**ChrF**	**TER**	**COMET**	**BLEU**	**ChrF**	**TER**	**COMET**
ft_whisper	google_mt	-	-	-	-	**64.22**	**76.06**	**29.78**	**87.03**
ft_whisper	microsoft_mt	-	-	-	-	20.49	43.92	69.42	76.69
google_stt	google_mt	4.23	18.38	88.81	54.02	44.16	63.36	42.97	82.21
google_stt	microsoft_mt	6.61	20.69	87.89	54.26	19.61	41.97	72.91	74.30
meta_mms	google_mt	-	-	-	-	42.17	61.40	44.77	81.56
meta_mms	microsoft_mt	-	-	-	-	18.67	40.70	73.16	73.20
microsoft_stt	google_mt	**25.96**	**47.43**	**64.43**	**77.50**	56.37	70.51	36.16	84.30
microsoft_stt	microsoft_mt	*21.36*	*42.87*	*70.84*	*75.13*	19.67	42.83	70.06	75.66
whisper	google_mt	9.11	27.85	90.45	57.21	*56.87*	*71.81*	*35.23*	*85.82*
whisper	microsoft_mt	8.39	27.07	91.60	55.09	19.44	43.27	70.35	76.22

Table 9: MT scores of all tested combinations of modules for Pashto and French (both directions). The best score in each column is in **bold** and the second one in *italics*. The pipelines are ordered alphabetically by name of ASR and then of MT. The ASR system from Meta does not support Pashto, and we did not have enough data to fine-tune Whisper for Pashto.

Arabizi *vs* LLMs: Can the Genie Understand the Language of Aladdin?

Perla Al Almaoui
Faculté de traduction et d'interprétation
Université de Genève
almaoui.perla@outlook.com

Pierrette Bouillon
Faculté de traduction et d'interprétation
Université de Genève
pierrette.bouillon@unige.ch

Simon Hengchen
Faculté de traduction et d'interprétation & iguanodon.ai
Université de Genève
simon.hengchen@unige.ch

Abstract

In this era of rapid technological advancements, communication continues to evolve as new linguistic phenomena emerge. Among these is Arabizi, a hybrid form of Arabic that incorporates Latin characters and numbers to represent the spoken dialects of Arab communities. Arabizi is widely used on social media and allows people to communicate in an informal and dynamic way, but it poses significant challenges for machine translation due to its lack of formal structure and deeply embedded cultural nuances. This case study arises from a growing need to translate Arabizi for gisting purposes. It evaluates the capacity of different LLMs to decode and translate Arabizi, focusing on multiple Arabic dialects that have rarely been studied up until now. Using a combination of human evaluators and automatic metrics, this research project investigates the models' performance in translating Arabizi into both Modern Standard Arabic and English. Key questions explored include which dialects are translated most effectively and whether translations into English surpass those into Arabic.

1 Introduction

Although there are approximately 420 million Arabic speakers worldwide, an intriguing linguistic paradox emerges: Modern Standard Arabic (MSA), the standardized form of the language, is the mother tongue of none. Instead, Arabs communicate through their regional dialects, which are vibrant linguistic hybrids influenced by Arabic and the historical languages of each region. These dialects have been honed by geographic, cultural, and historical factors, and can vary significantly even within a single country, resulting in a mosaic of over 60 distinct varieties. Arabizi (a fusion of "Arabic" and Englizi, the Arabic word for English) is an informal, non-standard writing system that emerged in the 1990s when Arabic keyboards were not widely available. It uses Latin characters and numbers, combining both transliteration and transcription mappings. Primarily used in online communication—such as short messages and comments on social media—Arabizi varies significantly across dialects and even within the same dialect (Harrat et al., 2019). For instance, the transcription of the following sentence in MSA أريد أن أكلّمك بموضوع (I want to talk to you about something) in Arabizi can be "badde e7kik bi mawdu3" in Levantine Arabic, or "rani hab nahdar m3ak f wahd sujet" in Algerian Arabic.

The idea of romanizing the Arabic language is not a new concept, as there have already been several attempts to do so over the last century. However, these efforts largely failed, as they were perceived as colonialist initiatives aimed at suppressing cultural and religious identity. More recently, the International Organization for Standardization (ISO) introduced two norms, ISO 233 in 1984 and ISO 233-2 in 1993, to standardize the romanization of Arabic. These standards aimed to facilitate the international exchange of information. Nevertheless, their adoption remained limited due to their impracticality, with usage restricted primarily to official contexts (Al Almaoui, 2024).

Conversely, Arabizi has become the dominant written form of communication among Arabic speakers in informal settings. Its rise reflects a crucial sociolinguistic reality: while MSA remains the language reserved for academic, religious, and formal settings, it is often perceived as inaccessible or overly formal for daily use. Arabizi, by contrast, offers a dynamic and flexible medium for self-expression that aligns with the fluidity of Arabic dialects (Allehaiby, 2013; Yushmanov, 1961).

Despite its widespread use across digital platforms, and the recent focus on informal language

Proceedings of Machine Translation Summit XX Volume 2, pages 28–41, June 23-27, 2025

and low-resource languages, Arabizi remains an unexplored area in natural language processing (NLP). It poses particular challenges due to its colloquial nature, variation across dialects and lack of standardization, as well as the scarcity of digital resources. In NLP, research on Arabizi has mainly focused on transliteration into Arabic (deromanization) at the character or word level, using different approaches (Guellil et al., 2017; Shazal et al., 2020), and on the creation of a parallel annotated corpus of SMS and chat messages written in Arabizi and their corresponding Arabic script transliterations by (Bies et al., 2014). Some studies explore interlinguistic machine translation (MT) techniques to and from Arabizi, employing various architectures and pipelines, mainly between English and Egyptian dialects (see Harrat et al. (2019) for a summary up until 2017). While some recent datasets for low resource language translation include romanization, they are not specifically focused on Arabizi. Flores benchmark (Goyal et al., 2022), for example, is limited to the romanized transcription of MSA or Arabic dialects in Arabic scripts. The TerjamaBench dataset (Momayiz et al., 2024) is an exception and includes entries in Darija, the Moroccan Arabic dialect, written in both Latin alphabet (Arabizi) and Arabic script, and their corresponding English translations.

Since there is a growing need to translate Arabizi into resource-rich languages on social media and other digital platforms, we conducted a case study to evaluate the feasibility of using large language models (LLMs) for out-of-the-box machine translation. The project began when the language technology company iguanodon.ai received a request from a client who wanted to know if short Arabizi texts could be translated for gisting purposes. The study involves a collaboration between the start-up and a professional translator with previous experience in Arabizi. Our contribution includes AladdinBench, an authentic dataset in Arabizi for three dialects publicly available on huggingface[1] and a comparative evaluation of five LLMs using different prompting strategies.

To our knowledge, this is the first study that has explored the direct translation from different dialects in Arabizi to MSA or English without prior deromanization.

The rest of this paper is organized as follows. We describe the data production methodology and resulting dataset in Section 2, followed by the experimental setup in Section 3 and the results in Section 4. Finally, discussion of results and the limitations of this study are presented in Section 5 and Section 6.

2 Data Collection and Dataset

2.1 Dialects

We decided to focus on the translation of three Arabic dialects from three distinct countries—Lebanon, Egypt, and Algeria—into two target languages: MSA, a less-resourced language, and English. These three countries were selected because their dialects represent distinct linguistic varieties. The Lebanese dialect aligns with the Levantine group and the Algerian dialect with the Maghrebi group, while the Egyptian dialect is exceptionally prominent due to its widespread use and cultural influence (Ayoubi, 2022).

The Lebanese dialect reflects a rich history and various cultural influences. Ancient languages such as Aramaic and Syriac, once dominant in northern Lebanon, had a notable impact on the dialect, particularly when it comes to phonological features like the use of silent vowels. Other regions, closer to major coastal cities, feature dialects more aligned with Classical Arabic, with fewer phonological deviations. Lebanon's Ottoman past also shaped its linguistic landscape, with Turkish loanwords becoming integral to Lebanese lexicon after four centuries of Ottoman rule (Iskandar, 2022; Al Almaoui, 2024).

Egyptian Arabic evolved through layers of historical migrations, demographic shifts, and ancient linguistic roots. It was heavily influenced by Coptic, the language of ancient Egypt, and later by Arabic after the Islamic conquest in the 7th century. Over time, Egyptian Arabic absorbed linguistic elements from Greek, Turkish, Italian, French, and English during various periods of occupation and cultural exchange. Regional variations within Egypt further enrich its linguistic diversity: northern regions, including the Delta and Cairo, feature subtle dialectal differences, while Upper Egypt's Sa'idi Arabic retains more conservative features. Additionally, Bedouin communities in the Western Desert speak Arabic varieties that are distinct from urban Egyptian Arabic (Souag, 2009; Magidow, 2021).

Algerian Arabic is a product of extensive histor-

[1] https://huggingface.co/datasets/palmaoui/AladdinBench

ical and cultural interactions. Indigenous Berber languages, particularly Tamazight, form its linguistic foundation, while successive occupations introduced other influences. The Roman era brought Latin, especially in administration and religion; the influence of this language was then further reinforced by Christian scholars such as Saint Augustine. The Arab conquest in the 7th century made Arabic the language of faith and the elite. Tamazight continued to be used in day-to-day life. Subsequent occupations by the Spanish, the Ottomans, and the French contributed lexical and structural elements to the dialect. French, in particular, had a profound impact during colonial rule, shaping Algeria's modern plurilingual society. Algerian Arabic is marked by significant regional variation. Western regions display a strong Spanish influence, while central areas, including Algiers, are heavily influenced by French. Eastern regions, such as Constantine, retain more Classical Arabic features. Southern regions, including the Sahara, exhibit notable Berber linguistic characteristics, reflecting the enduring presence of Berber-speaking populations (Saadane and Habash, 2015; Chami, 2009).

2.2 Participants

Thirty-one participants were recruited for the study through LinkedIn and targeted recruitment messages, with at least four participants per sub-dialect to ensure balanced representation. All participants were native Arabic speakers who represent the specific regional varieties outlined in the previous section. Lebanese participants were selected from both southern and northern regions of Lebanon. Similarly, Algerian participants were drawn from Algiers, the capital, and Constantine to reflect distinct linguistic traits within the country. For Egypt, participants were recruited from Cairo in the north and Luxor in the south.

Participants were asked to share WhatsApp conversations they had engaged in with peers of a similar age group (20–35 years) and from the same regions as them. These conversations revolved around a range of everyday topics, in order to reflect natural and spontaneous interactions. The focus on this age demographic provided a degree of consistency in communication styles, as participants shared a common digital literacy and texting culture.

All participants, including both recruits and their peers, signed consent forms explicitly detailing the use and processing of their data in accordance with Swiss law. After the corpus was collected, it was manually anonymized to ensure privacy, and all real names were removed and substituted with fictitious ones where necessary. Subsequently, a professional Arabic-speaking translator translated the corpus into MSA and English, with these translations serving as reference texts for automatic metrics. The translation into Arabic represents an intralingual transformation from a dialectal and informal variety of Arabic to a formal and standardized form.

Table 1 presents the collected corpora, including the number of segments and tokens, the average number of tokens per sentence and the percentage of foreign and mixed words (code-mixing). Mixed words are created by combining roots from one language with prefixes, suffixes, or morphological patterns from another language, reflecting linguistic creativity and contact-induced change.

3 Experimental Setup

We carried out a systematic evaluation of translation quality using an automated protocol. For each dialect, we created a combination of parameters defined as follows:

- target language ∈ [EN, MSA]
- prompt_language ∈ [EN, MSA]
- prompt_strategy ∈ [no-shot, one-shot, two-shot]
- prompt_variation ∈ [Lebanon, Egypt, Algeria][2]
- model ∈ [GPT-4o, Llama 3, Claude, Gemini, Gemma, Mistral, Jais].

All models were prompted with a temperature of 0.5. A discussion of the chosen models and prompts is available in 3.1 and in 3.2. Evaluation metrics are presented in 3.3. Our code is available.[3]

3.1 Models

The models used in the experiments are all decoder-only transformer (Radford et al., 2018) models generally called "generative LLMs". We used a range of instruction-tuned LLMs of different parameter sizes (from 27B for Gemma to at least 70B for Llama3, while proprietary models are expected to be much larger) to cover various models, from open weights to proprietary, general purpose or, in the case of Jais, ones that specifically target the English-Arabic pair (Sengupta et al., 2023).

In this paper, "Llama" refers `Llama 3.3 70B-Instruct` (Dubey et al., 2024), "GPT-4o" (OpenAI, 2024) is `gpt-4o-2024-08-06`,[4]

[2]More on this in Subsection 3.2.
[3]https://github.com/iguanodon-ai/ArabizivsLLMs
[4]https://arxiv.org/pdf/2203.02155

Country	Region	Number of segments	Number of tokens	Total tokens	Tokens per segment	English words	French words	Mixed words	% code-switching in corpus
Lebanon	North	127	508	1075	3.1	55	12	0	13.19%
	South	141	567			33	11	0	7.76%
Egypt	Cairo	117	601	1159	8.1	28	0	0	4.65%
	Luxor	42	558			3	0	0	0.5%
Algeria	Algiers	145	639	1164	3.8	59	3	8	10.95%
	Constantine	99	525			52	1	5	11%

Table 1: Summary of segment, token, and foreign word counts by region

"Claude" to Anthropic's 3.5 Sonnet,[5] "Gemma" to `gemma-2-27b-it` (Gemma Team et al., 2024), and, also from Google, "Gemini" to the latest Gemini 1.5 Pro version (Gemini Team et al., 2024).[6] "Mistral" is `Mistral Large 24.11` from the eponymous company and, finally, "Jais" refers to `jais-family-30b-16k-chat` (Sengupta et al., 2023).

3.2 Prompts

In order to achieve the best translation results, we built on He (2024)'s findings by assigning the role of a professional translator to our LLM. This approach outperformed both simpler prompts and those with excessive context. Furthermore, for each of the three main dialects, we used three prompt strategies: no-shot, one-shot, and two-shot, all written in English. These prompts were the same across regions, except for the specific mention of each dialect in the corresponding prompts. The examples used in the one- and two-shot configurations are not part of the evaluated set, and are from the Algerian and Lebanese dialects. We further refined and duplicated these prompt variations to cover two target languages: one set asked for translation into English and the other into MSA. Finally, all prompts were translated into Arabic by a native Arabic speaker who is also a professional translator. In total, we ran experiments with 36 unique prompts (3 regions * 3 strategies * 2 target languages * 2 prompt languages), or 18 per target language, which we used on all models. The prompts in English are available in Appendix A, while their equivalents in Arabic can be found here.

3.3 MT Evaluation

We used automatic metrics and evaluated the potential of using LLM-as-a-judge for direct assessment evaluation.

3.3.1 Automatic Evaluation

We used several metrics to quantify the quality of the generated translations. On the more classical side we use BLEU (Papineni et al., 2002), chrF (Popović, 2015) and TER (Snover et al., 2006). All scores were calculated using SacreBLEU (Post, 2018).[7] In order to avoid the usual pitfalls of word- and character-based metrics, especially since we were studying dialects without formal orthography, we further investigated the quality of the translations using techniques based on sub-word embeddings: BERTScore (Zhang et al., 2019) and two versions of COMET: COMET-22 (Rei et al., 2022a, `Unbabel/wmt22-comet-da`) and its reference-free version CometKiwi (Rei et al., 2022b, `Unbabel/wmt22-cometkiwi-da`). The latter three methods help alleviate two limitations of our work: the fact that only one reference translation is available for each sentence and the extremely short length of certain sentences.

3.3.2 Human Evaluation

Since no Arabizi-specific metric or resource exists for our dialect selection, we assessed whether LLMs in an "LLM-as-a-judge" setting (Zheng et al., 2023) can be used to mimic human evaluation to reduce the reliance on hard-to-source users of Arabizi.

For human evaluation, we adopted the direct assessment method, which evaluates translations based on a Likert scale ranging from 1 to 5 (higher is better) according to two key criteria: fluency and adequacy (See Appendix B). Due to time and human resource constraints, we did not manually annotate all translations. We instead sampled a random machine translation for both target languages and for each source sentence of our dataset. These machine translation outputs were sampled across all our variables, i.e. models, prompt languages,

[5]`anthropic.claude-3-5-sonnet-20240620-v1:0`

[6]December 2024 release.

[7]The relevant signatures are provided in Appendix D.

and prompt strategies. The resulting set, consisting of 671 segments (268 for Lebanon, 159 for Egypt and 244 for Algeria, see Table 1) for each target language, was then manually rated by two native speakers of Arabic who are professional translators, one of them being the first author of this study and the original translator of the dataset. We then calculated Cohen (1960) κ to measure their agreement in terms of fluency and accuracy (see Appendix E for results). Cohen (1960) κ results indicate moderate agreement for adequacy and lower agreement for fluency, with some variations across language pairs.

The set, which not only consisted of the reference and machine translation but also of the source sentence, was then iteratively fed into GPT-4o in an "LLM-as-a-judge" setting (Zheng et al., 2023), with a prompt in English tasking the LLM to follow the human annotation guidelines.[8] The LLM showed strong correlation with both human annotators, with Spearman (1904)'s ρs comprised in the range from 0.457 (annotator 2, fluency, Egypt to EN) to 0.844 (annotator 2, adequacy, Egypt to AR). These results indicate that an LLM can be used as an easy way to gauge translation quality during model development. The different correlations as well as all the data for direct assessment can be found in Appendix E.

4 Results

4.1 Qualitative Error Analysis

Due to space constraints, this section will only provide some examples of the main errors. Refer to the table for a more detailed overview of the main errors. Most models tend to mistranslate, especially when figurative language is used. A larger issue lies with Llama3 which tends to output words in another script when translating to MSA. An obvious example is the translation of the segment *Almatar da* (هذا المطار, "this airport") as المطر да – transforming the "da" in Arabic to Cyrillic. The problem is not limited to Cyrillic, as characters in Latin and Chinese scripts can also be found in the output. Another type of failure specific to a model is Jais' re-occuring hallucinations. The model often associates feelings of anger to an otherwise neutral message, leading to translations that are irrelevant and contain violent information.

[8]The prompt is shared in Appendix C.

4.2 Quantitative Analysis

See Appendix F for the complete set of results.

4.2.1 Effect of Prompting Techniques

On one hand, one-shot prompting for translations into English increased BLEU scores across all models. For example, in GPT-4o, the BLEU score improved from 17.386 for no-shot to 20.158 for one-shot, a 16% increase. Two-shot prompting, however, provided only a marginal gain or even slight variation. For instance, in GPT-4o, the BLEU score slightly dropped from 20.158 for one-shot to 19.771 for two-shot. On the other hand, the improvements to translations into Arabic were less pronounced, suggesting that few-shot prompting is less effective. In GPT-4o, BLEU increased from 8.395 for no-shot to 10.099 for one-shot, a 20% increase, but the shift from one-shot to two-shot (10.150) was minimal. Similarly, in the case of Claude-3, the BLEU score improved from 2.982 for no-shot to 4.009 for one-shot, a 34% increase, but two-shot promting (4.016) provided almost no additional benefit.

4.2.2 Effect of Target Language

English translations consistently outperformed Arabic translations across all metrics, indicating that models handle English more effectively. For instance, GPT-4o achieved higher BLEU scores in English (17.39 to 20.16) than in Arabic (8.40 to 10.15), with chrF scores following a similar trend (43.08 to 45.50 for English vs. 36.64 to 38.09 for Arabic). TER also confirmed that English translations required fewer edits, with scores of 70.29 for one-shot compared to 78.70 for Arabic. Other models, such as Claude-3 and Llama-3, exhibited similar disparities, with English BLEU scores nearly doubling those of Arabic. Both COMET metrics and BERTScore further highlighted this gap, although BERTScore pointed to different alignment characteristics between languages. While GPT-4o and Gemini were the strongest models for Arabic, their scores still lagged behind their English performance, reinforcing the overall trend of English translations being more accurate and consistent.

4.2.3 Effect of Source Dialect

The evaluation of translation performance across different dialects revealed notable variations in quality, as measured by the different translation metrics (cf Appendix 6). The Egyptian dialect demonstrated the highest translation quality, with an average BLEU score of 9.65 and a chrF score of 34.64, indicating the highest word- and character-level accuracy. Additionally, Egyptian achieved a BERTScore of 0.37 and a COMET score of 0.67, suggesting higher semantic similarity to reference translations. The Lebanese dialect followed with a BLEU score of 7.52 and a chrF score of 26.59, with a comparable COMET Kiwi score of 0.48 but a slightly lower COMET score of 0.65. The Algerian dialect ranked third, with a significantly lower BLEU score of 4.24 and a chrF score of 23.21, along with the lowest BERTScore of 0.33 and COMET score of 0.63.

The disparity in translation quality among the dialects could be explained by linguistic, sociocultural, and technological factors. Egyptian Arabic, the most widely spoken and documented dialect, aligns closely with MSA and is predominant in the media, ensuring better representation in training datasets. By contrast, Algerian Arabic's heavy code-switching (cf Table 1) with Berber, French, and Spanish, along with figurative word meanings, make translation more challenging. Its lack of representation in digital corpora further limits LLMs training, resulting in poorer translation performance.

4.2.4 Effect of Prompt Language

As seen in a prior article (Zhang et al., 2023), our results confirm that prompting in English generally yields better results across all models.

4.3 Metrics Correlation

Because traditional metrics such as BLEU and chrF quantify n-gram overlap with the reference, thereby rewarding surface-level similarity and penalizing deviations, they tend to produce correlated scores and inversely correlate with TER.

Meanwhile, embedding-based metrics such as BERT Score and COMET rely on learned contextual representations to gauge semantic similarity, thus capturing deeper nuances in meaning and tolerating surface-level variations, which often leads them to yield patterns that are distinct from n-gram-focused measures.

Across the different combinations, BLEU and chrF scores typically fluctuated in parallel. However, certain model-prompt settings revealed inconsistencies, where BLEU increased while BERT Score or COMET remained unchanged or declined, indicating improved n-gram overlap but not necessarily better semantic accuracy or fluency. Despite these inconsistencies, higher BLEU generally correlated with good embedding-based metrics scores.

5 Conclusion and Discussion

Models struggle significantly with Arabizi. GPT-4o is the best-performing translation model, followed by Gemini. Mistral Large and Gemma perform moderately well, while Llama 3 and Jais are the weakest models (see Appendix H). Interestingly, Gemma performed surprisingly well in translation tasks despite being a 27B parameter model. Its results, particularly in English, were competitive with larger models, suggesting that model size is not the only determinant of translation quality—architectural optimizations and training data also play a crucial role.

For model prompting, few-shot approaches improved performance but was more effective for English than for Arabic. English prompts worked better overall and in all prompting scenarios, though the difference was much less stark for GPT-4o and Gemini and, to a lesser extent, for Gemma.

Despite a large variation in average segment length between different dialects, no clear pattern emerged in terms of automatic scores. This hints that translation quality does not directly depend on segment length.

The LLM-as-a-Judge scenario aligned with expert human raters, making it a relevant tool in this setting. This study further shows that while far from perfect, using "out-of-the-box" LLMs to translate Arabizi is a viable solution for gisting, especially when combined with an LLM-as-a-judge.

6 Limitations

This study has several limitations. First, the dataset does not fully capture the diversity of Arabizi usage across different regions and social contexts. Second, it relies on translators who are non-native speakers of English. Third, the variety of text lengths may affect performance, as shorter or longer texts might yield varying results. Furthermore, no Arabizi-specific evaluation metric was used, which can affect the accuracy of the assessments. Lastly, the study was constrained by a relatively small corpus, which may limit the applicability of its findings.

7 Acknowledgements

We would like to thank the volunteers who donated their conversations, the translator, the reviewers for their helpful comments and suggestions. Finally, our thanks go to Dr. Thien for her proofreading assistance.

8 CO_2 Emission Related to Experiments

It is difficult to estimate the energy usage of models that were run in an "inference-as-a-service" setting, especially when the details of such models are proprietary. Using the tool provided by Lannelongue et al. (2021)[9] and basing our calcuations on model sizes of around 400B parameters for the proprietary models, we estimate that the energy usage of our experiments amounted to 6.99 kWh in a US datacenter, which corresponds to a carbon footprint of 2.97 $kgCO_2e$.

References

Perla Al Almaoui. 2024. ChatGPT comme outil de traduction automatique des discussions WhatsApp : évaluation de la traduction de différents dialectes en Arabizi. Master's thesis, Université de Genève.

Wid H Allehaiby. 2013. Arabizi: An analysis of the romanization of the arabic script from a sociolinguistic perspective. *Arab World English Journal*, 4(3).

Anthropic. The Claude 3 model family: Opus, Sonnet, Haiku.

Nur Ayoubi. 2022. Shou, shinou, ey: Five major arabic dialects and what makes them unique. *Middle East Eye*. Accessed: 31 March 2025.

Ann Bies, Zhiyi Song, Mohamed Maamouri, Stephen Grimes, Haejoong Lee, Jonathan Wright, Stephanie Strassel, Nizar Habash, Ramy Eskander, and Owen Rambow. 2014. Transliteration of Arabizi into Arabic orthography: Developing a parallel annotated Arabizi-Arabic script SMS/chat corpus. In *Proceedings of the EMNLP 2014 Workshop on Arabic Natural Language Processing (ANLP)*, pages 93–103, Doha, Qatar. Association for Computational Linguistics.

Abdelkarim Chami. 2009. A historical background of the linguistic situation in algeria.

Jacob Cohen. 1960. A coefficient of agreement for nominal scales. *Educational and psychological measurement*, 20(1):37–46.

Abhimanyu Dubey, Abhinav Jauhri, Abhinav Pandey, Abhishek Kadian, Ahmad Al-Dahle, Aiesha Letman, Akhil Mathur, Alan Schelten, Amy Yang, Angela Fan, et al. 2024. The llama 3 herd of models. *arXiv preprint arXiv:2407.21783*.

[9]`https://calculator.green-algorithms.org/ai`

Gemini Gemini Team, Petko Georgiev, Ving Ian Lei, Ryan Burnell, Libin Bai, Anmol Gulati, Garrett Tanzer, Damien Vincent, Zhufeng Pan, Shibo Wang, et al. 2024. Gemini 1.5: Unlocking multimodal understanding across millions of tokens of context. *arXiv preprint arXiv:2403.05530*.

Gemma Gemma Team, Thomas Mesnard, Cassidy Hardin, Robert Dadashi, Surya Bhupatiraju, Shreya Pathak, Laurent Sifre, Morgane Rivière, Mihir Sanjay Kale, Juliette Love, et al. 2024. Gemma: Open models based on gemini research and technology. *arXiv preprint arXiv:2403.08295*.

Naman Goyal, Cynthia Gao, Vishrav Chaudhary, Peng-Jen Chen, Guillaume Wenzek, Da Ju, Sanjana Krishnan, Marc'Aurelio Ranzato, Francisco Guzmán, and Angela Fan. 2022. The Flores-101 evaluation benchmark for low-resource and multilingual machine translation. *Transactions of the Association for Computational Linguistics*, 10:522–538.

Imane Guellil, Faiçal Azouaou, Mourad Abbas, and Sadat Fatiha. 2017. Arabizi transliteration of Algerian Arabic dialect into Modern Standard Arabic. In *Social MT 2017/ First workshop on Social Media and User Generated Content Machine Translation*, Prague, Czech Republic.

Salima Harrat, Karima Meftouh, and Kamel Smaili. 2019. Machine translation for arabic dialects (survey). *Information Processing & Management*, 56(2):262–273. Advance Arabic Natural Language Processing (ANLP) and its Applications.

Sui He. 2024. Prompting ChatGPT for translation: A comparative analysis of translation brief and persona prompts. In *Proceedings of the 25th Annual Conference of the European Association for Machine Translation (Volume 1)*, pages 316–326, Sheffield, UK. European Association for Machine Translation (EAMT).

Amine Jules Iskandar. 2022. À l'origine du parler libanais (parts 1 and 2). Part 1 available at: `https://terredecompassion.com/2022/03/01/a-lorigine-du-parler-libanais-1-2/`, Part 2 available at: `https://terredecompassion.com/2022/03/08/a-lorigine-du-parler-libanais-2-2/`. Accessed: 2025-01-01.

Philipp Koehn and Christof Monz. 2006. Manual and automatic evaluation of machine translation between European languages. In *Proceedings on the Workshop on Statistical Machine Translation*, pages 102–121, New York City. Association for Computational Linguistics.

Loïc Lannelongue, Jason Grealey, and Michael Inouye. 2021. Green algorithms: quantifying the carbon footprint of computation. *Advanced science*, 8(12):2100707.

Alexander Magidow. 2021. The old and the new: Considerations in arabic historical dialectology. *Languages*, 6(4):163. Accessed: 31 March 2025.

Imane Momayiz, Aissam Outchakoucht, Omar Choukrani, and Ali Nirheche. 2024. Terjamabench: A culturally specific dataset for evaluating translation models for moroccan darija.

OpenAI. 2024. Gpt-4o system card. *arXiv preprint arXiv:2410.21276*.

Kishore Papineni, Salim Roukos, Todd Ward, and Wei-Jing Zhu. 2002. Bleu: a method for automatic evaluation of machine translation. In *Proceedings of the 40th Annual Meeting of the Association for Computational Linguistics*, pages 311–318, Philadelphia, Pennsylvania, USA. Association for Computational Linguistics.

Maja Popović. 2015. chrF: character n-gram F-score for automatic MT evaluation. In *Proceedings of the Tenth Workshop on Statistical Machine Translation*, pages 392–395, Lisbon, Portugal. Association for Computational Linguistics.

Matt Post. 2018. A call for clarity in reporting BLEU scores. In *Proceedings of the Third Conference on Machine Translation: Research Papers*, pages 186–191, Brussels, Belgium. Association for Computational Linguistics.

Alec Radford, Karthik Narasimhan, Tim Salimans, Ilya Sutskever, et al. 2018. Improving language understanding by generative pre-training.

Ricardo Rei, José G. C. de Souza, Duarte Alves, Chrysoula Zerva, Ana C Farinha, Taisiya Glushkova, Alon Lavie, Luisa Coheur, and André F. T. Martins. 2022a. COMET-22: Unbabel-IST 2022 submission for the metrics shared task. In *Proceedings of the Seventh Conference on Machine Translation (WMT)*, pages 578–585, Abu Dhabi, United Arab Emirates (Hybrid). Association for Computational Linguistics.

Ricardo Rei, Marcos Treviso, Nuno M. Guerreiro, Chrysoula Zerva, Ana C Farinha, Christine Maroti, José G. C. de Souza, Taisiya Glushkova, Duarte Alves, Luisa Coheur, Alon Lavie, and André F. T. Martins. 2022b. CometKiwi: IST-unbabel 2022 submission for the quality estimation shared task. In *Proceedings of the Seventh Conference on Machine Translation (WMT)*, pages 634–645, Abu Dhabi, United Arab Emirates (Hybrid). Association for Computational Linguistics.

Houda Saadane and Nizar Habash. 2015. A conventional orthography for Algerian Arabic. In *Proceedings of the Second Workshop on Arabic Natural Language Processing*, pages 69–79, Beijing, China. Association for Computational Linguistics.

Neha Sengupta, Sunil Kumar Sahu, Bokang Jia, Satheesh Katipomu, Haonan Li, Fajri Koto, William Marshall, Gurpreet Gosal, Cynthia Liu, Zhiming Chen, et al. 2023. Jais and jais-chat: Arabic-centric foundation and instruction-tuned open generative large language models. *arXiv preprint arXiv:2308.16149*.

Ali Shazal, Aiza Usman, and Nizar Habash. 2020. A unified model for Arabizi detection and transliteration using sequence-to-sequence models. In *Proceedings of the Fifth Arabic Natural Language Processing Workshop*, pages 167–177, Barcelona, Spain (Online). Association for Computational Linguistics.

Matthew Snover, Bonnie Dorr, Rich Schwartz, Linnea Micciulla, and John Makhoul. 2006. A study of translation edit rate with targeted human annotation. In *Proceedings of the 7th Conference of the Association for Machine Translation in the Americas: Technical Papers*, pages 223–231, Cambridge, Massachusetts, USA. Association for Machine Translation in the Americas.

Lameen Souag. 2009. Siwa and its significance for Arabic dialectology. *Zeitschrift für arabische Linguistik = Journal of Arabic linguistics = Journal de linguistique arabe*, 51:51–75.

C. Spearman. 1904. The proof and measurement of association between two things. *The American Journal of Psychology*, 15(1):72–101.

Nikolai Vladimirovich Yushmanov. 1961. The structure of the arabic language.

Biao Zhang, Barry Haddow, and Alexandra Birch. 2023. Prompting large language model for machine translation: A case study. *Preprint*, arXiv:2301.07069.

Tianyi Zhang, Varsha Kishore, Felix Wu, Kilian Q Weinberger, and Yoav Artzi. 2019. BERTScore: Evaluating text generation with bert. *arXiv preprint arXiv:1904.09675*.

Lianmin Zheng, Wei-Lin Chiang, Ying Sheng, Siyuan Zhuang, Zhanghao Wu, Yonghao Zhuang, Zi Lin, Zhuohan Li, Dacheng Li, Eric Xing, et al. 2023. Judging llm-as-a-judge with mt-bench and chatbot arena. *Advances in Neural Information Processing Systems*, 36:46595–46623.

A Prompts in English for all Dialects, Target Languages, and Prompt Strategies

"ALG" stands for Algeria, "EG" for Egypt, and "LB" for Lebanon. For the experiments with a prompt in Arabic, all prompts were translated into Modern Standard Arabic by the first author of the study, who is a native speaker of Arabic and a professional translator.

```
{
    "ALG_AR": {
        "no-shot": "You are a professional Arabic translator with years of
            experience translating spoken language from various Arabic dialects.
            Translate the following text from the Algerian dialect to Modern
            Standard Arabic.",

        "one-shot": "You are a professional Arabic translator with years of
            experience translating spoken language from various Arabic dialects.

            Source text: "Ma 3am efham chu 3am te7ke"
            Target text in Arabic: "لا أفهم ما تقوله"

        Based on the example above, translate the following text from the Algerian
            dialect to Modern Standard Arabic.",

        "two-shot": "You are a professional Arabic translator with years of
            experience translating spoken language from various Arabic dialects.

            Source text: "Ma 3am efham chu 3am te7ke"
            Target text in Arabic: "لا أفهم ما تقوله"

            Source text: "M t7kilich 7yetk kho"
            Target text in Arabic: "لا تقص عليّ قصّة حياتك أخي"


        Based on the examples above, translate the following text from the Algerian
            dialect to Modern Standard Arabic."
    },
    "ALG_EN": {
        "no-shot": "You are a professional Arabic translator with years of
            experience translating spoken language from various Arabic dialects.
            Translate the following text from the Algerian dialect to English.",

        "one-shot": "You are a professional Arabic translator with years of
            experience translating spoken language from various Arabic dialects.

            Source text: "Ma 3am efham chu 3am te7ke"
            Target text in English: "I don't understand what you're saying."

        Based on the example above, translate the following text from the Algerian
            dialect to English.",

        "two-shot": "You are a professional Arabic translator with years of
            experience translating spoken language from various Arabic dialects.

            Source text: "Ma 3am efham chu 3am te7ke"
            Target text in English: "I don't understand what you're saying."

            Source text: "M t7kilich 7yetk kho"
            Target text in English: "Don't tell me your life story, bro"

        Based on the examples above, translate the following text from the Algerian
            dialect to English."
        },
    "EG_AR": {
        "no-shot": "You are a professional Arabic translator with years of
            experience translating spoken language from various Arabic dialects.
            Translate the following text from the Egyptian dialect to Modern
            Standard Arabic.",
```

```
    "one-shot": "You are a professional Arabic translator with years of
        experience translating spoken language from various Arabic dialects.

        Source text: "Ma 3am efham chu 3am te7ke"
        Target text in Arabic: "لا أفهم ما تقوله"

    Based on the example above, translate the following text from the Egyptian
        dialect to Modern Standard Arabic.",

    "two-shot": "You are a professional Arabic translator with years of
        experience translating spoken language from various Arabic dialects.

        Source text: "Ma 3am efham chu 3am te7ke"
        Target text in Arabic: "لا أفهم ما تقوله"

        Source text: "M t7kilich 7yetk kho"
        Target text in Arabic: "لا تقص عليّ قصّة حياتك أخي"

    Based on the examples above, translate the following text from the Egyptian
        dialect to Modern Standard Arabic."
},
"EG_EN": {
    "no-shot": "You are a professional Arabic translator with years of
        experience translating spoken language from various Arabic dialects.
        Translate the following text from the Egyptian dialect to English.",

    "one-shot": "You are a professional Arabic translator with years of
        experience translating spoken language from various Arabic dialects.

        Source text: "Ma 3am efham chu 3am te7ke"
        Target text in English: "I don't understand what you're saying."

    Based on the example above, translate the following text from the Egyptian
        dialect to English.",

    "two-shot": "You are a professional Arabic translator with years of
        experience translating spoken language from various Arabic dialects.

        Source text: "Ma 3am efham chu 3am te7ke"
        Target text in English: "I don't understand what you're saying."

        Source text: "M t7kilich 7yetk kho"
        Target text in English: "Don't tell me your life story, bro"

    Based on the examples above, translate the following text from the Egyptian
        dialect to English."
    },
"LB_AR": {
    "no-shot": "You are a professional Arabic translator with years of
        experience translating spoken language from various Arabic dialects.
        Translate the following text from the Lebanese dialect to Modern
        Standard Arabic.",

    "one-shot": "You are a professional Arabic translator with years of
        experience translating spoken language from various Arabic dialects.

        Source text: "Ma 3am efham chu 3am te7ke"
        Target text in Arabic: "لا أفهم ما تقوله"


    Based on the example above, translate the following text from the Lebanese
        dialect to Modern Standard Arabic.",

    "two-shot": "You are a professional Arabic translator with years of
        experience translating spoken language from various Arabic dialects.
```

```
        Source text: "Ma 3am efham chu 3am te7ke"
        Target text in Arabic: "لا أفهم ما تقوله"

        Source text: "M t7kilich 7yetk kho"
        Target text in Arabic: "لا تقص عليّ قصّة حياتك أخي"

    Based on the examples above, translate the following text from the Lebanese
        dialect to Modern Standard Arabic."
    },
    "LB_EN": {
    "no-shot": "You are a professional Arabic translator with years of
        experience translating spoken language from various Arabic dialects.
        Translate the following text from the Lebanese dialect to English.",

    "one-shot": "You are a professional Arabic translator with years of
        experience translating spoken language from various Arabic dialects.

        Source text: "Ma 3am efham chu 3am te7ke"
        Target text in English: "I don't understand what you're saying."

    Based on the example above, translate the following text from the Lebanese
        dialect to English.",

    "two-shot": "You are a professional Arabic translator with years of
        experience translating spoken language from various Arabic dialects.

        Source text: "Ma 3am efham chu 3am te7ke"
        Target text in English: "I don't understand what you're saying."

        Source text: "M t7kilich 7yetk kho"
        Target text in English: "Don't tell me your life story, bro"

    Based on the examples above, translate the following text from the Lebanese
        dialect to English."
    }
}
```

B Adequacy and Fluency

Score	Adequacy	Fluency
5	All Meaning	Flawless Language
4	Most Meaning	Good Language
3	Much Meaning	Non-native Language
2	Little Meaning	Disfluent Language
1	None	Incomprehensible Language

Table 2: Adequacy and Fluency Evaluation Scale (Koehn and Monz, 2006)

C LLM-as-a-judge

The system prompt was the following:

> You are a professional translator, expert in Arabic, English, and Arabic dialects. Your role here is to evaluate the quality of a translation using two dimensions: 'Adequacy' (scale of 1 to 5, higher is better) and 'Fluency' (scale of 1 to 5, higher is better). You will be given a source text in Arabic dialect, a reference translation into `{target_lang}`, and a machine translation. Return in this format, and NOTHING ELSE:
>
> `Adequacy:[your_score]`
> `Fluency:[your_score]`

I trust and count on you.

The prompt was the following:

Source from {country}: {source}
Reference translation: {ref}
Machine translation: {hyp}
Give scores from 1 to 5 for both Adequacy and Fluency using the template:

```
Adequacy:[your_score]
Fluency:[your_score]
```

Return nothing else.

D Metrics Signatures

```
BLEU: nrefs:1|case:mixed|eff:no|tok:13a|smooth:exp|version:2.5.1
chrF: nrefs:1|case:mixed|eff:yes|nc:6|nw:0|space:no|version:2.5.1
TER: nrefs:1|case:lc|tok:tercom|norm:no|punct:yes|
  asian:no|version:2.5.1
```

E Human-LLM-as-a-judge Correlation and Direct Assessment

Country	Fluency		Adequacy	
	LLM-Rater 1	LLM-Rater 2	LLM-Rater 1	LLM-Rater 2
Lebanon - EN	0.602	0.495	0.653	0.824
Lebanon - AR	0.685	0.601	0.820	0.795
Egypt - EN	0.631	0.457	0.667	0.781
Egypt - AR	0.637	0.611	0.677	0.844
Algeria - EN	0.642	0.536	0.683	0.800
Algeria - AR	0.678	0.485	0.760	0.770

Table 3: Correlation Scores (Spearman (1904)'s ρ) Between Human Annotators and LLM-as-a-Judge in Direct Assessment Scores per Country and Target Language.

Country	Fluency		Adequacy	
	Rater 1	Rater 2	Rater 1	Rater 2
Lebanon - EN	2.494	3.822	2.203	2.431
Lebanon - AR	2.782	3.430	2.362	2.662
Egypt - EN	2.560	3.340	2.082	2.679
Egypt - AR	2.956	3.538	2.497	2.887
Algeria - EN	2.534	3.773	1.853	2.315
Algeria - AR	2.721	3.500	2.225	2.335

Table 4: Average Direct Assessment Scores (1-5) for Both Human Raters, per Country and Target Language.

F Automatic Evaluation Results for all Models

Due to space constraints, we are presenting the results averaged over the two prompt languages. A more comprehensive overview of the results is available in the accompanying spreadsheet.

Model	TL	Prompt Tech	BLEU	chrF	TER	BERT	KIWI	COMET
GPT-4o	EN	no-shot	17.386	43.081	77.038	0.478	0.434	0.733
GPT-4o	EN	one-shot	**20.158**	45.232	**70.287**	**0.529**	**0.439**	**0.757**
GPT-4o	EN	two-shot	19.771	**45.496**	70.294	0.521	**0.439**	0.755
GPT-4o	AR	no-shot	8.395	36.637	86.501	0.558	0.422	0.757
GPT-4o	AR	one-shot	10.099	**38.221**	**78.701**	**0.586**	**0.423**	**0.776**
GPT-4o	AR	two-shot	**10.150**	38.090	79.775	0.585	0.421	0.774
claude3	EN	no-shot	5.603	25.565	150.074	**0.270**	0.540	0.620
claude3	EN	one-shot	8.795	30.356	97.400	0.191	0.536	0.605
claude3	EN	two-shot	**9.433**	**32.360**	**96.325**	0.225	**0.541**	**0.625**
claude3	AR	no-shot	2.982	22.957	122.794	0.367	0.428	0.657
claude3	AR	one-shot	4.009	28.169	**97.126**	0.420	**0.431**	**0.686**
claude3	AR	two-shot	**4.016**	**28.473**	98.488	**0.425**	0.427	**0.686**
Llama3	EN	no-shot	6.972	27.982	107.160	**0.293**	**0.526**	**0.620**
Llama3	EN	one-shot	**8.234**	**28.510**	101.095	0.290	0.518	0.618
Llama3	EN	two-shot	7.709	27.988	**99.623**	0.274	0.521	0.613
Llama3	AR	no-shot	2.196	17.748	160.334	0.243	0.412	0.587
Llama3	AR	one-shot	**2.862**	**20.763**	**118.675**	**0.343**	**0.425**	**0.623**
Llama3	AR	two-shot	1.139	17.728	218.553	0.286	**0.425**	0.610
gemma2	EN	no-shot	8.523	27.979	89.761	0.330	**0.548**	0.634
gemma2	EN	one-shot	9.866	28.977	88.589	**0.337**	0.543	0.639
gemma2	EN	two-shot	**9.925**	**29.258**	**87.319**	0.333	0.545	**0.640**
gemma2	AR	no-shot	3.583	23.098	99.113	0.358	**0.429**	**0.644**
gemma2	AR	one-shot	**4.070**	24.175	**94.968**	0.388	0.424	0.660
gemma2	AR	two-shot	3.959	**24.400**	96.123	**0.389**	0.426	**0.664**
mistrallarge	EN	no-shot	7.919	**29.002**	101.704	**0.285**	**0.524**	**0.627**
mistrallarge	EN	one-shot	**9.409**	28.445	91.376	0.263	0.518	0.610
mistrallarge	EN	two-shot	9.259	28.347	**91.020**	0.268	0.521	0.612
mistrallarge	AR	no-shot	4.019	**25.413**	103.042	**0.434**	**0.493**	**0.673**
mistrallarge	AR	one-shot	4.230	24.663	95.517	0.428	0.482	0.672
mistrallarge	AR	two-shot	**4.372**	25.162	**94.433**	0.426	0.481	0.669
jais	EN	no-shot	1.518	15.273	344.316	**0.065**	0.470	0.501
jais	EN	one-shot	**2.157**	15.667	**160.450**	0.016	**0.511**	0.507
jais	EN	two-shot	1.735	**15.958**	192.409	0.042	0.499	**0.508**
jais	AR	no-shot	0.750	**14.486**	208.837	0.241	**0.420**	**0.583**
jais	AR	one-shot	**0.847**	14.120	**196.811**	0.258	0.418	0.578
jais	AR	two-shot	0.704	14.418	202.979	**0.270**	0.418	0.579
gemini	EN	no-shot	11.317	36.950	94.146	0.379	0.493	0.672
gemini	EN	one-shot	16.119	41.023	78.911	0.451	0.493	0.713
gemini	EN	two-shot	**16.187**	**41.182**	**77.605**	**0.455**	**0.495**	**0.720**
gemini	AR	no-shot	5.174	31.319	90.174	0.502	**0.470**	0.729
gemini	AR	one-shot	6.636	33.513	84.945	0.536	0.468	0.752
gemini	AR	two-shot	**7.585**	**33.987**	**84.428**	**0.541**	**0.470**	**0.753**

Table 5: Automatic Evaluation Results for all Models, Averaged over Prompt Languages. TL = Target Language, BERT = BERTScore, KIWI = wmt22-cometkiwi-da, COMET = wmt22-comet-da. Best scores for every model, target language, and prompt strategy are indicated in bold.

G Average Metric Scores for Dialects

Country	BLEU	chrF	TER	BERTScore	KIWI	COMET
Lebanon	7.5212	26.5935	123.5180	0.3604	0.4799	0.6547
Egypt	9.6466	34.6404	102.8187	0.3699	0.4749	0.6749
Algeria	4.2445	23.2068	122.1789	0.3322	0.4642	0.6303

Table 6: Translation Quality Scores for the Arabic Dialects

H Model Ranking

Model	BLEU	chrF	TER	BERTScore	KIWI	COMET
GPT-4o	14.326	41.126	77.099	0.542	0.429	0.758
gemini	10.503	36.329	85.034	0.477	0.481	0.723
gemma2	6.654	26.314	92.645	0.355	0.485	0.646
mistrallarge	6.534	26.838	96.181	0.350	0.503	0.643
claude3	5.806	27.980	110.368	0.316	0.483	0.646
Llama3	4.851	23.453	134.240	0.287	0.471	0.611
jais	1.285	14.986	217.633	0.148	0.456	0.542

Table 7: Ranking of Translation Models from Best to Worst Based on Average Automatic Metric Scores

Cultural Transcreation in Asian Languages with Prompt-Based LLMs

Helena Wu[1,4], **Beatriz Silva**[1], **Vera Cabarrão**[1], **Helena Moniz**[2,3]
[1]Unbabel, Lisbon, Portugal
[2]University of Lisbon, Portugal
[3]CLUL, Lisbon, Portugal
[4]INESC-ID, Lisbon, Portugal
helenawu@edu.ulisboa,pt, {beatriz.silva, vera.cabarrao}@unbabel.com,
helena.moniz@edu.ulisboa.pt

Abstract

This research explores Cultural Transcreation (CT) for East Asian languages, focusing primarily on Mandarin Chinese (ZH) and the customer service (CS) market.[1] We combined Large Language Models (LLMs) with prompt engineering to develop a CT product that, aligned with the Augmented Translation concept, enhances multilingual CS communication, enables professionals to engage with their target audience effortlessly, and improves overall service quality. Through a series of preparatory steps, including guideline establishment, benchmark validation, iterative prompt refinement, and LLM testing, we integrated the CT product into the CS platform, assessed its performance, and refined prompts based on a pilot feedback. The results highlight its success in empowering CS agents, regardless of linguistic or cultural expertise, to bridge effective communication gaps through AI-assisted cultural rephrasing, thus achieving its market launch. Beyond CS, the study extends the concept of transcreation and prompt-based LLM applications to other fields, discussing its performance in the language conversion of website content and advertising.

1 Introduction

Transcreation, also known as creative translation, is a language conversion approach in which discussions remain relatively sparse and primarily emphasise manual approaches, with a focus on its application in fields such as advertising, marketing and literary translation (Díaz-Millón and Olvera-Lobo, 2023). The present research aims to expand this concept beyond human transcreation by developing an automatic transcreation product that incorporates cultural awareness through the adoption of prompt engineering and Large Language Models (LLMs), with a primary emphasis on Mandarin Chinese (ZH) — both Simplified (zh-CN-Hans) and Traditional (zh-TW-Hant) — along with Japanese (JA) and Korean (KO).

This research was carried out at Unbabel, which provides translation services widely used in industries such as customer support (CS) and e-commerce. The Cultural Transcreation (CT) product developed in this study is integrated into Unbabel's machine translation (MT) workflow as a pre-translation step, creating a new automated CT pipeline, as shown in Figure 1.

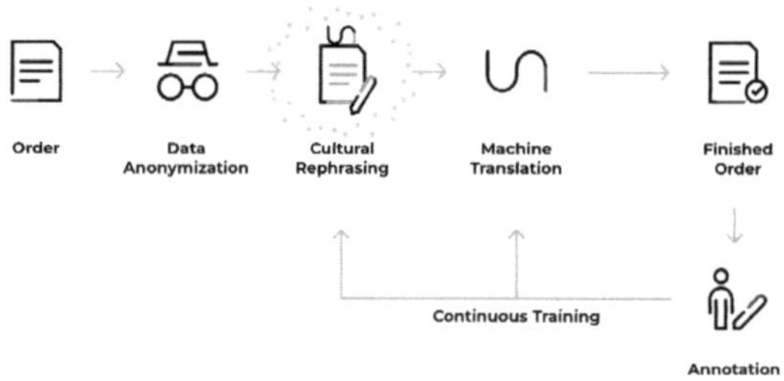

Figure 1: Automated CT Product Pipeline

The product is implemented on a CS platform, and is currently only available for use in the CS sector. The tickets (e-mails) produced by CS agents are first anonymised, and then undergo cultural adaptation within the source language to align with the target culture. Only after this cultural alignment are the tickets processed by the MT systems.

Notably, the principle of this product is aligned with the concept of Augmented Translation, which builds on Douglas Engelbart's (1962) vision of leveraging computational tools to enhance, rather than replace, human capabilities. In this context, our CT tool aims to equip CS agents — who communicate in the source language but lack cultural awareness of the target audience — with enhanced capabilities to effectively cross cultural and linguistic boundaries. Augmented Translation, as

[1]Part of this work was previously published in an international peer-reviewed venue, namely EAMT 2024. For the sake of clarity and ethical transparency, the following publication is integrated into the present work: Silva et al. (2024)

introduced by CSA Research and building upon Engelbart's integration of human expertise with AI-driven processes, represents a paradigm shift in the translation industry. It combines human expertise with advanced language technologies to enhance communication. Unlike traditional MT workflows, which rely solely on automation, this approach reinforces the role of human workers by integrating AI with human-in-the-loop processes. Rooted in Engelbart's (1962) vision of technology augmenting human capabilities, studies such as Lommel (2018) and O'Brien (2024) have further developed the concept, emphasising the necessity of a human-centered approach. Ultimately, our CT solution minimises misunderstandings caused by a single MT and the cultural differences that could lead to conflicts. It ensures that CS adheres more closely to the cultural conventions of the target language.

2 Literature Review

Transcreation, a portmanteau of "Translation" and "Creation", combines translation with creative adaptations to preserve the original message's essence while aligning it with specific target norms. This approach achieves a level of adaptation beyond what translation offers by addressing both creative and target-specific aspects. In the context of transcreation, the approach that focuses on cultural awareness can be called Cultural Transcreation, which is the central focus of this research.

In essence, transcreation bridges the gap between maintaining the source intention and addressing the cultural and audience-specific nuances. As Gaballo (2012) defines it: "Transcreation is an intra-/interlingual re-interpretation of the original work suited to the readers/audience of the target language, which requires the translator to come up with new conceptual, linguistic, and cultural constructs to make up for the lack (or inadequacy) of existing ones. It can be looked at as a strategy to overcome the limits of 'untranslatability'".

Along this line, we can develop the perspective that translation, localisation, and transcreation represent distinct yet overlapping approaches to language conversion, varying in their degree of adaptation and cultural sensitivity. While translation primarily emphasises on linguistic accuracy and fidelity to the source text, localisation adapts content to fit specific cultural and technical contexts, incorporating elements such as date formats and currencies (Pym, 2017, pp. 119, 131-132). Transcreation, by contrast, is a highly creative process that prioritises cultural adaptation, re-interpreting content to align with audience expectations while preserving the original intent. Though scholars such as Szasz and Olt (2018) and Rike (2013) clearly differentiate transcreation from other approaches, some (Mangiron and O'Hagan, 2006; Munday et al., 2022) consider it a subset of localisation.

Then, focusing on the perspective of distinguishing transcreation from the other two concepts, some theoretical frameworks, such as Juliane House's functionalism and Lawrence Venuti's critique, further elucidate these distinctions. House (1997, 2014, 2015) defines translation as a process to achieve functional equivalence between the source and the target, distinguishing between "overt" translations, which retain source-cultural elements, and "covert" translations, which adapt more seamlessly to the target culture. This functionalist perspective highlights that translation, though adaptive, primarily preserves the original content's intent and scope without significant creative re-interpretation. Localisation, aligning with skopos theory (Vermeer, 1978), extends beyond translation by embedding content within cultural, linguistic, and technical norms, ensuring usability without fundamentally altering the original's communicative intent. Transcreation, on the other hand, represents the most adaptive approach, focusing on emotional and cultural resonance over literal fidelity. Venuti's (2017) domestication theory is particularly relevant here, as transcreation prioritises audience engagement by reshaping content to align with target cultural expectations. From a functionalist perspective, transcreation aligns even more closely with skopos theory, as it prioritises intended impact, often requiring significant creative restructure.

In sum, distinguishing transcreation from the other two requires recognising their varying degrees of adaptation. While all three involve cross-cultural transformation, transcreation occupies the most dynamic end of this spectrum, ensuring content is not only translated but strategically reshaped to maximise cultural and emotional resonance.

In this way, transcreation, particularly CT, challenges the traditional boundaries of translation industry by addressing the need for cultural adaptation. The concepts of "high-context" and "low-context" cultures, introduced by Hall (1976), are vital for understanding cultural adaptation in language conversion. Low-context cultures, such as English-speaking countries, favour more explicit and direct communication. In contrast, languages of high-context cultures, such as Chinese and Japanese, rely heavily on implicit communication, shared assumptions, and contextual understanding. Effective translation between these frameworks requires more than linguistic accuracy, it demands cultural adaptation to ensure resonance with the target audience. Nida and Taber's (1969) concept of "dynamic equivalence" emphasises the impact over direct translation, particularly for high-context audiences. Katan (2015) notes that low-context information often requires adjustment to accommodate cultural subtleties, highlighting the critical role of CT in avoiding miscommunication.

The emergence and development of CT introduces several qualitative improvements compared to traditional translation methods. It enables creative adaptation that maintains the original message's essence while aligning with the cultural expectations of target audiences by prioritising key features of high-context cultures. Moreover, it mitigates the risks associated with hyper-literal translation, reducing potential misunderstandings and cultural misalignment. Beyond its academic value, transcreation holds significant economic potential for international markets. As noted by Carreira (2023), the rising demand for CT stems from non-language service provider companies addressing global communication challenges. It facilitates cross-cultural understanding, enhancing brand perception and customer engagement. Culturally sensitive communication strengthens customer relationships, ensuring content is engaging, relatable, and aligned with audience expectations. Moreover, integrating LLMs into transcreation workflows can amplify these benefits, enhancing cost and time efficiency while reducing reliance on manual transcreation, making it an economically viable solution for companies in global markets.

3 Methodology

This section outlines the systematic approach undertaken to develop a transcreative MT pipeline that incorporates cultural awareness into the translation workflow by leveraging prompt engineering and LLMs, and evaluates the effectiveness of prompt-based LLM transcreation. The research transitions from the theoretical aspects of transcreation to its practical implementation, addressing the current challenges in machine-generated cultural transcreation. After constructing guidelines and prompts tailored to the specific sector, these concepts will be integrated into the innovative product and applied in real-world scenarios to collect authentic data for evaluation and iterative optimisation of its market performance.

The core investigation and development area of this product is the CS sector. This field was chosen not only for the accessibility of relevant data but also because it offers pronounced cultural differences in communication between English-speaking CS agents and their international target audience. For this research, zh-CN-Hans, zh-CN-Hant, JA, and KO were identified as target languages, focusing specifically on Mandarin Chinese in this paper.

Considering English (EN) as the source working language, Mandarin Chinese as the target working language, and cultural transcreation as the research theme, we adopt a multi-stage experimental approach to achieve the study's objectives, where the outcomes of earlier experiments inform and support developing subsequent ones, creating an interconnected process. It is also worth mentioning that, in addition to all other responsibilities, the evaluation processes across all stages were also conducted manually and solely by the authors.

The first aim is establishing culturally aware guidelines based on shared assumptions within the target audience, manual observations of communication features, and real-world translation analysis. In addition, all actions were performed solely by the authors. Based on these guidelines, an initial version of the prompts was created to serve as the foundation for the subsequent experimental phases. The guidelines serve as the foundation for **benchmark analysis of MT cultural transcreation samples in the CS domain**, which assesses the effectiveness of initial prompts and LLM-generated outputs in the CS domain. By conducting a cultural assessment of automatic transcreation benchmarks, this stage improves prompt engineering strategies, which lead to establishing a formal Version 1.0 of the prompts, and inform subsequent experiments.

Then, the primary and central goal of this study — exploration and evaluation of the performance of the CT product generated by prompt-based LLM — will be achieved by conducting a **CT Clients Pilot**. This stage involves testing Version 1.0 of the prompts and refining it into Version 2.0 through seamlessly continuing data generation, real-time performance monitoring and adaptation.

Beyond CS, the study extends its last goal to assess the potential of prompt-generated LLM transcreation in other domains. By stepping beyond the primary focus on CS and cultural awareness, the exploration in **Website Content Generation and Advertising** aims to evaluate the adaptability and performance of automatic transcreation in distinct fields, contents, and text types, broadening the scope of its application and identifying future opportunities for research and development.

3.1 Basic Guidelines, Prompts, and LLM

We established a series of guidelines to implement the concept of cultural awareness, specifically for East Asian cultures. Since the initial target market is the CS sector, the guidelines were tailored to align with the cultural communication norms of this field. These guidelines included template examples, serving as strategic foundations to support the subsequent construction of prompts and experiments, enabling the LLM to generate culturally appropriate rephrasing more effectively.

The Chinese guidelines consist of three sections. The first section outlines specific communication methods and linguistic expressions to follow or avoid, with 16 suggestions for avoidance and 10 for compliance, comprising aspects such as text format, politeness, and emotional outputs.

The second section offers a more in-depth framework for CT in the CS field, covering key aspects such as e-mail formats, appropriate greetings and closings, and other practical expressions.

The final section presents real-world examples of manual cultural awareness annotations to further contextualise the guidelines. Native speakers of the target languages conducted culturally adapted rephrasing of actual CS e-mails, which were then used as templates for developing automatic transcreation. Furthermore, this section also includes additional resources, such as fictional CS e-mails designed as extreme case references for CT, as well as translation and rephrasing examples from chat interactions, offering a comprehensive foundation for refining the transcreation process.

Based on the established guidelines, the initial version of the prompts for e-mail rephrasing in the CS domain was successfully developed. These prompts were tailored for ZH, JA, and KO, reflecting each language's unique cultural requirements and were not shared across languages. Additionally, through iterative temperature tests, the optimal LLM temperature was identified as 0.7, adopting GPT-4 as the LLM. Notably, higher values tend to generate overly creative and unstable outputs, deviating from the prompts and becoming inconsistent with predefined expectations. In contrast, lower temperatures result in excessive rigidity, causing the LLM to either disregard prompts or fail to achieve the expected level of creativity.

3.2 Cultural Validation of MT Benchmarking

After establishing basic guidelines, prompts, and LLM settings, an MT benchmarking analysis was conducted to evaluate the initial version of the prompts. This step aimed to formalise the first production version of the prompts and assess the quality of culturally adapted transcreations generated by LLMs using the initial prompt.

The analysis is based on 21 MT benchmarking samples consisting of tickets provided by Unbabel clients across seven distinct industries, including social media platforms, food manufacturing, tourism, software development, electronic products, and gaming. Each sample includes both the original English text (Original EN), consisting of 166 segments, and the rewritten English text (Rephrased EN), comprising 174 segments. The Original EN represents the initial messages written by CS agents, while the Rephrased EN is produced by inputting the Original EN into an LLM, which rephrases the text to create a culturally sensitive and target-aligned EN version. This intermediary step ensures that the subsequent language translation process becomes more concise, clear, and tailored to the communication preferences of the target language audience. Moreover, this intermediate rephrasing step provides additional benefits beyond cultural alignment, strengthening the overall transcreation process in the CS domain. These aspects will be further elaborated in the next section, which focuses on the core client pilot experiment.

3.3 Cultural Transcreation Product Pilot

Following a brief benchmarking validation and the establishment of the first official prompts version for Asian languages, a three-month pilot was launched to gather authentic and real-time data, monitor product performance, and collect feedback for optimisation. The Cultural Transcreation concept was transformed as a cultural rephrasing feature, integrated into the CS platform via a "Rephrase" widget. This feature allows CS agents to click the button to access the CT service, which generates a rephrased EN version of the original text. The new version retains readability for CS agents while aligning with the target recipients' cultural context. They can then decide whether to edit the rephrased text before sending it to the MT system. Upon sending, the recipient receives the final version that is more in line with their culture and communication style.

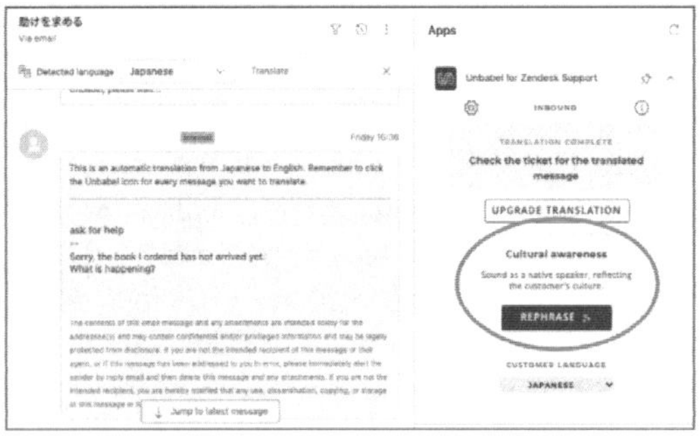

Figure 2: Interface of the CT Product Implemented in the CS Platform

In addition, the intermediate rephrasing step in the source language ensures greater accuracy and cultural relevance in subsequent translations while maintaining transparency of information and editability for the CS agents of the source language.

Figure 3: Pipeline of the CT product implemented in the CS Platform

This Live Pilot involved the CS teams of three Unbabel clients, selected for their high CS demands and frequent interactions with the international target groups. These companies represent three distinct industry sectors, providing a diverse dataset of email communications that reflect varied CS contexts and interactions. Specifically, **Client A**, **B**, and **C** belong to the Tourism, Internet and Electronics industries, respectively.

GPT-4 was initially selected as the LLM for the pilot, using a Few-Shot Prompting approach. The three-month pilot was divided into two phases. Phase I started on 26th January 2024. In the last week of this phase, we optimised the prompts based on collected feedback and re-evaluated alternative LLMs for rephrasing. Prompt Version 2.0 and the selected optimal model were deployed on 14 March, marking the start of Phase II, which continued until the pilot's official end on 29th April.

In terms of CT quality evaluation, the quality and performance of rephrased texts was assessed by the authors of the work through three key dimensions: (1) overall ticket quality, (2) errors caused by cultural rephrasing, and (3) the types and severity of rephrasing errors.

Firstly, the overall quality of the rephrased e-mails is classified into four categories: **Good** – successfully culturally transcreated e-mails without any error caused by LLM-generated rephrasing; **Minor issues** – contain minor errors with limited impact on clarity, yet culturally appropriate; **Major issues** – the rephrased text contains one or more notable errors, some of which affecting meaning or interpretation; **No change** – absence of meaningful cultural adaptation and lacks alignment with the communication norms of the target audience.

Secondly, we annotate errors from e-mails labelled "Minor Issues" or "Major Issues" in the previous step. It facilitates systematic data collection to inform the third dimension. Identified rephrasing errors are categorised into 11 types: **Greeting**, **Closing**, **Register**, **Added Information**, **Removed Information**, **Changed Information**, **Glossary Term**, **Emotion**, **Inconsistency**, **Grammar Issues**, and **Unidiomatic Expression**.

Then, errors are further assessed based on their severity: **Minor** (minimal impact on comprehension); **Major** (more pronounced issues that may alter meaning or reduce clarity); and **Critical** (causing misinterpretation or communication failure).

This structured evaluation framework ensures a consistent and rigorous assessment of LLM-generated rephrasings, enabling further optimisation of the transcreation process.

3.4 Discovering Transcreation on Website Content Generation

A preliminary investigation was conducted into another potential area for application: website content transcreation. This exploration aimed to evaluate whether transcreation, extending beyond cultural aspects to encompass broader bilingual transcreation, could be effectively applied to this field. As a side note, both this experiment and the subsequent supplementary advertising test were conducted exclusively in Simplified Chinese.

The source data for this exploration was provided by a cloud solution provider. For the trial dataset, based on more than 4,000 segments provided by the platform, we randomly selected 20 translation segments with human translation (HT) from each of seven different websites using the platform for content translation, with HT serving as the gold standard. This resulted in a dataset of 140 segments. Unlike the CS sector tests, this trial simplified the transcreation process by instructing the LLM to directly transcreate the source text into the target language, bypassing the intermediate EN rephrasing step, as shown in Figure 6.

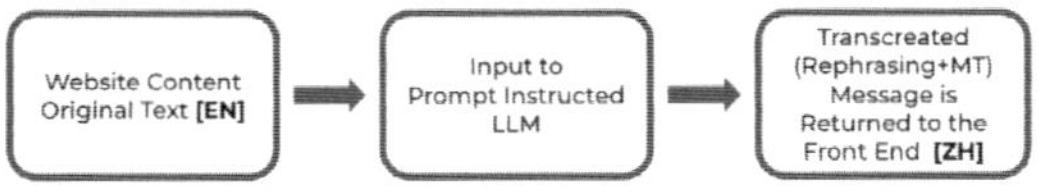

Figure 4: Pipeline of Transcreation Process Adopted in Website Content Generation

In terms of the seven websites from diverse industries, each presents distinct content features: Website A is an e-commerce platform offering contact lenses and selfie phones. Website B, a GPS tracker retailer, consists of marketing texts and product descriptions. Website C, a mattress store, provides product specifications and usage guidelines. Website D supports bio-pharmaceutical partnerships. Website E is a men's fashion retailer comprising product information and navigation-related content. Website F offers data science training content, and its dataset relies primarily on HT, with only two segments adopting MT.

Based on an initial review of the translation data, we developed a set of prompts for direct source-to-target (en > zh-CN) transcreation of multi-domain website content, employing the Few-Shot Prompting technique. GPT-4o, OpenAI's latest LLM at the time, was selected as the designated model for the transcreation tasks. This decision followed brief comparative tests with various LLMs, where GPT-4o displayed superior performance and optimal compatibility with the prompt. After testing different configurations, the model's temperature was set to 1.0 to achieve the desired balance between creativity and stability in the outputs.

As noted before, human translation for each data segment was defined as the gold standard for evaluating the quality of transcreated outputs generated by prompt-based LLM. This optimal reference enabled a comparative analysis, with quality evaluation annotations conducted by the author. The ratings were divided into five distinct categories, ranging from high to low, each accompanied by abbreviations for use in graphical representations in the Results and Discussion chapter:

1. Transcreation quality superior to human translation (**Tc > HT**)

2. Transcreation quality equal to human translation (**Tc = HT**)

3. Transcreation quality lower than human translation but higher than Machine Translation (**HT > Tc > MT**)

4. Transcreation quality equal to Machine Translation (**Tc = MT**)

5. Transcreation quality lower than Machine Translation (**Tc < MT**)

3.4.1 Additional Test in the Advertising Field

After completing the investigation on website content, a supplementary test was conducted. 20 segments in EN with creative potential of publicly available marketing slogans and advertising phrases were randomly selected. The aim was to evaluate whether the developed prompt, in conjunction with the same LLM (GPT-4o) and its configuration, could effectively perform automatic transcreation in the advertising domain, a field known for its complexity and creative demands, typically making it more suitable for human transcreation.

Additionally, given that some LLMs may inherently exhibit creative rewriting or translation skills that go beyond direct translation, it is crucial to attribute all transcreation results in this supplementary test solely to the prompt engineering developed in this research, rather than the LLMs' inherent abilities. To facilitate a clear comparison and highlight the impact of the developed prompt, the study also includes a baseline translation of the selected texts from EN to ZH without the use of prompts. Each translation/transcreation will include a hyperliteral EN back-translation of the Chinese output for additional clarity. However, it is important to note that these back-translations cannot fully convey the nuances and linguistic subtleties inherent in the Chinese text, as many differences in Chinese expression and phrasing are not directly translatable. This limitation should be considered when interpreting the results in the subsequent chapter.

4 Results and Discussion

4.1 MT Benchmarking for CT

As outlined in the Methodology chapter, this section examines 21 MT benchmarking samples from Unbabel clients across seven distinct industries. The samples were first culturally rephrased into EN to align with the cultural nuances of the target language, then translated into ZH, incorporating these cultural adaptations.

The analysis begins by categorising the types of modifications observed in the culturally rephrased text segments. Following this, a detailed examination will be conducted for each cultural rephrasing type, focusing on identifying cultural adjustments that remain absent or require further refinement, as highlighted through observations of the 21 samples. Note that these samples include 166 segments of Original EN and 174 segments of Rephrased EN.

The rephrased EN group demonstrated extensive modifications, including the addition of contextually relevant information to address gaps in the Original EN group. However, not all adjustments enhanced cultural adaptations. For statistical analysis, only culturally valid modifications contributing to cultural optimisation are considered.

Across all 21 tickets, 103 culturally rephrased segments were identified, representing approximately 59.20% of the total segments in the Rephrased EN tickets. As shown in Table 1, these 103 segments were categorised into four primary types of valuable rephrasing. It is essential to note that multiple rephrased segments may appear within a single ticket, and individual segments may exhibit several rephrasing types. Therefore, the Grand Total in the table reflects the total number of culturally adapted segments across all tickets, rather than the sum of rephrasing occurrences.

Main Category	Subcategory	No. of Segments	No. of Tickets
Politeness Adjustment	Courtesy Words	9	7
	Requests/Offers/Invitations	5	5
	Salutations and Valedictions	25	21
	Emotional Outputs	12	9
	Euphemism	0	0
	Total	**51**	**21**
Paraphrasing	Total	**56**	**19**
Grammatical Person Adjustment	Total	**3**	**3**
Functional Equivalence	Total	**4**	**3**
Grand Total		**103**	**21**

Table 1: Statistical Data of Rephrasing Types in Rephrased EN

Among the identified rephrasing types, **Politeness adjustment** emerged as a prominent cultural adaptation, with 51 segments across 21 tickets undergoing this modification.

While Politeness Adjustment was prevalent, **Paraphrasing** was the most common rephrasing type, observed in 56 segments across 19 tickets. This involved rewriting sentences to enhance clarity and cultural appropriateness. For example: Original EN – "Due to a system limitation, we can only reply in Chinese Simplified"; Rephrased EN – "Unfortunately, due to a system limitation, our reply will only be available in Chinese Simplified".

Another category, **Grammatical person adjustment**, was found in 3 segments across 3 tickets. These adjustments involved switching from singular to plural pronouns (e.g., "we" instead of "I") to align with CS conventions in ZH.

Functional equivalence accounted for 4 segments in 3 tickets. This category replaced idiomatic phrases in the source language with culturally appropriate equivalents in the target language. For instance: Original EN – "Consumer care channel"; Rephrased EN: "Customer service channel".

Furthermore, the analysis revealed 6 segments across 6 source tickets requiring cultural adaptation but left unaddressed: 1. **Functional equivalence** (4 segments); 2. **Emotional outputs** (1 segment); 3. **Paraphrasing** (1 segment).

Additionally, the structural analysis of the rephrased samples culminated in the creation of a mind map categorising all observed types of CT rephrasing. This framework offers a comprehensive overview of rephrasing types and their applications, serving as a foundation for future research and practical advancements in CT.

Figure 5: Linguistic-Based Classification of Transcreation Rephrases

4.2 Live Pilot Programme

As presented in the Methodology chapter, this pilot was divided into two phases. Phase I utilised the version 1.0 of the prompts, while Phase II introduced the optimised Prompt 2.0, developed from feedback in Phase I. The statistical data below summarises the culturally transcreated tickets produced during the three-month pilot. A total of 352 e-mails were reformulated using the CT product from EN to ZH, with 60.80% of the data collected during the first phase and 39.20% during the second phase. In addition, it should be noted that the decrease in data collection during Phase II was attributed to external factors such as the holiday season among CS agents and internal organisational restructuring.

	Target Language	No. of Segments	No. of Tickets	Total
Client A	zh-CN-Hans	3	9	12
	zh-TW-Hant	11	21	32
	Total	14	30	**44**
Client B	zh-CN-Hans	96	35	131
	zh-TW-Hant	26	12	38
	Total	122	47	**169**
Client C	zh-CN-Hans	8	6	14
	zh-TW-Hant	70	55	125
	Total	78	61	**139**
Grand Total		214	138	**352**

Table 2: CT Pilot Data Statistics – Number of Tickets

Despite these challenges, the comparative results between the two phases were promising. Following the two phases of pilot, using the same LLM but different prompt versions, a clear comparison is shown in Figure 6. While Prompt 1.0 already demonstrated outstanding performance, with no e-mails categorised as "No changes" (lacking cultural adaptation), the optimised Prompt 2.0 further improved the quality of automated CT. The percentage of e-mails rated as performing perfectly ("Good") increased from 40.65% to 57.97%, exceeding half of the total. Meanwhile, the proportion of e-mails with "Minor issues" and "Major issues" decreased significantly, from 42.06% to 32.61% and 17.29% to 9.42%, respectively. In other words, the percentage of e-mails achieving satisfactory quality ("Good" and "Minor issues") rose from 82.71% to 90.58%. These improvements underscore the success of the prompt optimisation process and highlight how well-designed prompts can significantly improve the performance of a product such as CT when used with consistent LLMs.

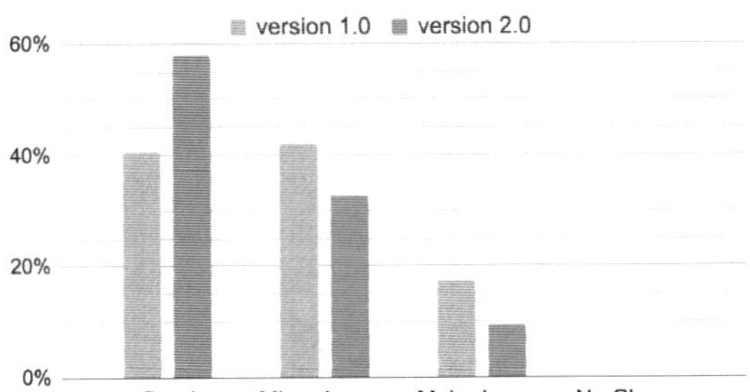

Figure 6: Rephrasing Quality of E-mails in Phase I & II

Regarding segments with rephrasing errors in the two phases, the results show a substantial reduction in errors from Prompt 1.0 to Prompt 2.0, particularly in categories such as *Greeting*, *Changed & Removed Information*, and *Unidiomatic Expression*. The error rate for *Greeting* decreased from 1 error per 23.78 tickets in Phase I to 1 error per 27.6 tickets in Phase II. Errors related to *Changed Information* dropped from 1 per 5.49 tickets to 1 per 34.5 tickets, while errors in *Removed Information* decreased from 1 per 15.29 tickets to 1 per 17.25 tickets. *Unidiomatic Expression* saw a significant decline, with errors reducing from 1 per 53.5 tickets to 1 per 138 tickets. Furthermore, errors in *Register*, *Added Information*, and *Emotion* were entirely eliminated in Phase II, improving from an initial rate of 1 error per 53.5 tickets, 214 tickets, and 53.5 tickets, respectively. Additionally, the number of "Major errors" saw a significant reduction, improving from an average of 1 error per 5.1 tickets in Phase I to 1 per 10.62 tickets in Phase II.

Then, by similarly calculating the average rephrasing error rate per ticket in both phases, the research reached the following result: in Phase I, the rephrasing error rate was 0.58 per ticket, which equates to 1 error for every 1.74 tickets. In Phase II, the rephrasing error rate decreased to 0.49 per ticket, meaning that an error occurred only once for every 2.06 tickets, while it is important to note that the probability of this being a "Major Error" is lower than in the previous phase.

In sum, the percentage of e-mails with optimal quality has increased substantially, while the occurrence of rephrasing errors has decreased. This not only an indicates the success of our prompt optimisation, but also illustrates how well-designed prompts can substantially improve the performance of products like CT when using the same LLM. Lastly, while this paper focuses on the results in ZH, similar improvements were observed in both JA and KO. Comparisons between the first and second versions of the prompts revealed notable progress and strong results across these languages.

4.3 Website Content Transcreation

The comparison of transcreated segments with the original website translations revealed that only 10 segments (7.14% of the total) exhibit quality between HT and MT, suggesting that the prompt-based transcreation approach introduced in this study outperforms standard MT. The remaining 92.86% (130 segments) were evenly distributed across the two highest levels. Of these, 65 segments (46.43%) exceeded the HT benchmark, indicating a quality level surpassing the defined gold standard. The other 65 segments (46.43%) matched HT quality. Notably, while *Tc > HT* is ranked above *Tc = HT* in quality evaluation, this does not imply that all segments can surpass HT. In some cases, *Tc = HT* represents the highest attainable quality, as the human-translated dataset already provides optimal translations. Therefore, segments matching HT further validate the effectiveness of the prompt-based LLM transcreation approach. These findings highlight that the prompt developed in this test, coupled with GPT-4o, has the potential to replace a substantial portion of HT in website content generation.

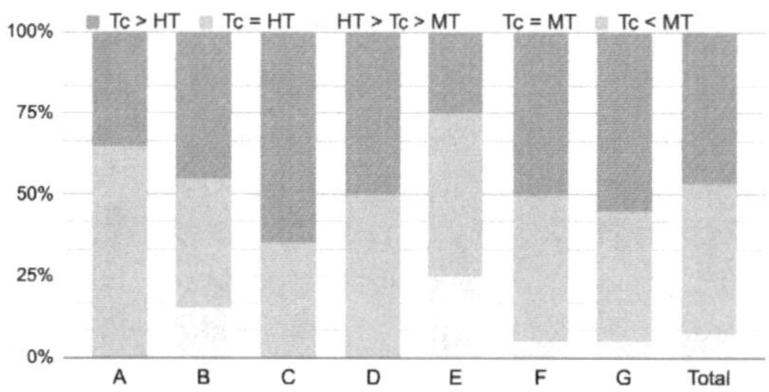

Figure 7: Quality of Transcreated Segments per Website

4.3.1 Transcreation in the Advertisement Industry

Owing to length constraints, Figure 9 shows only 3 of the 20 advertising segments of this test, where green-coloured segments highlight strong creative elements, red-coloured ones denote failed or awkward translations, and underlined sections indicate parts where the sentence is unnatural, lacks fluency, or does not align with the essential linguistic features of effective Chinese advertising. In the remaining unpresented slogans, prompt-based transcreation generally outperformed transcreation without prompts. Only 3 segments exhibited identical quality, as both represented optimal translation choices. This supplementary test clearly demonstrated the potential of integrating transcreation prompts with GPT-4o to achieve exceptional levels of creative adaptation and translation.

Brand	Original slogan	GPT-4o without prompt	GPT-4o with prompt
Esso	*Put a Tiger in Your Tank*	在你的油箱里加一只老虎 EN: "Add a tiger in your tank"	为您的油箱加点猛虎之力 EN: "Give your fuel tank the power of tiger"
Tide	*Tide's in, dirt's out.*	汰渍到，污渍跑。 EN: "Tide arrives, stains run."	汰渍到，污渍掉。 EN: "Tide arrives, stains wash out."
Dollar Shave Club	*Shave Time. Shave Money.*	省时间，省钱。 EN: "Save time, save money."	省时省钱，刮须无忧。 EN: "Save time save money, shave without worry."

Figure 8: Advertising Slogans' Transcreation Outputs

In conclusion, the success of the website content prompt developed at this stage is highly significant, demonstrating its ability to effectively process diverse content and text types across multiple fields.

5 Conclusions and Future Work

By bridging linguistics and AI, this research has made significant strides, foremost among them being developing an automated CT system for the CS sector. To achieve this, culturally aware guidelines were established for three Asian languages, followed by the evaluation of the initial version of the prompts through their automated transcreation outputs using MT benchmark samples. These prompts were then further refined, alongside the creation of a linguistically based classification for categorising transcreation rephrasing. The CT pilot test confirmed that the continuous optimisation of prompt-based LLMs significantly enhanced the cultural transcreation quality. This showed the product's potential as a valuable AI-assisted tool for real-world applications, increasing the productivity and efficiency of CS agents in their communication tasks. Beyond cultural adaptation, this study also explored the feasibility of prompt-based automated transcreation for website content and advertising. As a result, we developed a successful multi-purpose prompt adaptable across industries, content types, and text genres. These findings lay a solid foundation for future advancements and product innovation, with the goal of expanding transcreation applications beyond CS to drive broader industry adoption.

At present, efforts are underway to integrate Unbabel's proprietary TowerLLM (Alves et al., 2024) into the CT product to replace third-party LLMs. After optimising Prompt 3.0 and training the internal model, TowerLLM was tested with 21 EN-ZH ticket samples to generate CT outputs. These outputs were compared with GPT-4o outputs for the same samples to identify the best culturally adapted versions. The results showed that TowerLLM produced the best transcreated versions for 17 of 21 samples, with the remaining 4 being a tie between the two models. This progress indicates a potential shift to TowerLLM as the product's primary model soon. Additionally, development is underway for an automated CT quality monitoring programme, with ongoing efforts to explore broader areas of transcreation to expand Unbabel's services.

From a broader AI industry perspective, we believe that the sensible and responsible integration of AI into language services fosters human progress, as pursued by the CT product developed in this study. This aligns with the Augmented Translation concept, which views AI as a collaborator rather than a replacement for human translators, enhancing workflows and enabling creative problem-solving. In the CS sector, this means that CS agents are not replaced by automation but are instead empowered with AI-driven tools that support decision-making, refine translations, and adapt responses to align with cultural expectations. By leveraging this approach, the CT product not only facilitates the work of CS agents and enhances their efficiency, but also mitigates potential challenges arising from communication styles and cultural differences. Crucially, it adjusts tone, contextual appropriateness, and subtle linguistic distinctions vital for effective cross-cultural communication. To conclude, maximising AI's benefits requires a balanced strategy — leveraging its potential while maintaining human agency, ensuring AI enriches rather than disrupts professional and social progress.

Acknowledgments

This work was conducted as part of project no. 62 – "Center for Responsible AI", funded by European Funds under the "Recovery and Resilience Plan - Component 5: Agendas Mobilizadoras para a Inovação Empresarial", within the NextGenerationEU funding program. It received partial funding from FCT (Fundação para a Ciência e a Tecnologia) under project UIDB/50021/2020 (DOI:10.54499/UIDB/50021/2020). Additionally, the work was supported by the Centro de Linguística da Universidade de Lisboa (UID/00214).

References

Duarte M. Alves, José Pombal, Nuno M. Guerreiro, Pedro H. Martins, João Alves, Amin Farajian, Ben Peters, Ricardo Rei, Patrick Fernandes, Sweta Agrawal, Pierre Colombo, José G. C. de Souza, and André F. T. Martins. 2024. Tower: An open multilingual large language model for translation-related tasks. *Preprint*, arXiv:2402.17733.

Oliver Carreira. 2023. Surveying the economics of transcreation from the perspective of language professionals. *Across Languages and Cultures*, 24:127–144.

Mar Díaz-Millón and María Dolores Olvera-Lobo. 2023. Towards a definition of transcreation: a systematic literature review. *Perspectives*, 31(2):347–364.

Douglas C. Engelbart. 1962. Augmenting Human Intellect: A Conceptual Framework.

Viviana Gaballo. 2012. Exploring the boundaries of transcreation in specialized translation. *ESP Across Cultures*, 9:95–113.

Edward T. Hall. 1976. *Beyond Culture*. Anchor Books. Knopf Doubleday Publishing Group.

Juliane House. 1997. *Translation Quality Assessment: A Model Revisited*. Tübinger Beiträge zur Linguistik. G. Narr.

Juliane House. 2014. *Translation Quality Assessment: Past and Present*, pages 241–264.

Juliane House. 2015. *Translation: A Multidisciplinary Approach*. Palgrave Advances in Language and Linguistics. Palgrave Macmillan UK.

David Katan. 2015. Translation at the cross-roads: Time for the transcreational turn? *Perspectives*, 24:1–16.

Arle Lommel. 2018. Augmented translation: A new approach to combining human and machine capabilities. In *Proceedings of the 13th Conference of the Association for Machine Translation in the Americas (Volume 2: User Track)*, pages 5–12, Boston, MA. Association for Machine Translation in the Americas.

Carme Mangiron and Minako O'Hagan. 2006. Game localisation: Unleashing imagination with 'restricted' translation. *JOURNAL OF SPECIALISED TRANSLATION*, 6.

Jeremy Munday, Sara R. Pinto, and Jacob Blakesley. 2022. *Introducing Translation Studies: Theories and Applications*. Taylor & Francis.

Eugene A. Nida and Charles R. Taber. 1969. *The Theory and Practice of Translation*. Helps for translators. E. J. Brill.

Sharon O'Brien. 2024. Human-centered augmented translation: against antagonistic dualisms. *Perspectives*, 32(3):391–406.

Anthony Pym. 2017. *Exploring Translation Theories*. Online access with EBA: Taylor & Francis. Taylor & Francis.

Sissel M. Rike. 2013. Bilingual corporate websites-from translation to transcreation?

Beatriz Silva, Helena Wu, Yan Jingxuan, Vera Cabarrão, Helena Moniz, Sara Guerreiro de Sousa, João Almeida, Malene Sjørslev Søholm, Ana Farinha, and Paulo Dimas. 2024. Cultural transcreation with LLMs as a new product. In *Proceedings of the 25th Annual Conference of the European Association for Machine Translation (Volume 2)*, pages 57–58, Sheffield, UK. European Association for Machine Translation (EAMT).

Maria A. Szasz and Maria C. Olt. 2018. *Translation, Transcreation and Localization*. Editura U. T. Press.

Lawrence Venuti. 2017. *The Translator's Invisibility: A History of Translation*.

Hans J. Vermeer. 1978. Ein rahmen für eine allgemeine translationstheorie. *Lebende Sprachen*, 23(3).

A comparison of translation performance between DeepL and Supertext

Alex Flückiger, Chantal Amrhein, Tim Graf, Frédéric Odermatt, Martin Pömsl, Philippe Schläpfer, Florian Schottmann, Samuel Läubli

Supertext

`{firstname.lastname}@supertext.com`

Abstract

As strong machine translation (MT) systems are increasingly based on large language models (LLMs), reliable quality benchmarking requires methods that capture their ability to leverage extended context. This study compares two commercial MT systems – DeepL and Supertext – by assessing their performance on unsegmented texts. We evaluate translation quality across four language directions with professional translators assessing segments with full document-level context. While segment-level assessments indicate no strong preference between the systems in most cases, document-level analysis reveals a preference for Supertext in three out of four language directions, suggesting superior consistency across longer texts. We advocate for more context-sensitive evaluation methodologies to ensure that MT quality assessments reflect real-world usability.[1]

1 Introduction

After the transition from statistical to neural modelling roughly a decade ago (Kalchbrenner and Blunsom, 2013; Sutskever et al., 2014; Bahdanau et al., 2015), the field of MT is undergoing another paradigm shift towards leveraging LLMs (Xu et al., 2024; Wu et al., 2024b; Kocmi et al., 2024). LLM-based translation offers the potential for significantly improved translation quality, especially with respect to consistent translation of documents. Unlike neural machine translation (NMT) systems, which typically process documents as isolated sentences or paragraphs (Post and Junczys-Dowmunt, 2023), many LLMs operate with context windows that can span thousands of words, allowing them to maintain consistency throughout a document – for instance, by ensuring that a word's translation in the final sentence matches its previous forms (Wu et al., 2024b).

In the most recent shared task at the Conference on Machine Translation (WMT24) that focuses on evaluating the state of the art in general-domain translation quality, the majority of the 28 system submissions were already based on LLMs (Kocmi et al., 2024). Although without statistical significance and for the language direction English to German only, one system even outranked the human reference translations as evaluated by professional human annotators.

Despite this impressive achievement, findings of human-machine parity should be approached with caution. Similar claims already emerged with pre-LLM technology (Hassan et al., 2018), yet have subsequently been refuted due to limitations in the evaluation design focusing on single segments in isolation (Läubli et al., 2018; Toral et al., 2018; Freitag et al., 2021). The WMT24 shared task also highlights that evaluations based on automatic metrics (rather than human evaluation) can lead to wrong conclusions when comparing strong MT systems (Kocmi et al., 2024).

However, these insights are often overlooked in evaluations of commercial MT systems. For example, Intento's The State of Machine Translation 2024 report,[2] which assesses 52 providers across 11 language pairs, serves as a valuable resource for potential users in real-world settings, but its benchmarking methodology relies on automatic scoring of sentence-level data, and the authors acknowledge that 'you may need a human linguist' to ensure greater reliability.

In this paper, we evaluate two commercial translation systems (Section 2) under conditions that allow for leveraging the full-text capabilities of

[1]We release all evaluation data and scripts for further analysis and reproduction at `https://github.com/supertext/evaluation_deepl_supertext`

[2]`https://inten.to/machine-translation-report-2024`

LLMs. The segmentation of the source text is handled by the translation systems alone without any prior splitting (Section 3), and the resulting translations are rated by professional translators considering the full document context (Section 4). We find that while both systems translate a similar number of segments better than the other, the difference is more pronounced on the document level (Section 5), which we attribute to differences in how much context the systems consider during translation (Section 6). Our findings suggest that the adoption of LLMs creates opportunities for smaller players to challenge dominant industry leaders (Section 7).

2 Systems

We compare the free online offering of two commercial MT providers:

DeepL DeepL[3] is a widely used MT provider boasting 'unrivalled translations that set the standard'.[4] In the latest Intento report, it scores best among nine 'real-time engines' and, together with GPT-4, is found to 'consistently outperform other models'.[2] Due to its closed source, the technology behind DeepL's translation system is not publicly known.

Supertext Supertext[5] builds on an open, general-purpose LLM that has been specialised for the task of translation with proprietary methods and data. While the system can be adapted to specific domains, we use the freely available generic version. For the purpose of the evaluation described in this paper, we use both systems with default settings. For example, we do not specify politeness (formal/informal) although supported by both systems in some language combinations.

While both DeepL and Supertext provide target language variants for English (British and American), Supertext also provides target language variants for German (Austria, Germany, Switzerland), French (France, Switzerland), and Italian (Italy, Switzerland). As our use case is machine translation for people in Switzerland, we use the Swiss target language variant whenever available (Section 3.2).[6]

[3]https://www.deepl.com

[4]https://www.deepl.com/en/quality, see also Appendix A.

[5]https://www.supertext.com

[6]Compared to English variants, the Swiss variants of other languages differ minimally.

Language Direction	Texts	Segments	Words
de → en-GB	20	281	3336
de → fr-CH	20	276	3336
de → it-CH	20	265	3336
en → de-CH	20	211	3483
Total	80	1033	13491

Table 1: Evaluation data by language direction.

3 Data

3.1 Source Texts

We collect 20 texts each in two source languages: English (en) and German (de). All texts stem from news websites: New York Times[7] for English and Neue Zürcher Zeitung[8] for German, respectively. We select 10 FAQ pages and 10 recent news articles in the economy section from each website. Notably, these texts are only available in a single language; they are unlikely to be contained in the training data of either system we evaluate. To balance the distribution of text lengths, we trim the end of some texts by omitting their final paragraphs.

3.2 Target Texts

We create translations in four language directions (Table 1) directly in the respective online translation interface of each system as a regular user would.[9] We do not modify the texts before translation and paste them in their original formatting, including newlines. The translation systems may segment the text into smaller chunks internally.

After translation, we manually split and align the source texts and translations into sentences. If one of the systems merges two or more sentences into a single sentence, we ensure that the same content is merged for the other system, such that the raters are presented with parallel segments. Table 1 shows the resulting number of segments per language pair. The texts per source language are identical, differing only in how they were manually segmented for the A/B test after translation. Across the language pairs, the median number of segments per document is 13.

[7]https://www.nytimes.com

[8]https://www.nzz.ch

[9]All translations were produced on 27 January 2025.

4 Evaluation Setup

We conduct a blind A/B test in which professional translators rate DeepL and Supertext outputs with full document-level context.

4.1 Raters

We enrol 8 professional translators with experience in evaluating machine translation output, 1 to 3 per language direction. All raters have between 2 and 19 years of professional experience (average=8.6 years) in the language combination they are assigned to and are native in the respective target language.

4.2 Materials

We arrange all segments of a source document with their corresponding translations by both systems in a spreadsheet. The segments are presented in original document order, including formatting such as newlines, such that raters see the full source text and both translations side-by-side. We randomly assign the system outputs to columns labelled Translation A and Translation B for each text such that raters do not have any information about which translation stems from which system (a blind A/B test setting). System assignments are kept consistent within a text such that the document context remains natural.

4.3 Procedure

Documents are assigned to single raters. For each segment in each document, the assigned rater is asked to choose whether Translation A is better, Translation B is better, or whether both translations are of equal quality.

Our instructions explicitly state that 'equal' can mean that two translations are equally good or equally bad. Moreover, the raters were asked to focus on the content rather than punctuation to avoid that the results get biased because of specifics of a language variant.

5 Evaluation Results

Segment-level and text-level preference ratings are shown in Figures 1 and 2, respectively.

5.1 Segment-level

Across all language pairs, 9.5% of the segments generated by DeepL and Supertext are identical. The overlap is highest in de → en-GB, particularly in the FAQ texts where 26.1% of the segments were translated identically.

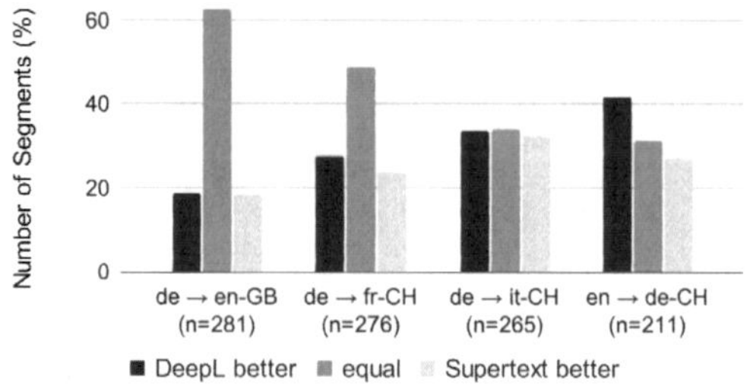

Figure 1: Segment-level ratings.

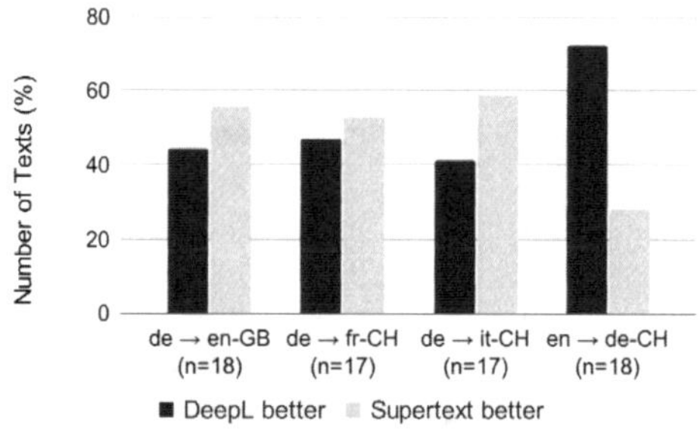

Figure 2: Aggregated segment-level ratings per text. Texts with the same number of preferred segments for both systems are excluded.

Participants rate most segments as equal in terms of translation quality in three out of four language directions. While the number of segments where one system is preferred over the other is similar for DeepL and Supertext in these language directions, raters show a preference for DeepL in en → de-CH (88 DeepL, 66 equal, 57 Supertext).

5.2 Document-level

We derive document-level preferences by aggregating the segment-level ratings of each evaluated document. For example, a text is counted as 'DeepL better' if the rater preferred DeepL's translations for more segments than Supertext's translations in that document.

In contrast to the pooled segment-level ratings (Section 5.1), raters show a preference for documents translated by Supertext in three out of four language directions, most notably in de → it-CH (7 DeepL, 3 equal, 10 Supertext). In en → de-CH, however, raters show a clear preference for documents translated by DeepL (13 DeepL, 2 equal, 5 Supertext).

6 Discussion

Our evaluation highlights that conclusions drawn from MT quality assessments may vary significantly depending on the unit of measurement. While raters in our study preferred a similar number of translated segments by DeepL and Supertext overall, the difference becomes more pronounced at the document level. This discrepancy suggests that segment-level assessments alone may not fully capture translation quality as perceived in real-world usage, where coherence and consistency across entire documents play a critical role.

Notably, while segment-level ratings indicate no strong preference between the two systems in most language directions, document-level aggregation reveals a more distinct pattern. Raters favour Supertext's translations at the document level in three out of four language directions, with the most pronounced difference observed in de $\rightarrow$ it-CH. This suggests that Supertext may provide better consistency or fluency across longer texts in these language directions. While we have yet to conduct a systematic qualitative comparison of system outputs, we find texts where the same word is translated differently by DeepL and consistently by Supertext across paragraphs. An example is shown in Table 2, where DeepL translates the German word *Startseite* as either *start page*, *home page*, or *Home page*.

In contrast, for en $\rightarrow$ de-CH, raters show a clear preference for DeepL at both the segment and document levels, indicating a potential strength of DeepL in handling this specific language combination. Our preliminary analysis is inconclusive at this point, but the Supertext outputs seem to contain a higher number of within-sentence errors such as wrong choices for individual words or omissions. Another hypothesis is that Supertext, which supports three different German target language variants, may introduce inconsistencies by mixing region-specific elements in translation outputs.

7 Conclusion

Our study highlights the growing significance of document-level evaluations in MT quality benchmarking, especially as LLM-based systems leverage broader context windows to enhance translation consistency. While segment-level assessments suggest no clear preference between DeepL and Supertext in most of the language directions we examined, document-level aggregation reveals notable differences. Supertext is preferred in three out of four language pairs, where its translations exhibit greater consistency. In contrast, en $\rightarrow$ de-CH shows a clear preference for DeepL, possibly due to fewer within-sentence errors or differences in regional language handling.

As LLM-based MT systems continue to evolve, future studies should further investigate the impact of context length on commercial MT benchmarking campaigns. Insights into how different systems leverage context and resolve ambiguities will be essential for advancing evaluation methodologies and ensuring that translation systems meet real-world user expectations.

Limitations

While A/B tests are commonly used for comparing two systems and a reliable basis for incrementally improving MT systems (Tang et al., 2010; Wu et al., 2024a), they provide no insight into the severity of errors within a translation or across different systems compared to MQM ratings (Freitag et al., 2021). Absent the use of more time-intensive evaluation frameworks, such limitations persist irrespective of whether preferences are aggregated at the system level or pooled by document.

During real-world usage, some mistakes may be harder to spot than others when not being shown contrastively against an alternative translation. Similarly, the preference in an A/B test may not correlate with the effort needed for post-editing the translation. To address these questions, we plan to extend our evaluation efforts.

The evaluation was carried out by professional translators working for Supertext. Since the A/B assignments were randomized and anonymized, we do not assume any bias. Additionally, in the interest of transparency, we publicly share the complete dataset, including the source text, translations from each system, and the corresponding ratings.

Finally, the scope of this study is not exhaustive but is limited to a subset of language pairs, two domains, and a limited number of documents. Yet, we are providing details that go beyond what DeepL is sharing publicly on their website.[4]

SID	Source text (de)	DeepL (en-GB)	Supertext (en-GB)
1	Wie kann ich die NZZ als Startseite festlegen?	How can I set the NZZ as my start page?	**How can I set NZZ as my homepage?**
2	Öffnen Sie Ihren Browser:	Open your browser:	Open your browser:
3	- Stellen Sie sicher, dass der Browser geöffnet ist, den Sie verwenden möchten (z.B. Google Chrome, Mozilla Firefox, Microsoft Edge, Safari).	- Make sure the browser you want to use is open (e.g. Google Chrome, Mozilla Firefox, Microsoft Edge, Safari).	- Make sure the browser you want to use is open (e.g., Google Chrome, Mozilla Firefox, Microsoft Edge, Safari).
4	Gehen Sie zu den Einstellungen:	Go to the settings:	Go to settings:
5	- In den meisten Browsern finden Sie die Einstellungen oder Optionen im Menü oben rechts, oft dargestellt durch drei Punkte (?) oder Striche (≡).	- In most browsers, you will find the settings or options in the menu at the top right, often represented by three dots (?) or dashes (≡).	- In most browsers, you'll find the settings or options in the menu in the top right corner, often represented by three dots (?) or lines (≡).
6	- Klicken Sie auf diese Punkte oder Striche, um das Menü zu öffnen, und wählen Sie dann Einstellungen.	- Click on these dots or dashes to open the menu and then select Settings.	- Click on these dots or lines to open the menu, and then select Settings.
7	Finden Sie die Option für die Startseite:	Find the option for the home page:	Find the option for the homepage:
8	- In den Einstellungen gibt es einen Abschnitt für die Startseite oder Beim Start.	- In Settings, there is a section for Home page or On startup.	**- In the settings, there is a section for the homepage or start page.**
9	- Suchen Sie nach einer Option wie „Startseite festlegen" oder „Beim Start" (je nach Browser kann der genaue Wortlaut unterschiedlich sein).	- Look for an option such as 'Set home page' or 'On startup' (the exact wording may vary depending on your browser).	**- Look for an option like "Set homepage" or "Start page" (the exact wording may vary depending on the browser).**
10	NZZ.de als Startseite festlegen:	Set NZZ.de as your start page:	**Set NZZ.de as your homepage:**
11	- Wenn Sie die Option „Bestimmte Seite öffnen" sehen, wählen Sie diese aus.	- If you see the option 'Open specific page', select it.	- If you see an option called "Open a specific page," select it.
12	- Geben Sie in das Eingabefeld https://www.nzz.de ein.	- Enter https://www.nzz.de in the input field.	- Enter https://www.nzz.de in the input field.
13	Einstellungen speichern:	Save settings:	Save settings:
14	- Die meisten Browser speichern die Änderung automatisch, sobald Sie das Feld verlassen.	- Most browsers save the change automatically as soon as you exit the field.	- Most browsers will save the change automatically as soon as you leave the field.
15	Sie können das Einstellungsfenster nun schließen.	You can now close the settings window.	You can now close the settings window.

Table 2: Example of a rated de → en-GB document. Better-rated translations are highlighted in bold; segments without any bold translation were rated as equal. System names are not shown during evaluation (Section 4).

Acknowledgments

We thank all the professional translators involved for their support with this evaluation.

References

Dzmitry Bahdanau, Kyunghyun Cho, and Yoshua Bengio. 2015. Neural Machine Translation by Jointly Learning to Align and Translate. In *Proceedings of ICLR*, San Diego, CA.

Markus Freitag, George Foster, David Grangier, Viresh Ratnakar, Qijun Tan, and Wolfgang Macherey. 2021. Experts, errors, and context: A large-scale study of human evaluation for machine translation. *Transactions of the Association for Computational Linguistics*, 9:1460–1474.

Hany Hassan, Anthony Aue, Chang Chen, Vishal Chowdhary, Jonathan Clark, Christian Federmann, Xuedong Huang, Marcin Junczys-Dowmunt, William Lewis, Mu Li, et al. 2018. Achieving human parity on automatic chinese to english news translation. *arXiv preprint arXiv:1803.05567*.

Nal Kalchbrenner and Phil Blunsom. 2013. Recurrent Continuous Translation Models. In *Proceedings of EMNLP*, pages 1700–1709, Seattle, WA.

Tom Kocmi, Eleftherios Avramidis, Rachel Bawden, Ondřej Bojar, Anton Dvorkovich, Christian Federmann, Mark Fishel, Markus Freitag, Thamme Gowda, Roman Grundkiewicz, Barry Haddow, Marzena Karpinska, Philipp Koehn, Benjamin Marie, Christof Monz, Kenton Murray, Masaaki Nagata, Martin Popel, Maja Popović, Mariya Shmatova, Steinthór Steingrímsson, and Vilém Zouhar. 2024. Findings of the WMT24 general machine translation shared task: The LLM era is here but MT is not solved yet. In *Proceedings of the Ninth Conference on Machine Translation*, pages 1–46, Miami, Florida, USA. Association for Computational Linguistics.

Samuel Läubli, Rico Sennrich, and Martin Volk. 2018. Has machine translation achieved human parity? a case for document-level evaluation. In *Proceedings of the 2018 Conference on Empirical Methods in Natural Language Processing*, pages 4791–4796, Brussels, Belgium. Association for Computational Linguistics.

Matt Post and Marcin Junczys-Dowmunt. 2023. Escaping the sentence-level paradigm in machine translation. *ArXiv*, abs/2304.12959.

Ilya Sutskever, Oriol Vinyals, and Quoc V. Le. 2014. Sequence to Sequence Learning with Neural Networks. In *Proceedings of NIPS*, pages 3104–3112, Montreal, Canada.

Diane Tang, Ashish Agarwal, Deirdre O'Brien, and Mike Meyer. 2010. Overlapping experiment infrastructure: more, better, faster experimentation. In *Proceedings of the 16th ACM SIGKDD International Conference on Knowledge Discovery and Data Mining*, KDD '10, page 17–26, New York, NY, USA. Association for Computing Machinery.

Antonio Toral, Sheila Castilho, Ke Hu, and Andy Way. 2018. Attaining the unattainable? reassessing claims of human parity in neural machine translation. In *Proceedings of the Third Conference on Machine Translation: Research Papers*, pages 113–123, Brussels, Belgium. Association for Computational Linguistics.

Guojun Wu, Shay B Cohen, and Rico Sennrich. 2024a. Evaluating automatic metrics with incremental machine translation systems. In *Findings of the Association for Computational Linguistics: EMNLP 2024*, pages 2994–3005, Miami, Florida, USA. Association for Computational Linguistics.

Minghao Wu, Thuy-Trang Vu, Lizhen Qu, George Foster, and Gholamreza Haffari. 2024b. Adapting large language models for document-level machine translation. *Preprint*, arXiv:2401.06468.

Haoran Xu, Young Jin Kim, Amr Sharaf, and Hany Hassan Awadalla. 2024. A paradigm shift in machine translation: Boosting translation performance of large language models. *Preprint*, arXiv:2309.11674.

A Appendix

For the sake of persistency, we share the archived link as well: `https://web.archive.org/web/20250215011944/https://www.deepl.com/en/quality`

Leveraging LLMs for Cross-Locale Adaptation: a Workflow Proposal on Spanish Variants

Vera Senderowicz Guerra
Welocalize
vera.senderowicz@welocalize.com

Abstract

Localization strategies often vary significantly across languages, but the necessity of developing entirely separate approaches for closely related language variants remains debatable. This paper investigates the potential of streamlining the development process of localization strategies across Spanish locales. Leveraging Large Language Models, prompting techniques, and specialized linguistic resources, we explore methods for adapting a chosen baseline translation —produced by a Neural Machine Translation engine and post-edited by professional linguists— into region-specific variants. Focusing on transformations from Latin American Spanish into Mexican and Argentine Spanish, we examine vocabulary, terminology, grammar, and stylistic differences. Our findings suggest that building from a high-quality baseline and applying a modular, mostly automated adaptation process can efficiently address locale-specific divergences. While this approach reduces the need for manual intervention, human linguistic review remains essential, especially to refine stylistic nuances.

1 Introduction

Many international enterprises operating in diverse markets worldwide translate their content into multiple languages and localize it to the specific variants spoken by their target audiences. Despite the overarching goal of effective engagement, localization strategies can vary significantly between languages and even among different variants of the same language, due to factors such as translation volume, data availability, audience size and potential clients in each region, with the ultimate objective being to choose the most efficient and best suited solution for each market (Dunne and Dunne, 2011).

In this paper, we investigate the extent to which localization strategies can be streamlined for different variants of the same language. We propose a standardized workflow based on a common, human reviewed Neural Machine Translation (NMT) root, and a set of optional AI-powered post-editing steps that utilize Large Language Models (LLMs), Retrieval-Augmented Generation (RAG), prompting techniques, and language resources. These steps are designed to address the divergences of each variant from the designated base and to make the necessary adjustments for adapting that base to different locales.

2 Experimental settings

This study is based on proprietary bilingual datasets provided by a commercial client in the entertainment industry. The source language is English (EN) —reflecting its centrality in both the client's operations and global markets— and the data comprise user interface segments and marketing copy. This content type is well-suited for the experiment because it constitutes a relatively low-risk domain, where minor regional inaccuracies are unlikely to cause significant consequences, and because it presents distinct localization challenges, as it often demands cultural specificity and audience engagement over linguistic neutrality. The same datasets are used throughout all stages of the experiment; they cannot be publicly released due to confidentiality agreements.

We focus on Spanish (ES), a language with numerous regional variants spoken in strategically important markets. Beyond its commercial relevance, ES offers a compelling case for this study due to the diversity of its variants across lexical, grammatical, and stylistic dimensions, each potentially requiring different adaptation strategies. The study examines three specific locales: Latin American (ES-LA), Argentine (ES-AR), and Mexican

Spanish (ES-MX). Due to the involvement of professional human translators in both comparison and evaluation tasks, the datasets are relatively small: 1637 segments for EN>ES-LA, 1635 for EN>ES-AR, and 1624 for EN>ES-MX. For cross-variant comparisons, only overlapping segments were retained: 1567 between ES-LA and ES-AR, 1495 between ES-AR and ES-MX, and 1474 between ES-LA and ES-MX. The ES-LA variant used is a commercially standardized form designed to be broadly accessible in pan-regional contexts when full regional localization is not feasible. The selection of only these three variants was guided by strategic relevance, data availability, and time constraints. While the approach is designed for potential reuse, its applicability to other locales and/or languages requires further specific testing and validation. It should also be noted that this approach is not intended for direct application to terminology-intensive domains such as legal or medical translation, which demand domain expertise, stricter quality controls, and accommodate more complex patterns of locale-specific terminology variation.

All LLM-based evaluations were conducted using OpenAI's GPT models, selected for their accessible fine-tuning capabilities (OpenAI). We chose GPT-4o mini due to its strong performance in automatic post-editing (Raunak et al., 2023) and its cost-efficiency relative to other OpenAI models (OpenAI, 2024). While we hypothesize that similar outcomes could be achieved with alternative models from other providers with minimal prompt adjustments (Uguet et al., 2024), model comparison was beyond the scope of this study, which focused on process development rather than tool benchmarking.

Prompting workflows were limited to three iterations per process and locale, following "Green AI" principles (Schwartz et al., 2020). Fine-tuning used no more than 55 examples per task. All experiments ran on 4 CPUs (Core i3-10350K) over 10h 30min, with an estimated carbon footprint of 276.37 gCO_2e (1.62 kWh), equivalent to 0.30 tree-months in Spain (calculated using Lannelongue et al., 2021).

3 The Spanish variations

To identify effective methods for transforming one ES locale into another, we first needed a clear understanding of what those transformations would entail. To this end, we conducted a contrastive linguistic analysis (Bennett, 2002; Ke, 2019) on reference translations from EN into ES-LA, ES-MX and ES-AR, all produced by the same NMT engine and post-edited by professional native linguists. This analysis led to the identification of the four categories of cross-locale divergences described below:

- **Terminological differences (client-specific terminology).** A subcategory of lexical changes, these terminological differences pertain to terms that primarily reflect the client's specific products and/or services and their preferred presentation to the target audience, rather than intrinsic characteristics of the ES variant itself.

- **Vocabulary differences (non-client-specific vocabulary).** Words and constructions that are preferred over others in different regions. Also a subcategory of lexical changes, these preferences are not dependent on the client's content but rather on the specific culture to which the content belongs. These preferences may include verbs (e.g., "regresar" is preferred over "volver" in ES-MX), nouns (e.g., "mamadera" is more commonly used than "biberón" in ES-AR), adjectives (e.g., while "small" tends to be translated as "chico" in ES-AR, "pequeño" is preferred in ES-LA), adverbs (e.g., "después" and "todavía" are more widely used in ES-AR than their corresponding "luego" and "aún"), and even different types of constructions (e.g., when used to convey a sense of duty, "tener que" is preferred over "deber" in ES-AR).

- **Grammatical differences.** While not all variants differ in this aspect, it is one of the most determining factors for recognizing ES locales: while certain words or terms might seem out of place if used in the context of a locale they don't belong to, verbs and pronouns conjugated according to the grammar rules of a different locale can lead to the entire text being identified as belonging to it. The primary difference usually lies in the second person: in this case, ES-LA and ES-MX don't present any differences, but ES-AR follows the "vos" conjugation ("vos amás", "vos querés", "vos partís"), instead of the widely used "tú" ("tú amas", "tú quieres", "tú partes").

- **Style differences.** The most complex category, it concerns how utterances sound "natural" within the cultural and communicative norms of each locale. Unlike grammar or terminology, style is less prescriptive: the rules governing it are highly context-dependent, often implicit, and nearly impossible to codify exhaustively. Additionally, style is shaped by overlapping factors such as client preferences, domain conventions, and regional usage, making style adaptation more intricate than other types of linguistic adjustment. Given this variability, it is challenging to provide universal examples, but some illustrative cases include the preference for the periphrastic future ("vas a venir") over the simple future ("vendrás") in ES-AR, and the use of constructions starting with "que lo" ("¡Que lo disfrutes!") instead of the imperative ("¡Disfrútalo!") in second person phrases expressing the speaker's wishes.

While this categorization is based on linguistic criteria, its primary purpose is to group elements according to the similarity or compatibility of the rules governing their transformation, thus enabling a shared adaptation approach.

3.1 Deciding the baseline locale

It was necessary to determine which locale would serve as the baseline for transformations. In this context, *baseline* does not imply neutrality, but rather refers to the more "in-between" variant, the most practical starting point for adaptation. To define it, we compared the reference samples mentioned above using two of the most widely recognized —and most commonly requested by clients— machine translation quality metrics that assess the distance between a hypothesis and a reference translation: BLEU (Papineni et al., 2002) and Levenshtein Edit Distance (Levenshtein, 1966), normalized by the number of characters in the MT output, as shown in Table 1 below.

ES locales	BLEU	PE Distance
LA-AR	84.53	7%
LA-MX	92.69	5%
MX-AR	83.84	6%

Table 1: Distance between ES samples measured by BLEU and Levenshtein Edit Distance.

The first significant observation from Table 1 is that the metrics support the primary hypothesis of our experiment: if minimal editing effort is required to convert one locale to another, all locales are relatively "close", which suggests that a strategy merge would not only be feasible but also sensible. Secondly, the results indicate that ES-AR might not be the best suited baseline candidate, as it is the most divergent from the other two locales. Additionally, it exhibits all four types of differences described when compared to both ES-MX and ES-LA, while these only display terminological and stylistic differences, which is reflected in their high similarity scores. Since the metrics indicate that both ES-MX and ES-LA are similarly suitable, we have chosen the latter as the baseline locale, based on our linguistic assessment: being a commercially constructed convention, it is better attained through human post-editing of NMT output following client-specific guidelines, as vocabulary and style-related uncertainties would be likely to arise during the adaptation process, with no underlying language community to inform such decisions beyond the client's specifications.

4 Adaptations

After defining the baseline locale, we proceeded to develop an automatic post-editing method for each of the previously defined categories of differences. We adopted a segment-level approach, iterating through segment pairs to individually perform automatic post-editing on each of them.

4.1 Terminology

To adapt client-specific terminology, we used a glossary stored in a CSV file, with EN source terms in the first column and corresponding terms for each target locale in subsequent columns. The replacement logic was as follows: when an EN term from the glossary appears in the EN source segment and the ES-LA term is present in the target segment, it is replaced with the appropriate ES-MX or ES-AR term based on the locale. If the ES-LA entry is missing in the glossary, we verify that the ES-MX or ES-AR term corresponding to that EN entry is present in the ES target segment.

While Regular Expressions (RegEx) efficiently identify character patterns for checking compliance with the conditions described in the replacement logic above (Chapman and Stolee, 2016), their contextual limitations make replacement challenging due to the morphological richness of Spanish (Moreno-Sandoval and Goñi-Menoyo, 2002).

Many glossary entries require a context-aware insertion into the target segment, in a manner that aligns them with any word sharing the same referent. To address this, we used LLMs, which excel at context-dependent tasks (Qureshi et al., 2024).

We combined the generative capabilities of LLMs with RegEx's pattern recognition through a Term-Augmented Generation (TAG) technique inspired by the work of Sara Zanzottera for the 2024 AMTA Tutorial Day (Zanzottera, 2024). Instead of loading the entire glossary for each segment, TAG retrieves only relevant entries, which are inserted into a "Translation Guide" and prompted to the LLM along with general instructions for terminology replacement. The final instructions were refined iteratively based on output errors. Templates of the prompts used are provided in Appendices A, B, and C.

4.2 Vocabulary

Like terminology, vocabulary replacements often require morphological adaptation to remain grammatical, so we followed a similar approach to that described in Section 4.1. In the long term, it would be feasible to create and maintain an ES cross-locale vocabulary table for reuse in various projects within the same content type. The contrastive analysis revealed differences between ES-LA and ES-AR, but not between ES-LA and ES-MX. Due to the limited number of entries, we prompted the full list without TAG. As the table grows, the process could mirror that of Section 4.1, minus the need to retrieve the EN term. Additionally, some entries require instructional notes to guide replacements based on context. For example, "deber" changes to "tener que" in ES-AR, unless used in its reflexive form, which expresses causal relationships rather than obligations or instructions in all ES variants. A sample prompt used for ES-AR is provided in Appendix D.

4.3 Grammar

LLMs are exposed to large sets of multilingual data and have the potential to process context and therefore appropriately conjugate words according to locale-specific grammar rules (Penteado and Perez, 2023; Uchida, 2024).

Table 2 shows the distance increase between the reference ES-AR translation and the baseline translation after asking GPT-4o mini to adapt the latter's grammar to ES-AR rules using a zero-shot and a few-shot approach (original distance metrics are in Table 1). The zero-shot prompt is included in Appendix E. Most errors were due to limited recall and issues with correctly applying the appropriate conjugations: many verbs and pronouns were incorrectly pluralized or converted into the first person instead of being adapted to the "vos" conjugation. Furthermore, even when verbs were correctly adapted, surrounding pronouns and adjectives were not always adjusted accordingly.

Prompting approach	BLEU	PE Distance
Zero-shot	81.20	9%
Few-shot	83.24	8%

Table 2: Quality metrics of ES-LA into ES-AR grammatical adaptations performed by GPT-4o mini.

Building on our previous research (Senderowicz, 2024) —which demonstrated that fine-tuning is particularly effective for grammatical conjugation adaptations— we fine-tuned GPT-4o mini for ES-LA to ES-AR grammar transformation. To enhance the model's capabilities beyond what few-shot prompting could achieve, we followed OpenAI's fine-tuning procedures (OpenAI; OpenAI, 2023). We constructed training and validation sets featuring a range of transformation examples drawn from the generic model's most significant errors, targeting the most challenging structures. To promote precision and avoid over-editing, we also included examples requiring no change. We conducted three fine-tuning iterations, evaluating performance after each and incorporating new examples that mirrored grammatical patterns in previously mishandled cases.

4.4 Style

As stated above, style is the most nuanced aspect of language, shaped by tone, register, and cultural norms, and rarely governed by fixed rules that allow for a single "correct" choice. In fact, our linguistic review showed that many stylistic differences across ES variants required no editing; not because style is minor, but because multiple renderings were equally appropriate within the client's context. This underscores the need for human evaluation: style's highly subjective and context-sensitive nature makes it especially difficult to automate. For this reason, we chose not to automate style adaptation, considering the process successful if it addresses grammar and terminology while leaving stylistic choices to human reviewers. This decision preserves style as a domain for expert input and allows linguists to focus on high-impact, creative work tied to brand voice and communicative intent.

4.5 Final workflow

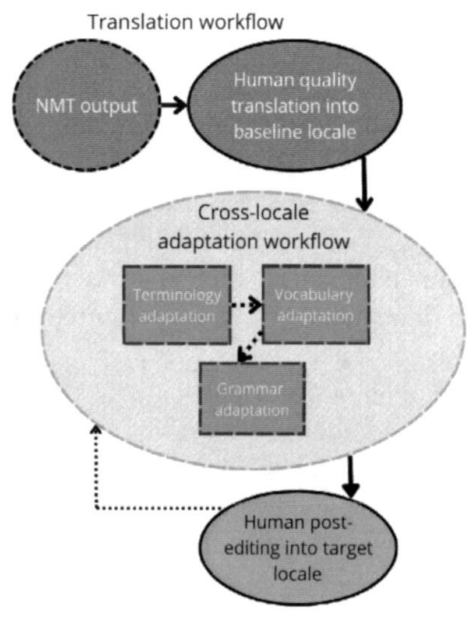

Figure 1: Schema of the proposed workflow. The optional steps are indicated with a discontinuous line.

The proposed workflow for cross-locale adaptation is illustrated in Figure 1. A human-quality translation of the baseline ES variant (with or without prior NMT involvement) goes through a modular cross-locale adaptation process. Depending on the specific types of divergence between the baseline and each target locale, one or more of its components come into play. The adaptation final output is reviewed by human linguists, whose primary focus is ideally on style. However, feedback on grammar or vocabulary can be reintegrated into the system for future use: new lexical items may be added to the vocabulary table with corresponding replacement rules, and grammatical error patterns found can be transformed into fine-tuning examples to improve the model's performance.

Locale	Steps needed	BLEU	PE Distance
MX	1	93.55	4%
AR	1, 2, 3	93.97	4%

Table 3: Adaptation steps needed for each locale transformation and their impact on editing effort. Step 1 corresponds to terminology, Step 2 to vocabulary and Step 3 to grammatical adaptations.

5 Results

To evaluate the results of our experiments, we compared them to the reference translations, also using BLEU and Levenshtein Edit Distance metrics, which let us assess the degree of improvement from the starting point (reflected in Table 1). As shown in Table 3, for ES-AR, the approach demonstrated a reduction in editing effort, with improvements of 9.44 in BLEU scores and 3% in Edit Distance for the chosen workflow. For ES-MX, the improvement is more modest: only 0.86 in BLEU, and 1% in Edit Distance.

To gain a deeper understanding of the results, we asked ES-AR and ES-MX native linguists to review the segments where the adaptation output differed from the reference translation. They were asked to classify each sentence into one of three categories: *acceptable differences* (alternative translations that are equally appropriate for the locale and content type), *minor errors* (slightly inadequate but still intelligible or contextually plausible translations), and *critical errors* (unacceptable mistakes that compromise correctness or clarity in the given context). This additional review and categorization was necessary because the translation metrics used capture deviation from a reference, but do not account for the possibility of multiple valid renderings. Therefore, a lower score does not necessarily indicate that a segment is incorrect or unsuitable.

As Figure 2 shows, from a sample of 1474 segments, out of the 262 ES-LA translations that initially differed from the ES-MX reference, 17% (46) were perfectly adapted to match the ES-MX translations, while 216 were not adapted to exactly match the reference. Among those, only 3% (7) were identified as critical errors, 10% (26) as minor er-

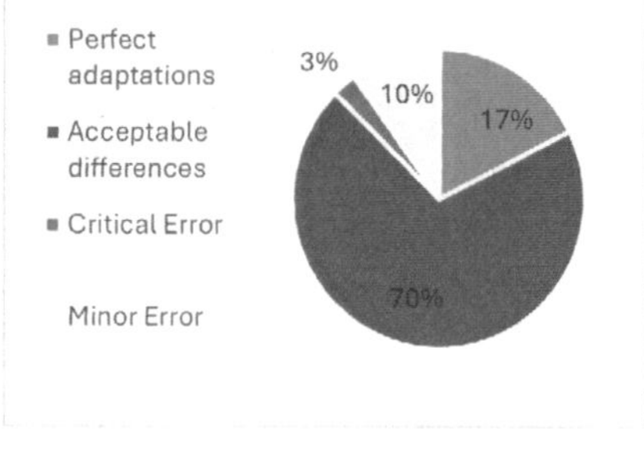

Figure 2: ES-LA segments adapted to ES-MX. The green and blue areas represent the segments that don't need further adaptation, while the red and yellow represent those that do.

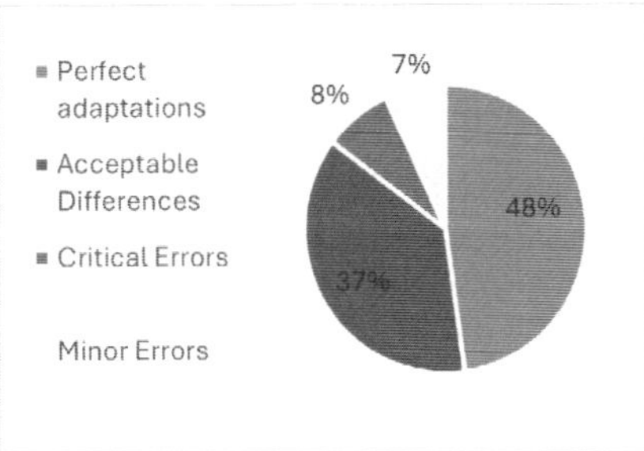

Figure 3: ES-LA segments adapted to ES-AR. The green and blue areas represent the segments that don't need further adaptation, while the red and yellow represent those that do.

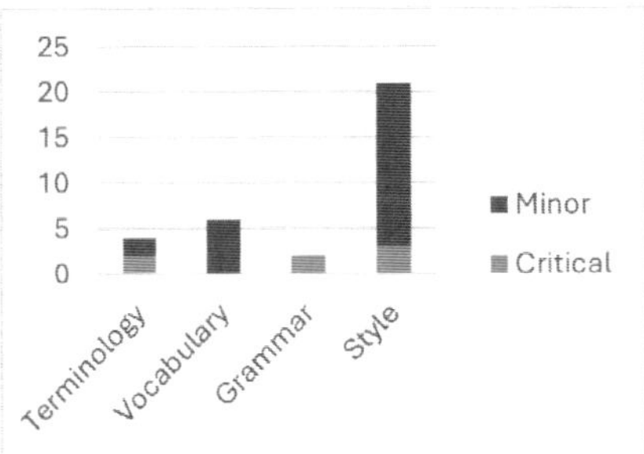

Figure 4: ES-LA into ES-MX error level and typology distribution. Out of the 33 segments with errors, 4 were related to terminology (2 critical, 2 minor), 6 to vocabulary (all minor errors), 2 to grammar (both critical), and 21 to style (3 critical, 18 minor).

rors, and 70% (183) as not requiring further adaptation. As for ES-AR, Figure 3 shows that from a sample of 1567 segments, out of the 625 ES-LA translations that initially differed from the ES-AR reference, 48% (299) were perfectly adapted to match the ES-AR translations, while 326 were not adapted to match the reference. Among those, 8% (49) were identified as critical errors, 7% (43) as minor errors, and 37% (234) as not requiring further adaptation. We also asked the linguists to classify the segments labeled as "errors", both critical and minimal, into the four categories defined in Section 3: terminology, vocabulary, grammar and style. Results for ES-MX and ES-AR can be found in Figure 4 and Figure 5 respectively, and they show that the objective stated in Section 4.4 was achieved: most of the fixes translators would have to perform pertain to the output's style.

In short, 87% of the ES-MX and 85% of the ES-AR automatically adapted segments would be ready for immediate publication, significantly reducing the amount of human post-editing effort involved.

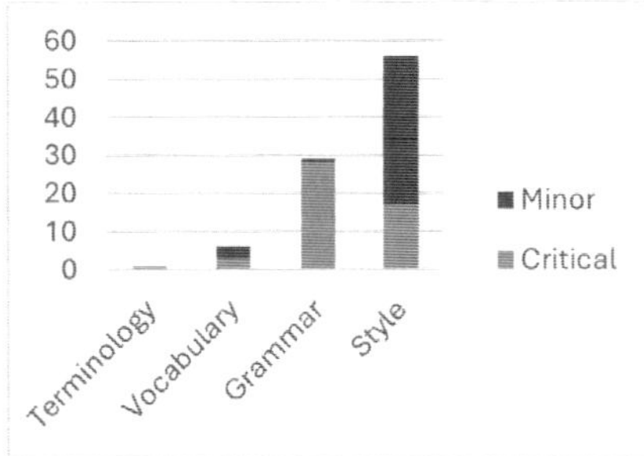

Figure 5: ES-LA into ES-AR error level and typology distribution. Out of the 92 segments with errors, 1 was related to terminology (critical), 6 to vocabulary (3 critical, 3 minor), 29 to grammar (28 critical, 1 minor), and 56 to style (17 critical, 39 minor).

6 Conclusions

In conclusion, this paper has introduced an innovative approach to same-language localization by leveraging the contextual understanding and generative capabilities of LLMs, along with linguistic resources and prompting techniques, to re-imagine the task as more akin to a specific type of post-editing rather than a completely separate process. This method provides a deeper understanding of translation and localization workflows, mitigating the need for developing and maintaining multiple localization strategies and translation models for the different locales of a language, and allowing us to understand the rich and complex relationships between them.

The results demonstrate that this approach is feasible for marketing and product/UI content in Spanish, both for variants that exhibit multiple types of divergences from the chosen baseline locale and for those presenting just one. While not perfect without subsequent human reviewing, these processes can significantly reduce the implicated human post-editing efforts in the more mechanical type of adjustments, allowing linguists and translators to concentrate almost exclusively on the more creative aspects of their work, mainly related to style and brand identity.

Future steps involve expanding the approach to more language pairs, particularly those comprising non-Romance languages, which would present very different challenges. Furthermore, final data collected through this process could be used to fine-tune an LLM, exploring whether style adaptations —which we did not succeed in automating— can be taught to the LLM through demonstration rather than explicit instructions.

References

Paul Bennett. 2002. Teaching contrastive linguistics for MT. In *Proceedings of the 6th EAMT Workshop: Teaching Machine Translation*, Manchester, England. European Association for Machine Translation.

Carl Chapman and Kathryn T. Stolee. 2016. Exploring regular expression usage and context in python. In *Proceedings of the 25th International Symposium on Software Testing and Analysis*, ISSTA 2016, page 282–293, New York, NY, USA. Association for Computing Machinery.

Keiran J. Dunne and Elena S. Dunne. 2011. *Translation and Localization Project Management: The art of the possible*. John Benjamins Publishing, Amsterdam, The Netherlands and Philadelphia, USA.

Ping Ke. 2019. *Contrastive Linguistics*. Peking University linguistics research. Springer, Singapore.

Loïc Lannelongue, Jason Grealey, and Michael Inouye. 2021. Green algorithms: Quantifying the carbon footprint of computation. *Advanced Science*, 8(12):2100707.

Vladimir I Levenshtein. 1966. Binary codes capable of correcting deletions, insertions and reversals. *Soviet Physics Doklady*, 10:707.

Antonio Moreno-Sandoval and José Miguel Goñi-Menoyo. 2002. Spanish inflectional morphology in datr. *Journal of Logic, Language and Information*, 11:79–105.

OpenAI. Fine-tuning. fine-tune models for better results and efficiency. `https://platform.openai.com/docs/guides/fine-tuning`. Accessed: 2025-02-06.

OpenAI. 2023. A survey of techniques for maximizing llm performance. `https://www.youtube.com/watch?v=ahnGLM-RC1Y`. Accessed: 2025-01-25.

OpenAI. 2024. Gpt-4o mini: advancing cost-efficient intelligence. Technical report, OpenAI.

Kishore Papineni, Salim Roukos, Todd Ward, and Wei-Jing Zhu. 2002. Bleu: a method for automatic evaluation of machine translation. In *Proceedings of the 40th Annual Meeting of the Association for Computational Linguistics*, pages 311–318, Philadelphia, Pennsylvania, USA. Association for Computational Linguistics.

Maria Carolina Penteado and Fábio Perez. 2023. Evaluating gpt-3.5 and gpt-4 on grammatical error correction for brazilian portuguese. *arXiv preprint arXiv:2306.15788*. Accepted to LatinX in AI (LXAI) Research at ICML 2023.

Rizwan Qureshi, Muhammad Usman Hadi, Qasem Al-Tashi, Abbas Shah, Amgad Muneer, Muhammad Irfan, Anas Zafar, Naveed Akhtar, Mohammed Al-Garadi, Muhammad Shaikh, Syed Hassan, Maged Shoman, Jia Wu, Seyedali Mirjalili, and Mubarak Shah. 2024. Large language models: A comprehensive survey of its applications, challenges, limitations, and future prospects. Accessed: 2025-01-30.

Vikas Raunak, Amr Sharaf, Yiren Wang, Hany Awadalla, and Arul Menezes. 2023. Leveraging GPT-4 for automatic translation post-editing. In *Findings of the Association for Computational Linguistics: EMNLP 2023*, pages 12009–12024, Singapore. Association for Computational Linguistics.

Roy Schwartz, Jesse Dodge, Noah A. Smith, and Oren Etzioni. 2020. Green ai. *Commun. ACM*, 63(12):54–63.

Vera Senderowicz. 2024. From “comment allez-vous?” to “comment ça va?”: Leveraging large language models to automate formality adaptation in translation. In *Proceedings of the 16th Conference of the Association for Machine Translation in the Americas (Volume 2: Presentations)*, pages 237–254, Chicago, USA. Association for Machine Translation in the Americas.

Satoru Uchida. 2024. Using early llms for corpus linguistics: Examining chatgpt's potential and limitations. *Applied Corpus Linguistics*, 4(1):100089.

Celia Uguet, Fred Bane, Mahmoud Aymo, João Torres, Anna Zaretskaya, and Tània Blanch Miró Blanch Miró. 2024. LLMs in post-translation workflows: Comparing performance in post-editing and error analysis. In *Proceedings of the 25th Annual Conference of the European Association for Machine Translation (Volume 1)*, pages 373–386, Sheffield, UK. European Association for Machine Translation (EAMT).

Sara Zanzottera. 2024. Controlling llm translations of invariant elements with rag. `https://drive.google.com/file/d/1BvcNbsAGWp25EDpiQ5ljYos3_eneo3wu/view?t=3`. Accessed: 2025-02-07.

A Appendix A. Example prompt to generate terminology adaptations when an equivalent term in ES-LA is available

You are a Spanish-speaking linguist from *Mexico/Argentina*. You are instructed to:

1. Read the original English text: $'original - text'$. Can you find any EN terms from the Translation Guide below in it? If you can't, stop reading the instructions and don't do anything else. If you do, go on to step 2 below.

2. Read the Spanish translation: $'spanish - translation'$. If $'en - term'$ is translated as $'esLA - term'$ in the Spanish translation, replace it for $'esMX - term' \backslash 'esAR - term'$. The replacement should be case-insensitive but

should respect the original capitalization of the term in the text.

Follow these general instructions:

A. Watch out! Don't do a "search and replace" type of job. The terms from the Translation Guide might have a different gender, number or capitalization in the text and still be the same. Example 1: if the Translation Guide includes the term "phones", and you find "phone" in the English text, you can consider them a match. Example 2: if the Translation Guide includes the term "callejón" and you find "Callejones" in the Spanish translation, you can consider them a match, even if the word is in plural and capitalized. Be smart about that when you're editing.

B. Morphology matters a lot in Spanish: When you replace Spanish word for another, make sure all articles and adjectives related are adapted accordingly. Don't produce outputs like "El chica" or "Las guapos altas", which are agrammatical in Spanish. The same goes for verbs: when you do replacements, make sure the original conjugation from the text in Spanish is respected.

C. After applying only those changes, return the final version of the translation, without any extra words, explanations, or headers.

Translation Guide:

EN term -> esLA term -> esMX term | esAR term

B Appendix B. Example prompt to generate terminology adaptations when no equivalent term in ES-LA is available

You are a Spanish-speaking linguist from *Mexico/Argentina*. You are instructed to:

1. Read the original English text: $'original - text'$. Can you find any EN terms from the Translation Guide below in it? If you can't, stop reading the instructions and don't do anything else. If you do, go on to step 2 below.

2. Read the Spanish translation: $'spanish - translation'$. Make sure $'en - term'$ is translated as $'esMX - term'$|$'esAR - term'$ in the Spanish text, and make necessary adjustments if it's not.

Follow these general instructions:

A. Watch out! Don't do a "search and replace" type of job. The terms from the Translation Guide might have a different gender, number or capitalization in the text and still be the same. Example 1: if the Translation Guide includes the term 'phones', and you find "phone" in the English text, you can consider them a match. Example 2: if the Translation Guide includes the term "callejón" and you find "Callejones" in the Spanish translation, you can consider them a match, even if the word is in plural and capitalized. Be smart about that when you're editing.

B. Morphology matters a lot in Spanish: When you replace Spanish word for another, make sure all articles and adjectives related are adapted accordingly. Don't produce outputs like "El chica" or "Las guapos altas", which are agrammatical in Spanish. The same goes for verbs: when you do replacements, make sure the original conjugation from the text in Spanish is respected.

C. After applying only those changes, return the final version of the translation, without any extra words, explanations, or headers.

Translation Guide:

EN term -> No-term -> esMX term | esAR term

C Appendix C. Example prompt to generate terminology adaptations when the Translation Guide includes more than one term

You are a Spanish-speaking linguist from *Mexico/Argentina*. You are instructed to:

1. Read the original English text: $'original - text'$. Can you find any EN terms from the Translation Guide below in it? If you can't, stop reading the instructions and don't do anything else. If you do, go on to step 2 below.

2. Read the Spanish translation: $'spanish - translation'$. Make sure that every EN term is translated as its corresponding esMX term in the Spanish translation, and not as its esLA term. Make the necessary replacements to make that true. The replacement should be case-insensitive but should respect the original capitalization of the term in the text.

Follow these general instructions:

A. Watch out! Don't do a "search and replace" type of job. The terms from the Translation Guide might have a different gender, number or capitalization in the text and still be the same. Example 1: if the Translation Guide includes the term "phones", and you find "phone" in the English text, you can consider them a match. Example 2: if the Translation Guide includes the term "callejón" and you find "Callejones" in the Spanish translation, you can consider them a match, even if the word is in plural and capitalized. Be smart about that when you're editing.

B. Morphology matters a lot in Spanish: When you replace Spanish word for another, make sure all articles and adjectives related are adapted accordingly. Don't produce outputs like "El chica" or "Las guapos altas", which are agrammatical in Spanish. The same goes for verbs: when you do replacements, make sure the original conjugation from the text in Spanish is respected.

C. After applying only those changes, return the final version of the translation, without any extra words, explanations, or headers.

Translation Guide:

EN term -> No-term -> esMX term | esAR term

EN term -> esLA term -> esMX term | esAR term

EN term -> No-term -> esMX term | esAR term

D Appendix D. Example prompt to generate ES-AR vocabulary adaptations

You are a Spanish-speaking linguist from Argentina, specialized in Spanish locale adaptation. Adapt the given Spanish translation according to the following steps:

Approach this task step-by-step, in the specified order, take your time and do not skip steps.

1. Read the Spanish translation carefully: $'spanish - translation'$.

2. Change any future tense verbs to the "ir a" + infinitive form.

3. Change any present perfect form (verb "haber" + past participle) into simple past.

4. Change specific words. Convert:

- "aquí" to "acá",
- "aún" to "todavía",
- "luego" to "después",
- the verb "presionar" into "tocar",
- the verb "permitir" into "dejar",
- the verb "utilizar" into "usar",
- the verb "deber" into the construction "tener que", when applicable, respecting the original conjugation.

After applying the listed changes, make sure the result is still a good translation of $'original - text'$. Then return the final version of the translation. If no changes are applicable, return "No response". Do not add any extra words, explanations, or headers. Do not translate any content into English.

E Appendix E. Example prompt to generate ES-AR grammatical adaptations

You are a Spanish-speaking linguist from Argentina, specialized in Spanish locale adaptation. Adapt the given Spanish translation according to the following steps:

Approach this task step-by-step, in the specified order, take your time and do not skip steps.

1. Read the Spanish translation carefully: $'spanish - translation'$. 2. Transform any second person verbs and pronouns to their Argentine Spanish form using "vos"/"ustedes". 3. After applying the listed changes, make sure the result is still a good translation of $'original - text'$. Then return the final version of the translation.

If no changes are applicable, return "No response". Do not add any extra words, explanations, or headers. Do not translate any content into English.

SpeechT: Findings of the First Mentorship in Speech Translation

Yasmin Moslem[✩] **Juan Julián Cea Morán**[*] **Mariano Gonzalez-Gomez**[*]

Muhammad Hazim Al Farouq[*] **Farah Abdou**[*] **Satarupa Deb**[*]

Abstract

This work presents the details and findings of the first mentorship in speech translation (SpeechT), which took place in December 2024 and January 2025. To fulfil the mentorship requirements, the participants engaged in key activities, including data preparation, modelling, and advanced research. The participants explored data augmentation techniques and compared end-to-end and cascaded speech translation systems. The projects covered various languages other than English, including Arabic, Bengali, Galician, Indonesian, Japanese, and Spanish.

1 Introduction

At the beginning of the mentorship on speech translation, the participants were provided with the following descriptions and guidelines for each task:

Data: Define, collect, and process bilingual speech data in a chosen language. Your dataset should consist of "train", "dev/validation", and "test" splits. By the end of the task, each participant should share a Hugging Face link to their datasets. The dataset page metadata should include sections for data sources, processing steps you applied in detail, and credits/citations of the original datasets.

Modelling: Choose one of the popular models, e.g. Whisper (Radford et al., 2022) or Wav2Vec (Baevski et al., 2020), and fine-tune it on the data prepared in the first task. Experimenting with different fine-tuning approaches and hyperparameters is encouraged. By the end of the task, the participants should share their fine-tuned models, and evaluation scores on the test dataset.

Advanced Research: Enhance the quality of your model through experimenting with advanced approaches, including creating synthetic data (Lam et al., 2022; Moslem, 2024), comparing end-to-end systems to cascaded systems (Agarwal et al., 2023), using language models (e.g. n-grams) (Baevski et al., 2020), domain adaptation (Samarakoon et al., 2018), or any other valid approach. By the end of the task, the participants should share their advanced models. They should also clarify how the advanced approach improved the speech translation quality compared to the original fine-tuned model.

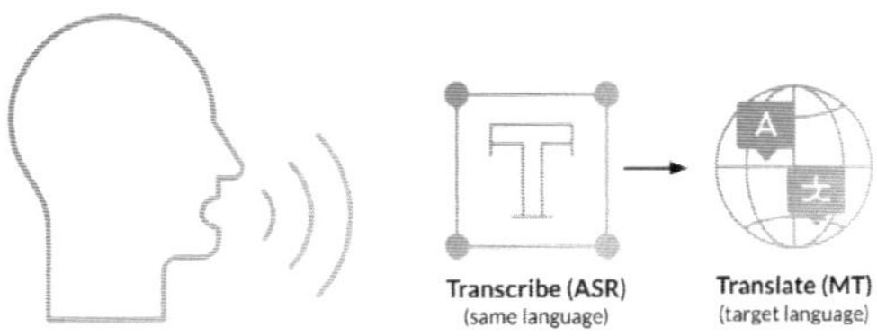

Figure 1: Cascaded Speech-to-Text System: Two models are trained, one for ASR, and one for MT of the transcriptions.

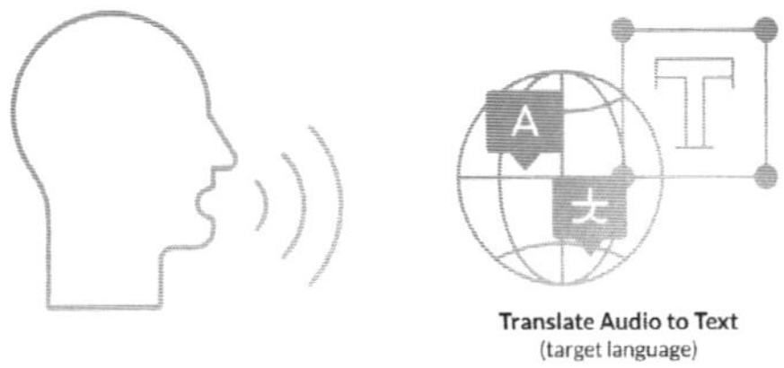

Figure 2: End-to-End Speech-to-Text System: One model is trained to generate the translation directly.

Release & Publication: Write the project details to publish as a paper. Moreover, the outcomes of all the projects are publicly accessible.[1]

2 End-to-End vs. Cascaded systems

Speech translation systems can be (a) "cascaded" systems, or (b) "end-to-end" systems (Agarwal et al., 2023; Ahmad et al., 2024). Cascaded speech translation systems use two models, one for auto-

[✩]Correspondence: `yasmin[at]machinetranslation.io`
[*]Participant in the mentorship

[1]`https://huggingface.co/SpeechT`

matic speech recognition (ASR) and one for textual machine translation (MT) (cf. Figure 1). End-to-end speech translation systems use one model for the whole process (cf. Figure 2).

2.1 Cascaded Speech Translation

Cascaded speech systems involve sequential modules for Automatic Speech Recognition (ASR), Machine Translation (MT), and optionally Text-to-Speech (TTS), simultaneously combined to deliver the output to the end user. The ASR system generates transcriptions from the input audio, and then the MT model translates the transcriptions into the target language. Among the advantages of building "cascaded" systems are:

- Better quality in production.
- Each component (ASR, MT, TTS) can be individually optimized.
- Domain-specific (e.g. legal or medical) MT can be easily integrated.

2.2 End-to-End (E2E) Speech Translation

In end-to-end (E2E) speech systems, one model produces the whole process. E2E systems can also be extended with "cascaded" components. Among the advantages of building E2E systems are:

- Simpler deployment
- Better performance (lower latency)

3 Approaches to synthetic data

When the data is limited for the language or domain, synthetic data can be used to augment the authentic data. Synthetic data for speech translation systems can be generated in diverse methods, including:

- Using TTS models to generate synthetic source audio for authentic translations (Moslem, 2024)
- Using MT models to generate translations of audio transcriptions
- Sampling, translating, recombining: Lam et al. (2022) used an advanced approach to create synthetic data, by first chunking segments and transcriptions, creating a memory of prefix-suffix chunks based on part-of-speech tagging. Then they retrieve chunks from the memory to augment prefix chunks with similar suffix chunks. Finally, they translate the new transcription with MT. Tools such as WhisperX (Bain et al., 2023) (based on Whisper) can be used for creating alignments based on word-level timestamps.

4 Projects

Most of the projects used a mix of data augmentation of authentic data with synthetic data, fine-tuning models, and comparing the performance of "end-to-end" speech systems to "cascaded" systems (cf. Section 2).

Participants used the Hugging Face Transformers library to fine-tune pretrained models. They fine-tuned Whisper (Radford et al., 2022) for "end-to-end" speech translation, and for ASR in the "cascaded" system. Moreover, they fine-tuned NLLB-200 (Costa-jussà et al., 2022) for text-to-text translation as part of "cascaded" speech translation systems. For evaluation, they used the sacreBLEU library (Post, 2018) to obtain BLEU (Papineni et al., 2002) and ChrF++ (Popović, 2017) scores. In addition, one of the participants calculated COMET scores (Rei et al., 2020). For inference, they either used the Transformers library or Faster-Whisper (based on CTranslate2 (Klein et al., 2020)) for audio translation and transcription with Whisper. For text-to-text translation with OPUS and NLLB-200 models, some of them used the Transformer library directly while others used CTranslate2 with *float16* quantization, which is more efficient. For synthetic data generation, they used ChatGPT (OpenAI, 2023) and OPUS (Tiedemann and Thottingal, 2020) models.

Given that each participant chose a language pair, we dedicate a section for each project based on the language pair, including Galician-to-English, Indonesian-to-English, Spanish-to-Japanese, Arabic-to-English, and Bengali-to-English. Each language section describes data, modelling, and evaluation of each project.

4.1 Galician-to-English

4.1.1 Data [GL-EN]

In this project, two different Galician-to-English Speech Translation datasets have been curated. First, we compiled the dataset *OpenHQ-SpeechT-GL-EN* from the *crowdsourced high-quality Galician speech data set* by Kjartansson et al. (2020). After deduplicating the Galician audio-transcription pairs, we have applied a machine translation step to generate the corresponding English translations. More specifically, we have used

Language Pair	Train	Dev	Test	Dataset
AR-EN	2,228	278	279	*farahabdou/FLEURS-AR-EN-split*
BN-EN	41,984	9,000	1,000	*satarupa22/indic-en-bn*
ES-JA	9,972	1,440	1,345	*Marianoleiras/voxpopuli_es-ja*
GL-EN	4,798	507	282	*juanjucm/OpenHQ-SpeechT-GL-EN*
GL-EN	2,742	496	212	*juanjucm/FLEURS-SpeechT-GL-EN*
ID-EN	1,243	792	844	*cobrayyxx/COVOST2_ID-EN*

Table 1: Data Statistics

GPT-4o (Brown et al., 2020; OpenAI, 2023) with the following prompt:

> [{"role":"system", "content": "You are a helpful assistant that translates Galician (gl-ES) to English (en-XX).", },
>
> {"role": "user", "content": {source_text}}]

Given the absence of reference translation, we assessed the translation quality using CometKiwi (*wmt23-cometkiwi-da-xl*) (Rei et al., 2023), measuring an average score of 0.75. In total, this dataset contains approximately ten hours and twenty minutes of audio.

The second dataset is *FLEURS-SpeechT-GL-EN*. This is a subset of the *FLEURS* (Conneau et al., 2023) dataset, which contains two thousand parallel audio-transcription pairs in a hundred and two languages. For assembling our dataset, each Galician audio-transcription pair has been aligned with the corresponding English text. For this dataset, we used the same method for measuring translation quality, achieving an average score of 0.76. After cleaning and deduplication, this dataset contains around ten hours of audio. Table 1 shows more details about the data.

4.1.2 Modelling [GL-EN]

We first employed Whisper to train an "end-to-end" speech translation system. Whisper is a set of strong automatic speech recognition (ASR) architectures, trained on multilingual and multitask audio data. They can be further fine-tuned for speech translation. It supports Galician audio and text, making it a good choice for our data. Given our compute limitations, we experimented with two different backbones: *whisper-small* and *whisper-large-v3-turbo*, a simplified architecture of *whisper-large* with fewer parameters in the decoder section. We fine-tuned both models over our two datasets (cf. Section 4.1.1).

To further improve our "end-to-end" results, we trained a "cascaded" system which splits the speech translation task into two consecutive steps (cf. Section 2). Intuitively, this separation allows each model to specialise in a specific step of the pipeline, while adding one extra level of explainability to the whole process. The first module consists of a *whisper-large-v3-turbo*, this time in transcription mode, for generating Galician text given the input audio. Thereafter, on the same train split, we fine-tuned the MT model *NLLB-200-distilled-600M* on Galician-to-English text translation.

Inference was performed using the Transformers library. More specifically, we used its pipeline functionality to encapsulate pre-processing and post-processing steps. Training and inference were run on one RTX 4090 GPU.

4.1.3 Evaluation [GL-EN]

For the *FLEURS-SpeechT-GL-EN* dataset, the most performant "end-to-end" system was based on *whisper-small*, achieving a BLEU score of 22.62 and a ChrF++ score of 46.11. For the *OpenHQ-SpeechT-GL-EN* dataset, *whisper-large-v3-turbo* was better, with a BLEU score of 55.65 and a ChrF++ score of 72.19. Regarding our cascaded system for *FLEURS-SpeechT-GL-EN*, after using the MT model to translate the transcription generated by the ASR model, we obtained a BLEU score of 37.19 and a ChrF++ score of 61.33. For *OpenHQ-SpeechT-GL-EN*, the cascaded approach resulted in a BLEU score of 66.05 and a ChrF++ score of 79.58. Hence, the cascaded approach, despite being more computationally demanding, allows for a better specialization for each part of the system, hence generating significantly better results (cf. Table 2).

4.2 Indonesian-to-English

4.2.1 Data [ID-EN]

The dataset was compiled by extracting the English and Indonesian datasets from CoVoST2 (Wang et al., 2021b), a speech dataset in 21 languages, including Indonesian. Columns besides the index,

Indonesian audio with its transcription, and English transcription were removed. The next preprocessing step was checking duplicate indices within each split and identifying overlapping indices across the splits. This dataset was first used to train an "end-to-end" speech-translation system. For speech translation using a "cascaded" system, two models were trained: an automatic speech recognition (ASR) model and a machine translation (MT) model. Hence, the audio and transcription columns were used to train the ASR model, while textual source and target columns were used to train the text-to-text MT model.

4.2.2 Modelling [ID-EN]

We employed different approaches for the speech-translation tasks, an "end-to-end" system and a "cascaded" system (cf. Section 2). The pretrained model *whisper-small* was used for training the "end-to-end" system. We fine-tuned the model with the Indonesian audio and English transcription directly. Meanwhile, in the "cascaded" system, the model was fine-tuned to predict the audio transcription in the same language, which is Indonesian. As a "cascaded" system requires an MT model for translating Indonesian transcription into English, we fine-tuned *nllb-200-distilled-600M*, with batch size of 2 and gradient accumulation steps of 8 to simulate the effect of larger batch sizes. The model was trained for 10 epochs, saving the best epoch in the end.

For inference, we used Faster-Whisper for both translation and transcription with Whisper after converting the model into the CTranslate2 formate with float16 quantization, with a batch size 5 and the VAD filter enabled.[2] Similarly, for textual translation with NLLB-200, we used CTranslate2 with float16 quantization. Training was run on the T4 GPU from Google Colab, while inference used an RTX 2000 Ada GPU.

4.2.3 Evaluation [ID-EN]

The evaluation result of the "cascaded" system outperforms the "end-to-end" system on the *CoVoST2* test set. The "end-to-end" system achieved a BLEU score of 37.02 and ChrF++ score of 56.04 after fine-tuning Whisper Small, considerably improving the baseline (whose scores were BLEU 25.87 and ChrF++ 43.79). The "cascaded" system which fine-tuned both Whisper for transcription and NLLB-200 for translation achieved 48.60 BLEU score and 65.10 ChrF++ score, which outperforms both the baseline (BLEU 38.24 and ChrF++ 56.88) and the fine-tuned end-to-end model (cf. Table 2).

4.3 Spanish-to-Japanese

4.3.1 Data [ES-JA]

The foundational dataset is *VoxPopuli* (Wang et al., 2021a), from which we extracted audio and Spanish transcriptions. We generated Japanese translations using OPUS models (Tiedemann and Thottingal, 2020), initially translating from Spanish to English and then from English to Japanese. While multilingual options existed, this two-step approach was chosen due to the strong performance of high-resource language pairs. Post-processing was necessary to refine the dataset. First, we removed blank spaces, which are not typical in Japanese writing, ensuring proper formatting and consistency. Then, we eliminated empty texts and employed quality estimation with a threshold of 0.7 to filter out low-quality translations, using the CometKiwi (*wmt23-cometkiwi-da-xl*) model. This process helped maintain alignment between the audio, transcriptions, and translations, resulting in a final dataset of approximately 12.7k rows. Regarding content, the dataset consists of European Parliament event recordings featuring various Spanish accents. As a result, models trained on this data are likely to perform better in similar parliamentary or formal discourse scenarios (cf. Table 1).

4.3.2 Modelling [ES-JA]

We built two systems for the Spanish-to-Japanese (ES-JA) speech translation task, an "end-to-end" system and a "cascaded" system (cf. Section 2). The backbone of the "end-to-end" model is *whisper-small*, which has been trained on the ES-JA VoxPopuli dataset 4.3.1. This *whisper-small* model has been fine-tuned specifically for direct speech-to-text translation, meaning that the Spanish audio is encoded and directly decoded into Japanese, without requiring any intermediate transcription step. This approach offers a simpler architecture and a lower computational cost, since only one model is used, training and inference are more efficient.

On the contrary, the "cascaded" approach involves two separate models, (i) the *whisper-small* for transcribing Spanish audio into text, and (ii) the *nllb-200-distilled-600M* for translating the transcribed Spanish text into Japanese. While this method is more resource-intensive, it allows independent optimization of each component.

[2]Voice Audio Detection (VAD) removes low-amplitude samples from an audio signal, which might represent silence or noise.

For inference, both approaches process Spanish audio inputs into Japanese text output. In the "end-to-end" approach, the model directly translates Spanish speech into Japanese in a single step (only one model is executed, taking less time and resources). However, in the "cascaded" approach there is a sequential process: The output of the model that transcribes Spanish into text is the input to the model that translates Spanish into Japanese (Two models are used, making it possible to optimize each of them but using more resources), providing a higher quality in terms of translation quality metrics. For this, we used the Hugging Face Transformers library pipelines: "automatic-speech-recognition" and "translation". As for infrastructure, we conducted both training and inference of the models on one RTX 4090 GPU.

4.3.3 Evaluation [ES-JA]

The evaluation of the Spanish-to-Japanese translation models reveals a performance gap between the "end-to-end" and "cascaded" approaches. The "end-to-end" model scores on the test split indicate room for improvement, achieving a BLEU score of 20.86, a ChrF++ score of 23.36, and a COMET score of 77.7. This suggests that while the translations maintain some coherence, they lack the precision and fluency. In contrast, the "cascaded" approach outperforms the "end-to-end" model across all metrics. This system reaches a BLEU score of 35.32, a ChrF++ score of 32.82, and a COMET score of 89.86, demonstrating superior lexical and syntactic alignment with reference translations (cf. Table 2).

4.4 Arabic-to-English & Bengali-to-English

Due to the similarity of the projects of the Arabic-to-English and Bengali-to-English language pairs, we combine them in one section. Unlike the aforementioned projects that fine-tuned models for all systems, these two projects fine-tuned models for the "end-to-end" system. In addition, the Bengali-to-English project fine-tuned Whisper for the "cascaded" system. However, both project used the baseline of NLLB-200 600M without fine-tuning.

4.4.1 Data [AR-EN & BN-EN]

The dataset used in the Arabic-to-English project is a subset of the FLEURS dataset (Conneau et al., 2023), while the Bengali-to-English project used the IndicVoices dataset after filtering out segments whose mining scores are less than 0.7 (Jain et al., 2024; Javed et al., 2024). The data is split into training and test sets to facilitate model training and evaluation. As the datasets include both the transcriptions and translations, it is useful for "end-to-end" speech translation tasks, as well as "cascaded" systems that involve separate speech recognition and machine translation models. Table 1 illustrates more details about the used data.

4.4.2 Modelling [AR-EN & BN-EN]

Two approaches were employed for the Arabic-to-English and Bengali-to-English translation tasks:

End-to-End Model: The model utilizes whisper-small model, which is a pre-trained speech-to-text model capable of handling "end-to-end" speech translation. This model directly translates Arabic or Bengali speech into English text without intermediate steps. While the Arabic model was fine-tuned on the FLEURS dataset, the Bengali models were fine-tuned with the IndicVoices dataset.

Cascaded Model: This approach combines two models: (i) Automatic Speech Recognition (ASR) using the Whisper model to transcribe Arabic speech into Arabic text, and (ii) Machine Translation (MT) using NLLB-200 to translate the transcribed Arabic or Bengali text into English.

For Arabic-to-English inference, the Hugging Face Transformers library was used for both speech-to-text transcription and text translation tasks, as well as "end-to-end" speech translation. For Bengali-to-English "end-to-end" translation, the FasterWhisper library (based on CTranslate2) was used after converting the model with float16 quantization, while translation with NLLB-200 600M used CTranslate2. Training and inference utilized Google Colab, as well as GPU P100 on Kaggle and a multi-GPU setup comprising two NVIDIA T4 GPUs on Kaggle.

4.4.3 Evaluation [AR-EN & BN-EN]

As in the case of other projects, the results of English-to-Arabic and Bengali-to-English speech translation indicate that the "cascaded" model outperforms the "end-to-end" model in terms of translation quality (cf. Table 2).

5 Conclusions

The SpeechT mentorship brought together several practitioners and students from diverse companies and institutions across the world to explore speech translation. The participants have diverse backgrounds, ranging from generic software knowledge to text-to-text MT experience. Ultimately, five participants have made successful submissions and contributed to this work (cf. Section 6).

Language Pair	System	Model	Type	Dataset	BLEU	ChrF++
GL-EN	End-to-End	Whisper Small	Baseline	Fleurs	16.01	44.99
	End-to-End	Whisper Large Turbo	Baseline	Fleurs	5.09	26.59
	Cascaded	+ NLLB-200 600M	Baseline	Fleurs	34.47	59.29
	End-to-End	Whisper Small	Fine-tuned	Fleurs	22.62	46.11
	End-to-End	Whisper Large Turbo	Fine-tuned	Fleurs	18.96	46.00
	Cascaded	+ NLLB-200 600M	Fine-tuned	Fleurs	**37.19**	**61.33**
	End-to-End	Whisper Small	Baseline	OpenHQ	21.46	41.12
	End-to-End	Whisper Large Turbo	Baseline	OpenHQ	3.38	21.82
	Cascaded	+ NLLB-200 600M	Baseline	OpenHQ	43.01	64.52
	End-to-End	Whisper Small	Fine-tuned	OpenHQ	50.96	69.24
	End-to-End	Whisper Large Turbo	Fine-tuned	OpenHQ	55.64	72.19
	Cascaded	+ NLLB-200 600M	Fine-tuned	OpenHQ	**66.05**	**79.58**
ID-EN	End-to-End	Whisper Small	Baseline	CoVoST2	25.87	43.79
	Cascaded	+ NLLB-200 600M	Baseline	CoVoST2	38.24	56.88
	End-to-End	Whisper Small	Fine-tuned	CoVoST2	37.02	56.04
	Cascaded	+ NLLB-200 600M	Fine-tuned	CoVoST2	**48.60**	**65.10**
ES-JA	End-to-End	Whisper Small	Baseline	VoxPopuli	0.48	3.18
	Cascaded	+ NLLB-200 600M	Baseline	VoxPopuli	21.34	23.21
	End-to-End	Whisper Small	Fine-tuned	VoxPopuli	20.86	23.36
	Cascaded	+ NLLB-200 600M	Fine-tuned	VoxPopuli	**35.32**	**32.82**
AR-EN	End-to-End	Whisper Small	Baseline	Fleurs	5.65	31.75
	End-to-End	Whisper Small	Fine-tuned	Fleurs	15.06	39.03
	Cascaded	+ NLLB-200 600M	Baseline	Fleurs	**24.38**	**51.79**
BN-EN	End-to-End	Whisper Small	Baseline	IndicVoices	6.33	24.60
	End-to-End	Whisper Small	Fine-tuned	IndicVoices	10.08	30.97
	Cascaded	+ NLLB-200 600M	Baseline	IndicVoices	**20.42**	**42.51**

Table 2: Results: Cascaded systems outperform end-to-end systems in speech translation across all language pairs.

Successful submissions incorporated a range of techniques. In particular, participants experimented with synthetic data generation with large language models (e.g. GPT4) and MT models (e.g. OPUS). The focus of most of the experiments was comparing the speech translation performance of "end-to-end" systems with "cascaded" systems (cf. Section 2). For this purpose, the participants fine-tuned pretrained models, including Whisper and NLLB-200. While the "end-to-end" systems fine-tuned Whisper for direct speech translation, building the "cascaded" systems involved two steps, namely fine-tuning Whisper for ASR, and then employing an MT model (e.g. NLLB) for translation of the generated transcription. As Table 2 illustrates, "cascaded" systems outperformed "end-to-end" across all language pairs. In conclusion, this mentorship has enabled the participants to experiment with various system designs and fine-tuning strategies, deepening their understanding of the speech translation area through hands-on practice.

6 Contributions

- **Yasmin Moslem:** Organizer and mentor of *SpeechT* mentorship in Speech Translation

Participants (alphabetically ordered)

- **Farah Abdou:** Participant, Arabic-to-English Speech Translation
- **Juan Julián Cea Morán:** Participant, Galician-to-English Speech Translation
- **Mariano Gonzalez-Gomez:** Participant, Spanish-to-Japanese Speech Translation
- **Muhammad Hazim Al Farouq:** Participant, Indonesian-to-English Speech Translation
- **Satarupa Deb:** Participant, Bengali-to-English Speech Translation

References

Agarwal, M., Agrawal, S., Anastasopoulos, A., Bentivogli, L., Bojar, O., Borg, C., Carpuat, M., Cattoni, R., Cettolo, M., Chen, M., Chen, W., Choukri, K., Chronopoulou, A., Currey, A., Declerck, T., Dong, Q., Duh, K., Estève, Y., Federico, M., Gahbiche, S., Haddow, B., Hsu, B., Mon Htut, P., Inaguma, H., Javorský, D., Judge, J., Kano, Y., Ko, T., Kumar, R., Li, P., Ma, X., Mathur, P., Matusov, E., McNamee, P., P. McCrae, J., Murray, K., Nadejde, M., Nakamura, S., Negri, M., Nguyen, H., Niehues, J., Niu, X., Kr. Ojha, A., E. Ortega, J., Pal, P., Pino, J., van der Plas, L., Polák, P., Rippeth, E., Salesky, E., Shi, J., Sperber, M., Stüker, S., Sudoh, K., Tang, Y., Thompson, B., Tran, K., Turchi, M., Waibel, A., Wang, M., Watanabe, S., and Zevallos, R. (2023). FINDINGS OF THE IWSLT 2023 EVALUATION CAMPAIGN. In Salesky, E., Federico, M., and Carpuat, M., editors, *Proceedings of the 20th International Conference on Spoken Language Translation (IWSLT 2023)*, pages 1–61, Toronto, Canada (in-person and online). Association for Computational Linguistics.

Ahmad, I. S., Anastasopoulos, A., Bojar, O., Borg, C., Carpuat, M., Cattoni, R., Cettolo, M., Chen, W., Dong, Q., Federico, M., Haddow, B., Javorský, D., Krubiński, M., Kim Lam, T., Ma, X., Mathur, P., Matusov, E., Maurya, C., McCrae, J., Murray, K., Nakamura, S., Negri, M., Niehues, J., Niu, X., Ojha, A. K., Ortega, J., Papi, S., Polák, P., Pospíšil, A., Pecina, P., Salesky, E., Sethiya, N., Sarkar, B., Shi, J., Sikasote, C., Sperber, M., Stüker, S., Sudoh, K., Thompson, B., Waibel, A., Watanabe, S., Wilken, P., Zemánek, P., and Zevallos, R. (2024). FINDINGS OF THE IWSLT 2024 EVALUATION CAMPAIGN. In *Proceedings of the 21st International Conference on Spoken Language Translation (IWSLT 2024)*, pages 1–11, Stroudsburg, PA, USA. Association for Computational Linguistics.

Baevski, A., Zhou, H., Mohamed, A., and Auli, M. (2020). Wav2Vec 2.0: A Framework for Self-supervised Learning of Speech Representations. In *Proceedings of the 34th International Conference on Neural Information Processing Systems*, number Article 1044 in NIPS '20, pages 12449–12460, Red Hook, NY, USA. Curran Associates Inc.

Bain, M., Huh, J., Han, T., and Zisserman, A. (2023). WhisperX: Time-Accurate Speech Transcription of Long-form Audio. In *Proceedings of Interspeech 2023, the 24th Annual Conference of the International Speech Communication Association*, pages 4489–4493.

Brown, T. B., Mann, B., Ryder, N., Subbiah, M., Kaplan, J., Dhariwal, P., Neelakantan, A., Shyam, P., Sastry, G., Askell, A., Agarwal, S., Herbert-Voss, A., Krueger, G., Henighan, T., Child, R., Ramesh, A., Ziegler, D. M., Wu, J., Winter, C., Hesse, C., Chen, M., Sigler, E., Litwin, M., Gray, S., Chess, B., Clark, J., Berner, C., McCandlish, S., Radford, A., Sutskever, I., and Amodei, D. (2020). Language Models are Few-Shot Learners. In *Advances in Neural Information Processing Systems (NeurIPS 2020)*, volume 33, pages 1877–1901, Virtual. Curran Associates, Inc.

Conneau, A., Ma, M., Khanuja, S., Zhang, Y., Axelrod, V., Dalmia, S., Riesa, J., Rivera, C., and Bapna, A. (2023). FLEURS: FEW-shot learning evaluation of universal representations of speech. In *2022 IEEE Spoken Language Technology Workshop (SLT)*, pages 798–805. IEEE.

Costa-jussà, M. R., Cross, J., Çelebi, O., Elbayad, M., Heafield, K., Heffernan, K., Kalbassi, E., Lam, J., Licht, D., Maillard, J., Sun, A., Wang, S., Wenzek, G., Youngblood, A., Akula, B., Barrault, L., Gonzalez, G. M., Hansanti, P., Hoffman, J., Jarrett, S., Sadagopan, K. R., Rowe, D., Spruit, S., Tran, C., Andrews, P., Ayan, N. F., Bhosale, S., Edunov, S., Fan, A., Gao, C., Goswami, V., Guzmán, F., Koehn, P., Mourachko, A., Ropers, C., Saleem, S., Schwenk, H., and Wang, J. (2022). No Language Left Behind: Scaling human-centered machine translation. arXiv [cs.CL].

Jain, S., Sankar, A., Choudhary, D., Suman, D., Narasimhan, N., Khan, M. S. U. R., Kunchukuttan, A., Khapra, M. M., and Dabre, R. (2024). BhasaAnuvaad: A Speech Translation Dataset for 13 Indian Languages. arXiv [cs.CL].

Javed, T., Nawale, J. A., George, E. I., Joshi, S., Bhogale, K. S., Mehendale, D., Sethi, I. V., Ananthanarayanan, A., Faquih, H., Palit, P., Ravishankar, S., Sukumaran, S., Panchagnula, T., Murali, S., Gandhi, K. S., R, Ambujavalli, M, Manickam K, Vaijayanthi, C. V., Karunganni, K. S. R., Kumar, P., and Khapra, M. M. (2024). IndicVoices: Towards building an inclusive multilingual speech dataset for Indian languages. arXiv [cs.CL].

Kjartansson, O., Gutkin, A., Butryna, A., Demirsahin, I., and Rivera, C. (2020). Open-Source High Quality Speech Datasets for Basque, Catalan and Galician. In *Proceedings of the 1st Joint Workshop on Spoken Language Technologies for Under-resourced languages (SLTU) and Collaboration and Computing for Under-Resourced Languages (CCURL)*, pages 21–27.

Klein, G., Zhang, D., Chouteau, C., Crego, J., and Senellart, J. (2020). Efficient and high-quality neural machine translation with OpenNMT. In *Proceedings of the Fourth Workshop on Neural Generation and Translation*, pages 211–217, Stroudsburg, PA, USA. Association for Computational Linguistics.

Lam, T. K., Schamoni, S., and Riezler, S. (2022). Sample, translate, recombine: Leveraging audio alignments for data augmentation in end-to-end speech translation. In *Proceedings of the 60th Annual Meeting of the Association for Computational Linguistics (Volume 2: Short Papers)*, pages 245–254, Stroudsburg, PA, USA. Association for Computational Linguistics.

Moslem, Y. (2024). Leveraging Synthetic Audio Data for End-to-End Low-Resource Speech Translation. In *Proceedings of the 21st International Conference on Spoken Language Translation (IWSLT 2024)*, pages 265–273.

OpenAI (2023). GPT-4 Technical Report. arXiv [cs.CL].

Papineni, K., Roukos, S., Ward, T., and Zhu, W.-J. (2002). Bleu: a Method for Automatic Evaluation of Machine Translation. In *Proceedings of the 40th Annual Meeting of the Association for Computational Linguistics*, pages 311–318, Philadelphia, Pennsylvania, USA. Association for Computational Linguistics.

Popović, M. (2017). chrF++: words helping character n-grams. In *Proceedings of the Second Conference on Machine Translation*, pages 612–618, Copenhagen, Denmark. Association for Computational Linguistics.

Post, M. (2018). A Call for Clarity in Reporting BLEU Scores. In *Proceedings of the Third Conference on Machine Translation: Research Papers*, pages 186–191, Brussels, Belgium. Association for Computational Linguistics.

Radford, A., Kim, J. W., Xu, T., Brockman, G., McLeavey, C., and Sutskever, I. (2022). Robust Speech Recognition via Large-Scale Weak Supervision. arXiv [eess.AS].

Rei, R., Guerreiro, N. M., Pombal, J., van Stigt, D., Treviso, M., Coheur, L., C. de Souza, J. G., and Martins, A. (2023). Scaling up CometKiwi: Unbabel-IST 2023 submission for the quality estimation shared task. In *Proceedings of the Eighth Conference on Machine Translation*, pages 841–848, Stroudsburg, PA, USA. Association for Computational Linguistics.

Rei, R., Stewart, C., Farinha, A. C., and Lavie, A. (2020). COMET: A Neural Framework for MT Evaluation. In *Proceedings of the 2020 Conference on Empirical Methods in Natural Language Processing (EMNLP)*, pages 2685–2702, Online. Association for Computational Linguistics.

Samarakoon, L., Mak, B., and Lam, A. Y. S. (2018). Domain adaptation of end-to-end speech recognition in low-resource settings. In *2018 IEEE Spoken Language Technology Workshop (SLT)*, pages 382–388. IEEE.

Tiedemann, J. and Thottingal, S. (2020). OPUS-MT — Building open translation services for the World. In *Proceedings of the 22nd Annual Conferenec of the European Association for Machine Translation (EAMT)*, Lisbon, Portugal.

Wang, C., Riviere, M., Lee, A., Wu, A., Talnikar, C., Haziza, D., Williamson, M., Pino, J., and Dupoux, E. (2021a). VoxPopuli: A Large-Scale Multilingual Speech Corpus for Representation Learning, Semi-Supervised Learning and Interpretation. In *Proceedings of the 59th Annual Meeting of the Association for Computational Linguistics and the 11th International Joint Conference on Natural Language Processing (Volume 1: Long Papers)*, pages 993–1003.

Wang, C., Wu, A., and Pino, J. (2021b). CoVoST 2 and Massively Multilingual Speech-to-Text Translation. In *Proceedings of Interspeech 2021, 22nd Annual Conference of the International Speech Communication Association*, pages 2247–2251.

ZuBidasoa: Participatory Research for the Development of Linguistic Technologies Adapted to the Needs of Migrants in the Basque Country

Xabier Soto[1,2], Ander Egurtzegi[2], Maite Oronoz[1], Urtzi Etxeberria[2]
[1]HiTZ Center - Ixa, University of the Basque Country UPV/EHU,
[2]CNRS - IKER UMR5478
xabier.soto@ehu.eus

Abstract

Recent years have witnessed the development of advanced language technologies, including the use of audio and images as part of multimodal systems. However, these models are not adapted to the specific needs of migrants and Non-Governmental Organizations (NGOs) communicating in multilingual scenarios. In this project, we focus on the situation of migrants arriving in the Basque Country, nearby the western border between Spain and France. For identifying migrants' needs, we have met with several organisations helping them in different stages, including: sea rescue; primary care in refugee camps and *in situ*; assistance with asylum demands; other administrative issues; and human rights defence in retention centres. In these interviews, Darija has been identified as the most spoken language among the under-served ones. Considering this, we have started the development of a Machine Translation (MT) system between Basque and Darija (Moroccan Arabic), based on open-source corpora. In this paper, we present the description of the project and the main results of the participatory research developed in the initial stage.

1 Introduction

ZuBidasoa project aims to use MT as a bridge for improving the communication between migrants and NGOs. The project, developed between HiTZ - UPV/EHU and CNRS - IKER UMR5478, will last 3-4 years (from 2024 up to 2028) and is funded by the Basque government (project reference: POS_2023_1_0035).

The first stage of this project focuses on the participatory research carried out with 12 NGOs assisting migrants in the Basque Country, based in the cross-border cities of Donostia, Irun, Hendaia and Baiona.

For the first phase of this project, we have defined the following research questions[1]:

1. Among the NGOs working with migrants in the Basque Country, what is the knowledge and use of language technologies?

2. Are current Natural Language Processing (NLP) tools enough to meet the language needs of migrants and related NGOs?

3. How can we use MT to improve the communication between migrants and NGO members, as well as the internal work of NGOs?

2 Related Work

Recently, Maher et al. (2024) have broadly covered translation and migration research.

Extant work geographically closer to ours is done in Spain by Rico et al. (2020), describing a project developed with Caritas[2] and CEAR[3] to translate their documents from Spanish to English, French, Russian, Arabic and Chinese using *ad hoc* Neural Machine Translation (NMT) systems.

More specifically, Macken et al. (2024) presents a platform to be used in asylum reception centres in Belgium "to translate English, French or Dutch text messages into a set of at least 14 languages, including low-resourced languages such as Pashto, Somali and Tigrinya".

Compared to the previous work, the contributions of this project are the following:

1. We work in a cross-border location, where Basque, Spanish and French are spoken by many people, especially NGO members.

2. We consider the diglossic situation in the Basque Country, where Basque is minoritised with respect to Spanish and French.

[1]Adapted from Tesseur et al. (2022)
[2]https://www.caritas.es/
[3]https://www.cear.es/

Proceedings of Machine Translation Summit XX Volume 2, pages 75–76, June 23-27, 2025

3. We plan to develop MT systems for translating between two under-served languages, in our case Basque and Darija (Moroccan Arabic).

3 Main Results

Regarding the above research questions, from the NGO members interviewed we conclude that:

1. their knowledge and use of language technologies can be defined as basic. Most of the groups make use of Google Translate[4], one of the interviewed mentioned difficulties to use it, while another one used an MT tool and a dictionary better suited for Basque[5].

2. the current NLP tools are not enough to satisfy the needs of migrants and organisations working with them. Some NGOs prefer interpretation for dealing with medical or juridical issues, while others mention that automatic tools may suffice provided that these work better for specific domains and languages.

3. in all the cities under study, there is a linguistic/cultural gap between NGOs and Darija speaking migrants. Thus, a way to improve communication between migrants and NGO members would be the development of a Basque/Darija MT system, considering the possibility of translating audio and images.

The election of Darija as a language is confirmed by a recent study[6] by Gaindegia[7], stating that Morocco is the most common country of origin for migrants arriving in the Basque Country (after Spain and France). Even if Modern Standard Arabic is the main written language in Morocco, Darija is the most spoken language (HCP, 2024). When written, Darija uses both Arabic and Latin scripts.

During this initial research, we have identified a dataset (Outchakoucht and Es-Samaali, 2024)[8] with around 50,000 Darija/English sentences. In addition, both Basque and Darija are included in FLORES+[9], making it easier to evaluate future systems in a standardised way.

[4] `https://translate.google.com/`

[5] Elia: `https://elia.eus/` and Elhuyar hiztegia: `https://hiztegiak.elhuyar.eus/`, respectively.

[6] `https://shorturl.at/bIkTc`

[7] `https://www.gaindegia.eus/`

[8] Darija Open Dataset: `https://github.com/darija-open-dataset/dataset`

[9] `https://huggingface.co/datasets/openlanguagedata/flores_plus`

4 Conclusion and Future Work

Based on these and newly created corpora, we plan to develop MT models between Basque and Darija, using encoder-decoder NMT systems and instruction-tuned language models derived from Latxa (Etxaniz et al., 2024). In the future, we plan to adapt the systems to the legal domain and extend them to other languages. We will also explore the possibility of translating audio and images using visual and multimodal language models.

Acknowledgments

Xabier Soto is a researcher supported by the postdoctoral improvement program offered by the Basque Government (POS_2023_1_0035).

References

Julen Etxaniz, Oscar Sainz, Naiara Perez, Itziar Aldabe, German Rigau, Eneko Agirre, Aitor Ormazabal, Mikel Artetxe, and Aitor Soroa. 2024. Latxa: An open language model and evaluation suite for Basque. In *Proceedings of the 62nd Annual Meeting of the Association for Computational Linguistics (Volume 1: Long Papers)*, pages 14952–14972, Bangkok, Thailand. Association for Computational Linguistics.

Haut Commissariat au Plan du Maroc HCP. 2024. Recensement général de la population et de l'habitat 2024.

Lieve Macken, Ella Hest, Arda Tezcan, Michaël Lumingu, Katrijn Maryns, and July Wilde. 2024. MaTIAS: Machine translation to inform asylum seekers. In *Proceedings of the 25th Annual Conference of the European Association for Machine Translation (Volume 2)*, pages 6–7, Sheffield, UK. European Association for Machine Translation (EAMT).

Brigid Maher, Loredana Polezzi, and Rita Wilson, editors. 2024. *The Routledge Handbook of Translation and Migration (1st ed.)*. Routledge.

Aissam Outchakoucht and Hamza Es-Samaali. 2024. The evolution of darija open dataset: Introducing version 2. *Preprint*, arXiv:2405.13016.

Celia Rico, María Del Mar Sánchez Ramos, and Antoni Oliver. 2020. INMIGRA3: building a case for NGOs and NMT. In *Proceedings of the 22nd Annual Conference of the European Association for Machine Translation*, pages 469–470, Lisboa, Portugal. European Association for Machine Translation.

Wine Tesseur, Sharon O'Brien, and Enida Friel. 2022. Language diversity and inclusion in humanitarian organisations: Mapping an ngo's language capacity and identifying linguistic challenges and solutions. *Linguistica Antverpiensia, New Series–Themes in Translation Studies*, 21.

Machine Translation to Inform Asylum Seekers: Intermediate Findings from the MaTIAS Project

Lieve Macken, Ella van Hest, Arda Tezcan, Michaël Lumingu, Katrijn Maryns and July De Wilde
Department of Translation, Interpreting and Communication
Ghent University
Belgium
`{firstname.lastname}@ugent.be`

Abstract

We present interim findings from the MaTIAS project, which focuses on developing a multilingual notification system for asylum reception centres in Belgium. This system integrates machine translation (MT) to enable staff to provide practical information to residents in their native language, thus fostering more effective communication. Our discussion focuses on three key aspects: the development of the multilingual messaging platform, the types of messages the system is designed to handle, and the evaluation of potential MT systems for integration.

1 Introduction

The MaTIAS project aims to develop a multilingual notification tool for asylum reception centres in Belgium. The prototype will consist of a web platform that allows staff to send practical messages via WhatsApp in the residents' preferred language. The project started in July 2023 and will finish in December 2025. The project is carried out by two research groups from Ghent University[1] in collaboration with Fedasil, the federal agency responsible for the reception of asylum seekers in Belgium. It has been funded by the EU Asylum, Migration and Integration Fund (AMIF).

2 The multilingual messaging platform

The web platform is based on Django (a Python-based web framework). The platform's interface will be available in Dutch, French and English, which are also the three source languages for writing messages. Residents will receive messages and their translations via WhatsApp. The main functionalities of the platform are (1) the registration of users (i.e. residents), (2) the writing and sending of messages, and (3) the viewing of previously sent messages. A link to a Fedasil database containing information on residents will make it possible to send messages to specific groups of residents (e.g. only residents on the 2nd floor, only residents with children). For user registration, staff can enter the resident's unique Fedasil identification number, the centre in which the resident lives, the preferred language for receiving messages and the resident's telephone number. To send a message, staff use an interface similar to traditional e-mail programs. Fields include subject, source language (Dutch, English or French), department (e.g. social services, reception), recipient type (entire centre or groups of residents), resident centre, resident groups (if applicable) and scheduled delivery. For viewing previously sent messages, centres can use settings options to determine which staff members have access to this functionality.

3 Inventory of messages

Based on observations in four asylum reception centres (Macken et al., 2024), an inventory of about 400 Dutch messages was compiled. The inventory includes content on house rules, hygiene and safety, administration and services, opening hours and public holidays, appointments, work and classes, etc.

This list of messages was narrowed down to 200 based on the criteria of variation, frequency, and length[2]. The messages were then manually translated into English and French by staff at Ghent University. The English messages (6711 words) were then sent to a translation agency to obtain human translations into 14 languages[3] (Albanian, Ara-

[1]MULTIPLES (`https://research.flw.ugent.be/en/multiples`) and LT3 (`https://research.flw.ugent.be/en/lt3`)

[2]In addition, content that was available on www.fedasilinfo.be was not retained as we already have high quality translations available in 14 languages.

[3]Fedasil determined the target languages on the basis of current needs.

Proceedings of Machine Translation Summit XX Volume 2, pages 77–78, June 23-27, 2025

bic, Armenian, Farsi, Georgian, German, Pashto, Portuguese, Romanian, Russian, Somali, Spanish, Tigrinya, and Turkish). The set of 200 translated messages was used for MT evaluation (see the section below) and will also serve as a context-specific translation memory to customize the selected MT system prior to its integration into the messaging platform.

4 MT evaluation

The MT evaluation was conducted in two phases: a preliminary evaluation from May to August 2024 and a subsequent evaluation in December 2024 to January 2025. These evaluations aimed to determine the usefulness of existing automatic evaluation metrics for low-resourced languages, assess the translation quality of different MT systems, and investigate the impact of source language (English versus French or Dutch) on translation quality.

The first evaluation was based on a fully parallel test set of 577 sentences (6226 English words) in 14 languages extracted from the Fedasil website (Macken et al., 2024). The source languages tested were English, French and Dutch, while the target languages included a diverse set of 11 languages (the languages listed in section 3, with the exception of Armenian, Georgian and Romanian). We evaluated three commercial systems (Google Translate, Microsoft Translator and ModernMT), and one open-source model (Meta AI's No Language Left Behind Model[4]).

In the second evaluation, we selected the 100 odd-numbered English messages (3518 English words) from the message inventory described above and translated them into the 14 target languages using the three commercial systems. As ModernMT is an adaptive system that can be easily customised by uploading a translation memory, we saved the remaining 100 even-numbered messages (3193 English words) in a translation memory to adapt ModernMT to our domain.

We looked at all the automatic evaluation metrics available in MATEO (Vanroy et al., 2023), but quickly ruled out the neural metrics as they either lacked support for certain target languages[5] or had not been sufficiently tested on them. We faced tokenization issues with word-based metrics (BLEU and TER) in several languages. For instance, in Tigrinya, the Ge'ez punctuation mark isn't properly stripped during preprocessing. Thus, the character-based metric ChrF is the only robust metric across all target languages.

The results of the first test indicate that, across all language pairs, the three commercial systems consistently outperformed the open-source model. Among the commercial systems, Google Translate ranked first, followed by Microsoft Translator and ModernMT, although the rankings varied depending on the language pair. In the first dataset, translations from English consistently achieved higher scores compared to those from Dutch or French. In the second test, ModernMT with translation memory performed better than its counterpart without translation memory, except for Georgian. For 9 language pairs the customised version of ModernMT achieved the highest ChrF scores; Google Translate achieved the highest scores for 3 language pairs; MicrosoftTranslator scored best for one language.

ModernMT's use of translation memory for adaptation demonstrated a positive impact on translation quality. Based on the evaluation results and ModernMT's adaptability, this system was selected for integration into the MaTIAS project. Its ability to efficiently incorporate domain-specific translations meets the project's objectives. In a follow-up study, we will manually evaluate the usability of automated translations for all target languages and correlate available automated metrics with manual scores.

Acknowledgments

This project is co-financed by the European Commission under the Asylum, Migration and Integration Fund (AMIF 093-133).

References

Lieve Macken, Ella Hest, Arda Tezcan, Michaël Lumingu, Katrijn Maryns, and July Wilde. 2024. MaTIAS: Machine translation to inform asylum seekers. In *Proceedings of the 25th Annual Conference of the European Association for Machine Translation (Volume 2)*, pages 6–7, Sheffield, UK. European Association for Machine Translation (EAMT).

Bram Vanroy, Arda Tezcan, and Lieve Macken. 2023. MATEO: MAchine translation evaluation online. In *Proceedings of the 24th Annual Conference of the European Association for Machine Translation*, pages 499–500, Tampere, Finland. European Association for Machine Translation.

[4]We used nllb-200-3.3B, as this was the only version we could run on our GPU.

[5]BERTScore does not support Pashtu, Somali, Tigrinya and COMET and BLEURT-20 do not support Tigrinya.

CAT-GPT: A Skopos-Driven, LLM-Based Computer-Assisted Translation Tool

Paşa Abdullah Bayramoğlu
Üsküdar University / Istanbul
pasa.bayramoglu@uskudar.edu.tr

Abstract

This paper introduces CAT-GPT, an innovative Computer-Assisted Translation (CAT) tool designed to address context-awareness and terminological consistency challenges often encountered in standard CAT workflows. Grounded in Skopos theory and powered by a Large Language Model (LLM) backend, CAT-GPT integrates context-sensitive segmentation, automatically generated and adjustable translation instructions, and an advanced machine translation component. Comparative observations with a widely used CAT tool (RWS Trados Studio) suggest that CAT-GPT reduces post-editing effort and improves text-level coherence, especially in specialized or domain-specific scenarios.

1 Introduction

CAT tools form a cornerstone of modern translation workflows, providing features such as translation memories, terminology management, and built-in machine translation (O'Brien et al., 2017). However, many of these systems rely on sentence-level segmentation without robust methods for maintaining broader context (Läubli et al., 2020). Consequently, translations can become fragmented, leading to increased post-editing and potential inconsistencies in specialized content (Kappus & Ehrensberger-Dow, 2020). Furthermore, texts requiring high terminological precision and clear functional alignment—such as legal or technical documentation—can suffer when each sentence is treated in isolation.

To address these gaps, I present CAT-GPT, a tool that combines GPT-4o with context-sensitive segmentation and user-defined instructions grounded in Skopos theory. By allowing translators to specify functional goals and revise guidelines throughout the process, CAT-GPT aligns the final product with the intended communicative purpose (Vermeer, 2014).

2 Product Description

2.1 Key Features

CAT-GPT employs context-sensitive segmentation that determines segment boundaries by analyzing linguistic structure, discursive flow, and paragraph-level cues rather than relying solely on sentence breaks. This design ensures that long or syntactically dense sentences—commonly found in highly regulated documents—remain coherent, minimizing the risk of fragmenting essential information (Läubli et al., 2020). A specialized prompt-based routine merges semicolon-ended lines, preserves bullet-list integrity, and avoids superficial breaks, reflecting the document's actual structure and communicative logic.

Before translation begins, the system automatically generates a set of translation instructions incorporating user preferences on style, terminology, and overall communicative goals. Crucially, these instructions remain active throughout the workflow, so if the translator later updates stylistic or terminological choices, subsequent segments are re-translated accordingly. Rooted in Skopos theory (Vermeer, 2014), the instructions can be updated at any point, giving translators the flexibility to adjust as project needs evolve.

Once the instructions are finalized, an LLM-based engine (GPT-4o) references them to provide on-demand machine translation suggestions. This approach allows domain-specific terminology to be applied consistently from one segment to another, a common challenge in texts where certain expressions, roles, or designations recur. By continuously aligning the LLM's output with both

Proceedings of Machine Translation Summit XX Volume 2, pages 79–80, June 23-27, 2025

the text's purpose and the user's evolving instructions, CAT-GPT aims to reduce repetitive corrections, streamline the revision process, and produce more coherent target texts (Vieira et al., 2023).

2.2 User Interface

Developed in PyQt5, the CAT-GPT interface presents source–target segments with real-time status indicators (e.g., "Not Translated," "Draft," "Approved") and machine translation suggestions. Figure 1 shows a partial view of the editor, where translators can merge or split segments, edit or refine their instructions, and track overall progress.

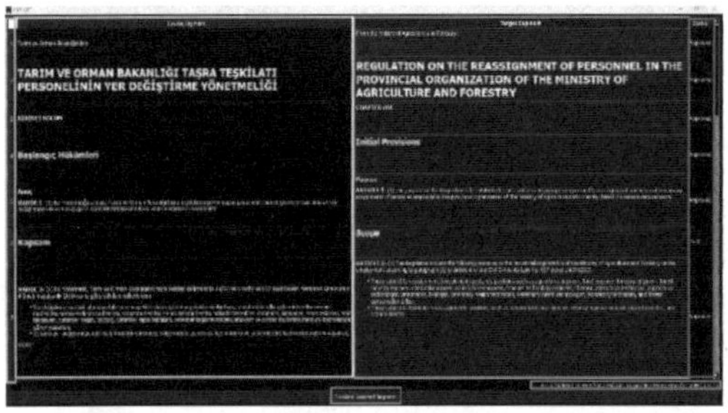

Figure 1: A partial screenshot of CAT-GPT's editor. Segment numbers are highlighted in pink, source text segments are marked in yellow, target text segments are indicated in orange, segment statuses are displayed in red, the 'Translate Segment' button is marked in blue, and the character count for each segment's status is shown in green.

2.3 Pricing, Licensing, and Availability

CAT-GPT will be released as open-source software on GitHub once development is complete. The tool itself incurs no license fee or subscription, and users only pay for GPT-4o API usage directly to OpenAI on a "pay as you go" basis.

3 Comparison with Existing CAT Tools

A mainstream sentence-based CAT tool (RWS Trados Studio 2022) was observed alongside CAT-GPT for a project that contained repeated references to specific articles and multiple official titles across several paragraphs. The sentence-based system often broke up closely related items, forcing minor inconsistencies to accumulate whenever a role or article name recurred (Kappus & Ehrensberger-Dow, 2020; O'Brien et al., 2017). For instance, designations might appear in slightly varied translations across different sentences, requiring corrections each time.

CAT-GPT's paragraph-level segmentation, by contrast, preserved the logical structure of these references, enabling them to be rendered consistently each time they appeared. Once the translator or reviewer introduced updated guidelines—for example, a new stylistic approach to referencing articles—CAT-GPT immediately integrated these changes into subsequent machine translation output. As a result, the text maintained a uniform presentation of repeated terms from one paragraph to another, reducing editing passes and aligning with the text's overall communicative objectives (Läubli et al., 2020). Future work will expand testing against other LLM-based CAT tools.

4 Conclusion

By merging GPT-4o with context-sensitive segmentation and Skopos-focused instructions, CAT-GPT addresses key deficienciés in conventional CAT workflows. Early outcomes suggest that it reduces post-editing demands, enhances terminological consistency, and preserves the text's communicative purpose. Future development plans include scaling up to larger projects, expanding language support, and refining the interface to meet varied professional and academic needs.

References

Kappus, M., & Ehrensberger-Dow, M. (2020). The ergonomics of translation tools: Understanding when less is actually more. *The Interpreter and Translator Trainer, 14*(4), 386–404.

Läubli, S., Simianer, P., Wuebker, J., Kovacs, G., Sennrich, R., & Green, S. (2020). The impact of text presentation on translator performance. *Target.*

O'Brien, S., Ehrensberger-Dow, M., Connolly, M., & Hasler, M. (2017). Irritating CAT tool features that matter to translators. *HERMES–Journal of Language and Communication in Business, 56*, 145–162.

Vermeer, H. J. (2014). The priority of purpose (Skopos theory). In *Towards a general theory of translational action* (pp. 85–94). Routledge.

Vieira, N. R., Zelenka, N. R., Youdale, R. L., Zhang, X., & Carl, M. (2023). Translating science fiction in a CAT tool: Machine translation and segmentation settings. *Translation & Interpreting, 15*(1), 216–235.

MTUOC server: integrating several NMT and LLMs into professional translation workflows

Antoni Oliver
Universitat Oberta de Catalunya
aoliverg@uoc.edu

Abstract

In this paper, we present the latest version of MTUOC-server and MTUOC-multiserver, a robust tool capable of launching one or more translation servers. It supports a wide range of NMT systems and LLM models, both commercial and open-source, and is compatible with several communication protocols, broadening the range of tools it can work with. This server is a component of the MTUOC project and is distributed under a free license.

1 Introduction

The number of available machine translation (MT) systems has significantly increased in recent years, and with the successful integration of Large Language Models (LLMs) for translation, the variety of options is higher than ever. However, not all of these systems are suitable for professional translation environments, as they cannot be easily integrated with existing translation tools. While some of these systems offer impressive quality, they may lack essential features, such as the restoration of XML tags, which are crucial in real-world translation scenarios. Even more, the combination of several MT tools in a single workflow is not always straightforward.

Taking all these factors into account, and in line with objectives of the MTUOC (**M**achine **T**ranslation at **U**niversitat **O**berta de **C**atalunya) project[1], which aims to make advanced MT technologies more accessible to everyone, we have developed new versions of the MTUOC server and a companion program called MTUOC-multiserver. The MTUOC-server is a software application designed to interface with a single MT or LLM translation system, supporting multiple communication protocols to ensure compatibility with a wide range of client applications. It can integrate with an extensive array of translation services and tools, a capability that continues to expand with each new version. The MTUOC-multiserver is a software application capable of connecting with multiple MTUOC-servers, aggregating translation candidates from each server, and ranking them based on predefined metrics or criteria. This ensures that the top-ranked translation candidate is the best among all received options.

2 Main features

2.1 Multiplatform Support

The MTUOC-server is designed to maximize compatibility with major operating systems, including Linux, Windows, and macOS. However, running the translation service locally may not always be feasible, as some engines run only on specific operating systems.

2.2 Hardware requirements

The MTUOC server is designed to work on any computer provided it has enough memory to load the required models. No powerful servers are needed and the MT systems and LLMs models can be used in systems with no GPU available, with the consequent decrement of translation speed. This enables access to advanced translation systems for any user.

2.3 Implemented communication protocols

MTUOC can be configured to communicate with client applications using one of the following protocols: the MTUOC protocol (specific to the MTUOC project), Moses, ModernMT, OpenNMT, or NMTWizard.

[1] https://mtuoc.github.io/

2.4 Available MT systems and LLMs

The MTUOC-server currently supports a wide range of MT systems, encompassing both open-source and commercial options. Accessing commercial systems requires an API key. The currently supported MT systems include Marian, OpenNMT, Moses, OpusMT, NLLB, ctranslate2, Transformers, Aina, Softcatalà, Apertium, Google Translate, DeepL, and Lucy. We are now integrating LLMs for translation, with the following models slated for inclusion: Salamandra[2], both instruct and translation models; Bloom[3], as it has demonstrated good translation performance (Bawden and Yvon, 2023); ChatGPT, as it's being used for translation (Peng et al., 2023), DeepSeek, accessed either with the API or querying the full model downloaded from HuggingFace using the transformers library. When using LLMs the user can specify the prompt for the translation and, if needed, a regular expression to retrieve the translation from the answer. We plan to include additional NMT systems or LLM models as they become available in the future. The integration of new models is straightforward, as it can be achieved through the adaptation of the existing MTUOC modules, which are implemented as specific Python classes initialized when the MTUOC-server starts.

2.5 Restoration of XML tags

Some MT engines cannot accurately retrieve the positions of XML tags in the target segment that are present in the source. This limitation is critical when translating complex formats, such as DOCX files. The MTUOC-server includes a tag restoration algorithm that utilizes word (or subword) alignments. When the MT system provides these alignments, MTUOC uses them for tag restoration. For MT systems that do not supply this information, MTUOC can rely on external fast_align models to calculate the word alignments.

2.6 Reordering of candidates

Some MT and LLM models can provide a set of translation candidates ranked by an internal measure. Using the MTUOC-Multiserver, it is possible to retrieve multiple translations from various MT systems or LLMs. In both cases, the server can reorder these candidates based on external quality estimation metrics, such as SBERT cosine similarity or COMET, ensuring that the first candidate provided is the one with the highest value for the chosen metric.

[2]https://huggingface.co/collections/BSC-LT/
[3]https://huggingface.co/bigscience/bloom

2.7 Use of translation memories

MTUOC-server can integrate translation memories and return retrieved translations if the match score is higher than a predefined threshold. It can be configured to return either only the match or the match integrated into the MT candidates, positioned according to the match score.

2.8 Plugins for CAT Tools

We provide plugins for the following popular CAT tools: OmegaT[4] and RWS Trados Studio[5]. These plugins are designed to work with the MTUOC communication protocol. Additionally, if the MTUOC-server is started using a different protocol, it can also be compatible with other tools. For instance, starting the server with the ModernMT protocol enables seamless compatibility with Okapi tools such as Rainbow or Tikal. We also provide a desktop application, MTUOC-Translator[6], which can be used to translate documents using the MTUOC-server. Additionally, a web application[7] is available for translating documents through MTUOC-server.

3 Conclusions and future work

We have presented a tool that allows to integrate several MT and LLM into professional translation workflows. The tool holds a free license (GNU-GPL) and it can be downloaded from Github.[8] As a future work, we plan to explore more efficient ways to query LLMs, as ollama or llama.cpp.

References

Rachel Bawden and François Yvon. 2023. Investigating the translation performance of a large multilingual language model: the case of Bloom. *arXiv preprint arXiv:2303.01911.*

Keqin Peng, Liang Ding, Zhong, et al. 2023. Towards making the most of ChatGPT for machine translation. In *Findings of the Association for Computational Linguistics: EMNLP 2023*, pages 5622–5633.

[4]https://github.com/mtuoc/MTUOC-OmegaT-plugin
[5]https://github.com/mtuoc/MTUOC-Trados-plugin
[6]https://github.com/mtuoc/MTUOC-Translator
[7]https://github.com/mtuoc/MTUOC-web-translator
[8]https://github.com/mtuoc/MTUOC-server

OPAL Enable: Revolutionizing Localization Through Advanced AI

Mara Nunziatini, Konstantinos Karageorgos, Aaron Schliem, Mikaela Grace
Welocalize
mara.nunziatini@welocalize.com
konstantinos.karageorgos@welocalize.com
aaron.schliem@welocalize.com
mikaela.grace@welocalize.com

Abstract

This paper discusses the capabilities and benefits of OPAL Enable, an advanced AI suite designed to modernize localization processes. The suite comprises Machine Translation (MT), AI Post-Editing (AIPE), and AI Quality Estimation (AIQE) tools, integrated into renowned Translation Management Systems (TMS). The paper provides an in-depth analysis of these features, detailing their procedural order and the time and cost savings they offer. It emphasizes the customization potential of OPAL Enable to meet client-specific requirements, increase scalability, and expedite workflows.

1 Introduction

OPAL Enable[1], globally available since the third quarter of 2024, is an advanced suite of AI tools designed to modernize the localization process, accelerate the time-to-market for our clients and deliver significant savings. The AI tools that constitute OPAL Enable are MT, AIPE and AIQE. The OPAL Enable suite is accessible via proprietary API endpoints and can be integrated into the TMS. We currently support XTM[2] and Phrase[3]. The following offers an overview of the AI features that construct OPAL Enable, accompanied by a description of the procedural order these attributes follow. To conclude the paper, we present the time and cost savings that can be achieved.

2 Customizing MT and leveraging clients' TMs

As part of OPAL Enable configuration, our AI Enablement team fine-tunes MT engines with clients' specific translation memories (TMs) and glossaries. Different MT engines are trained (from different MT services providers[4]) and the best performing engine per language and content type is selected based on the results of automatic scoring and human evaluations. By customizing MT, we align with specific client requirements, therefore minimizing the risk of errors in domain and client-specific terminology, as well as brand voice. This results in a raw MT output that exhibits superior quality compared to the output from generic engines. The client's TM is also leveraged in production: in the TMS, MT is applied only to those segments that do not have a high fuzzy TM match, typically those below 75%. Fuzzy matches and MT suggestions are then submitted to AIPE for review, while 100% matches skip AIPE going directly to AIQE. ICE (In Context Exact)[5] matches are locked and go directly to delivery.

3 AIPE

At the heart of OPAL Enable lies the AIPE feature, which enhances MT output and TM fuzzy matches following language-specific conventions and critically selected historical human-approved translations. Acting as a human post-editor, AIPE edits MT output and TM fuzzy matches as needed by correcting errors, restructuring sentences, and refining linguistic flow and style. Our AIPE feature utilizes state-of-the-art technology, incorporating secure publicly available Large Language Models (LLMs) as well as a refined, augmented retrieval strategy that selectively uses human-reviewed segments from past projects and language-specific

[1]Operating Platform for AI-enabled Language Services. https://www.welocalize.com/platform/

[2]https://xtm.cloud/

[3]https://phrase.com/

[4]Providers of MT models that can be customized such as Google, Microsoft, Systran.

[5]An ICE match is a 100% match where the preceding and the following segments that are in the TM are the same as the previous and next segment in the translation. Since the segment matched as well as the segments before and after that match are identical to the earlier translation, the translation quality has already been verified.

Proceedings of Machine Translation Summit XX Volume 2, pages 83–85, June 23-27, 2025

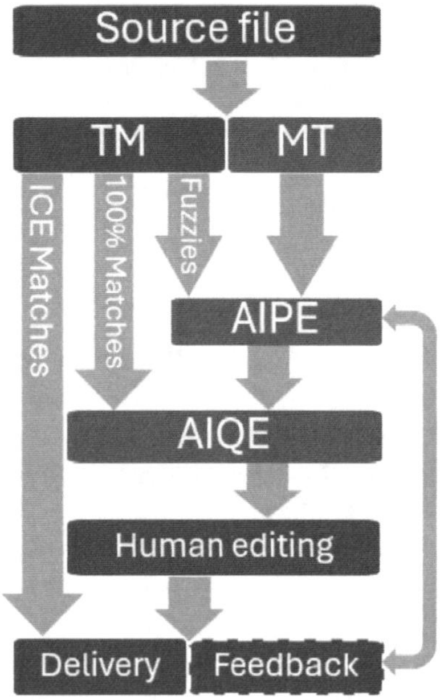

Figure 1: OPAL Enable workflow

rules into the prompt for each segment. This ensures that translations are not only accurate but also maintain the client's style and brand voice, appropriately applying terminology in a contextually-aware fashion.

4 AIQE

At this point, the AIQE feature, based on open-source software which we have modified to incorporate locale-specific knowledge, detects and locks the translated segments that meet a predefined quality threshold, thereby safely reducing the scope of the human review. The acceptability threshold is adjusted in accordance with client's quality requirements: the higher the threshold, the stricter the quality requirements, and therefore the smaller the number of segments that are locked and approved without human review. Finally, the Human in the Loop (HITL) reviews the translated text, only focusing on the segments below the established AIQE threshold and refining text for consistency, fluency, and accuracy. The key strength of the system is the ability to provide adaptable quality thresholds for each combination of language and content type, according to the needs of the client. After human editing, OPAL Enable ensures the expected translation quality is met through automated Quality Assurance checks via TMS, while internal quality audits are run in line with ISO specifications. The final post-edited output is collected and utilized to feed and improve the models for the next projects.

5 Why OPAL Enable?

By reducing the number of segments that need human review (thanks to AIPE and AIQE), clients can benefit from reduced turnaround time and costs, which allows them to send more volumes for translation. However, OPAL Enable's unique strength lies in its unparalleled adaptability: while AIPE and AIQE features are commonly found among competitors, our distinctive edge is our ability to extensively customize solutions to align with each client's specific needs. Indeed, every one of our AI features can be personalized to meet the client's requirements: we customize MT using the client's TMs and glossaries, we meticulously adjust the AIPE feature to ensure translations align with the client's historical translations and locale conventions, while the quality threshold of the AIQE feature can be elevated or lowered based on the client's quality expectations. This tailored approach guarantees delivery of superior results that transcend the capabilities of standard offerings, ensuring our solutions are not just effective, but also personalized to clients' unique business needs.

6 Costs and time savings

In terms of time savings and productivity, post-edit throughput in the OPAL Enable environment has been observed to increase by up to 60% compared to traditional post-editing thanks to an improved base translation, and up to 99% compared to human-only workflow. In terms of cost reduction, OPAL Enable offers approximately 35% cost savings compared to a human-only workflow with traditional word rate models.

7 Availability and fees

OPAL Enable is readily accessible to clients globally, and it can be deployed in XTM and Phrase. It is currently available for 21 languages[6] but it is constantly expanding. The licensing model is designed to cater to businesses of varying sizes, and consists of standard elements (annual product licensing fee, data usage fee) plus elements that vary per client (number of languages used, volumes, use of other services, etc.). The annual product licensing fee includes feature configuration and customization

[6]ar, pt-BR, zh-CN, zh-TW, nl, fr-CA, fr-FR, de, id, it, ja, ko, es-419, no, pl, pt-PT, ru, es-ES, sv, th, tr (with en-US or en-UK as the source).

of MT engines. The data usage fee is based on the actual number of words processed.

8 Conclusion

In conclusion, OPAL Enable is a cutting-edge AI solution that streamlines the localization process, enhancing productivity, reducing costs, and ultimately speeding up the time-to-market for our clients without jeopardizing quality.

UniOr PET: An Online Platform for Translation Post-Editing

Antonio Castaldo[1,2], **Sheila Castilho**[3], **Joss Moorkens**[3], **Johanna Monti**[1]
[1]University of Naples "L'Orientale", [2]University of Pisa, [3]Dublin City University
antonio.castaldo@phd.unipi.it, sheila.castilho@adaptcentre.ie,
joss.moorkens@dcu.ie, jmonti@unior.it

Abstract

UniOr PET is a browser-based platform for machine translation post-editing and a modern successor to the original PET tool. It features a user-friendly interface that records detailed editing actions, including time spent, additions, and deletions. Fully compatible with PET, UniOr PET introduces two advanced timers for more precise tracking of editing time and computes widely used metrics such as hTER, BLEU, and ChrF, providing comprehensive insights into translation quality and post-editing productivity. Designed with translators and researchers in mind, UniOr PET combines the strengths of its predecessor with enhanced functionality for efficient and user-friendly post-editing projects.

1 Introduction

The emergence of machine translation (MT) technologies has reshaped the translation industry, with post-editing becoming a critical task for translation productivity. Post-editing tools, however, often fail to meet the practical needs of translation researchers. UniOr PET addresses this gap by offering a browser-based platform optimized for simplicity while guaranteeing accurate data collection.

We release UniOr PET as an open-source tool, under the MIT License, encouraging collaboration and further development by the translation and research communities. Developers and researchers are invited to contribute enhancements, report issues, and propose new features, ensuring that UniOr PET evolves alongside the needs of its users. UniOr PET is designed with a strong focus on user privacy. Data is collected in compliance with GDPR standards and encrypted to safeguard sensitive information.

2 Product Description

UniOr PET is a lightweight, web-based tool that eliminates the need for users to download or install software. This feature directly addresses concerns raised by research participants about the inconvenience of downloading external applications. The platform features detailed tracking of editing activities, such as additions, deletions, and segment-level editing times. The tool is designed for scalability, as it provides automatic progress saving and a flexible interface for revisiting previously edited segments at any given time. The interface offers flexibility, with small or large editing areas, and a configurable editing layout that may be both vertical or side-by-side, displaying the source text, the MT output, and an editable field for the post-edited translation, as displayed in Figure 1.

UniOr PET also includes a dedicated management dashboard for project managers. This dashboard allows managers to oversee the entire post-editing workflow by tracking translator progress and comparing different post-editing outputs. The dashboard provides summary statistics, progress charts, and detailed comparisons of editing and quality metrics.

Recognizing the importance of context in translation post-editing and evaluation (Nelson Jr., 1989; House, 2006; Castilho and Knowles, 2024), UniOr PET allows translators to view a configurable number of preceding and following segments alongside the current one. This ensures consistency in tone, style, and narrative flow, which is essential when translating richly detailed texts such as literature. Real-time analytics are integrated into the management dashboard to enable assessment of post-editing productivity and effort.

The platform is designed to be an update to the already established PET Tool (Aziz et al., 2012), ensuring that the collected data, including editing times, are directly comparable between the two platforms. This compatibility allows researchers to leverage existing datasets and compare results across both tools seamlessly, making UniOr PET a valuable tool for academic and, potentially, professional use.

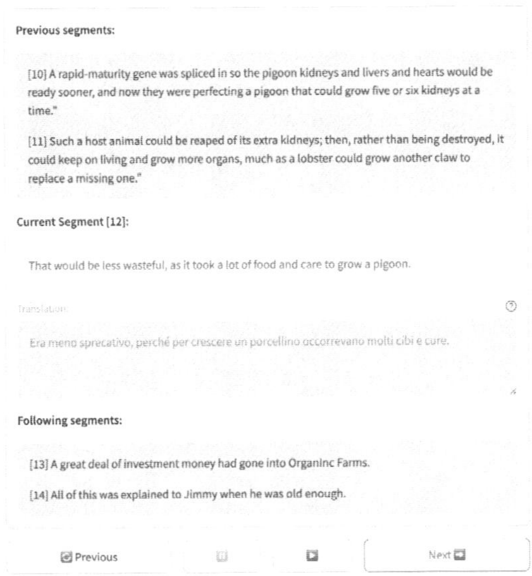

Figure 1: UniOr PET user interface, featuring PET Timer and contextual segments.

3 Data Collection

UniOr PET collects detailed interaction data during the post-editing process. This data includes information on editing actions, such as insertions, deletions, and substitutions. It also records time spent on each segment and on the overall task. Additionally, translation metadata, such as segment length and the source of the MT, is collected.

The platform includes two timers for tracking editing time, each tailored to different user needs. The first is a modern timer that begins recording automatically as soon as a segment is displayed and stops when the user moves to the next segment. This timer incorporates an idle time detection feature triggered after 30 seconds of inactivity, ensuring that only active editing time is logged, even if the translator steps away from the task. The second timer, known as the PET Timer, mirrors the functionality of the PET Tool. It offers a more traditional, manual approach to time tracking, giving translators precise control over when editing time is recorded to accommodate specific project requirements.

UniOr PET also computes hTER (Snover et al., 2006), BLEU (Papineni et al., 2002), and ChrF (Popović, 2015) scores, using the post-edited translation as the reference and the initial MT output as the hypothesis. This helps researchers assess the effectiveness of the MT models used for the initial translations.

4 Conclusion

UniOr PET is a newcomer post-editing tool, offering a streamlined browser-based platform designed to meet the needs of translators and researchers. By building on the foundation of the established PET tool, UniOr PET ensures data compatibility and comparability, while introducing contemporary features such as automated editing time tracking with idle time detection and integrated quality metrics in a browser-based, server-hosted user interface.

Acknowledgments

Part of this work has been funded by the National PhD programme in Artificial Intelligence, through a doctoral grant No. I51J23000540007. The second and third authors benefit from being members of the ADAPT SFI Research Centre at Dublin City University, funded by the Science Foundation Ireland under Grant Agreement No. 13/RC/2106_P2.

References

Wilker Aziz, Sheila Castilho, and Lucia Specia. 2012. PET: a Tool for Post-editing and Assessing Machine Translation. In *Proceedings of the Eighth International Conference on Language Resources and Evaluation (LREC'12)*, pages 3982–3987, Istanbul, Turkey. European Language Resources Association (ELRA).

Sheila Castilho and Rebecca Knowles. 2024. A survey of context in neural machine translation and its evaluation. *Natural Language Processing*, pages 1–31.

Juliane House. 2006. Text and context in translation. *Journal of Pragmatics*, 38(3):338–358.

Lowry Nelson Jr. 1989. Literary Translation. *Translation Review*, 29(1):17–30. Publisher: Routledge.

Kishore Papineni, Salim Roukos, Todd Ward, and Wei-Jing Zhu. 2002. Bleu: a Method for Automatic Evaluation of Machine Translation. In *Proceedings of the 40th Annual Meeting of the Association for Computational Linguistics*, pages 311–318, Philadelphia, Pennsylvania, USA. Association for Computational Linguistics.

Maja Popović. 2015. chrF: character n-gram F-score for automatic MT evaluation. In *Proceedings of the Tenth Workshop on Statistical Machine Translation*, pages 392–395, Lisbon, Portugal. Association for Computational Linguistics.

Matthew Snover, Bonnie Dorr, Rich Schwartz, Linnea Micciulla, and John Makhoul. 2006. A Study of Translation Edit Rate with Targeted Human Annotation. In *Proceedings of the 7th Conference of the Association for Machine Translation in the Americas: Technical Papers*, pages 223–231, Cambridge,

Massachusetts, USA. Association for Machine Translation in the Americas.

FLORES+ Mayas: Generating Textual Resources to Foster the Development of Language Technologies for Mayan Languages

Andrés Lou, Juan Antonio Pérez-Ortiz, Felipe Sánchez-Martínez, Miquel Esplà-Gomis, Víctor M. Sánchez-Cartagena

Transducens Research Group, Universitat d'Alacant, Spain

{and_lou,japerez,fsanchez,miquel.espla,vm.sanchez}@ua.es

Abstract

A significant percentage of the population of Guatemala and Mexico belongs to various Mayan indigenous communities, for whom language barriers lead to social, economic, and digital exclusion. The Mayan languages spoken by these communities remain severely underrepresented in terms of digital resources, which prevents them from leveraging the latest advances in artificial intelligence. This project addresses that problem by means of: 1) the digitisation and release of multiple printed linguistic resources; 2) the development of a high-quality parallel machine translation (MT) evaluation corpus for six Mayan languages. In doing so, we are paving the way for the development of MT systems that will facilitate the access for Mayan speakers to essential services such as healthcare or legal aid. The resources are produced with the participation of indigenous communities: native speakers provide the necessary translation services, QA, and linguistic expertise. The project is funded by the Google Academic Research Awards and carried out in collaboration with the Proyecto Lingüístico Francisco Marroquín Foundation in Guatemala.

1 Introduction

Recent advances in natural language processing (NLP) and artificial intelligence (AI) come with the caveat of needing a sufficiently large amount of data. These data are far from being available for the indigenous Mayan languages, which cover a historical region comprising Guatemala, Belize, and southern Mexico. Our project "Generating Textual Resources to Foster the Development of Language Technologies for Mayan Languages" aims at creating textual resources for Mayan languages as a first step for their language communities to take advantage of recent AI advances. Our two concrete goals are: digitising multiple printed linguistic resources and releasing them as data artefacts; and creating a parallel corpus, FLORES+ Mayas, to establish a high-quality benchmark for the development and evaluation of machine translation (MT) systems for some Mayan languages. This corpus will be obtained by translating the Spanish side of the FLORES+ corpus[1] (Goyal et al., 2022; NLLB Team et al., 2022), a de-facto standard for low-resource MT. Recognising the importance of indigenous participation, summarised in the epigram "Nothing about us without us", the Universitat d'Alacant has signed a formal collaboration agreement with the Proyecto Lingüístico Francisco Marroquín Foundation[2] (FPLFM), an indigenous, non-government organization from Guatemala with a long history in terms of language documentation and preservation. They provide us with the physical media to be digitised and are also our main liaison with the Mayan translation community in Guatemala.[3]

The project is funded by the Google Academic Research Award (GARA), a program open to professors at degree-granting institutions who are conducting research in the field of technology and computing.[4] The project started at the beginning of 2025 and plans to be completed by year-end. All developments will be hosted on `https://github.com/transducens/floresmayas` under open licenses: CC BY-SA 4.0 for FLORES+ Mayas and a yet-to-be-decided license for digitised resources.

2 Description of the proposed work

2.1 Digitisation of Mayan linguistic resources

FPLFM and INALI provided our research group with a number of physical copies of several text

[1] `https://oldi.org`

[2] `https://plfm.org`

[3] There is also an ongoing collaboration with the National Institute of Indigenous Languages (INALI) in Mexico.

[4] `https://research.google/programs-and-events/google-academic-research-awards`

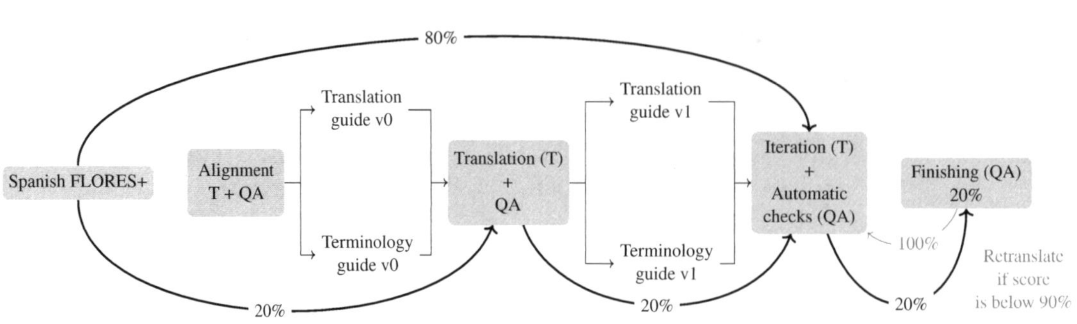

Figure 1: Workflow for developing FLORES+ Mayas (see main text for details).

sources, namely Mayan-Spanish bilingual dictionaries, grammar books, and bilingual narratives, in the following languages: Awakatek, Chuj, Jakaltek, Kaqchikel, Mam, Q'eqchi', Tz'utujil, K'iche', and Yucatec Mayan.[5] We digitised approximately 30 000 bilingual entries, 135 200 words of monolingual grammar descriptions, and 188 500 words from narratives. The digitisation was supported by the Miguel de Cervantes Virtual Library,[6] one of the largest open repositories of digitised Spanish-language historical texts. We are currently exploring the use of pure OCR engines, such as Tesseract (Smith, 2007), the use of multimodal LLMs, such as Google Gemini, and the combination thereof. The resulting documents will be further curated in order to be released as textual resources that may be used to train MT systems or language models (Tanzer et al., 2024). Given the historical lack of standardization of Mayan orthography (López Raquec, 1989), we will transcribe each resource into the corresponding modern standards.

2.2 FLORES+ Mayas

The development of FLORES+ Mayas involves the manual translation of the Spanish dev and devtest fractions (around 2 000 sentences and 50 000 words) of the the FLORES+ corpus into K'iche', Kaqchikel, Ixil, Mam, Q'anjob'al, and Q'eqchi'; these languages were selected on the criteria of availability of resources, number of speakers, and language taxonomy. We plan to organize an on-site translation task in Guatemala in the context of our agreement with FPLFM, where teams of indigenous native speakers will translate the corpus sentences. We will follow the methodology described by NLLB Team et al. (2022) (see Figure 1) consisting of the following stages: 1) **Alignment**: teams get acquainted with the nature of the data and the task, e.g. preparing lists of neologisms, discussing spelling and orthography, etc. 2) **Translation**: 150 sentences are translated for each language and sent to the QA analyst for review and feedback. 3) **Iteration**: Adjustments based on feedback are made and then the full translation of all the sentences is performed. 4) **Completion**: A sample (20%) of the translated sentences is assessed by the QA analyst, which will determine whether the quality is acceptable or retranslation is needed.

[5] The parallel data currently available ranges from a few thousand words (Awakatek) to a few million (Yucatec Mayan).

[6] https://www.cervantesvirtual.com

Acknowledgments

Project funded by Google through the 2024 Google Academic Research Awards program (Society-Centered AI RFP).

References

Naman Goyal et al. 2022. The FLORES-101 evaluation benchmark for low-resource and multilingual machine translation. *Transactions of the Association for Computational Linguistics*, 10:522–538.

Margarita López Raquec. 1989. *Acerca de los alfabetos para escribir los idiomas mayas de Guatemala: proyecto lingüístico Francisco Marroquín, Antigua Guatemala, Julio 1988.* Ministerio de Cultura y Deportes.

NLLB Team et al. 2022. No language left behind: Scaling human-centered machine translation. *ArXiv*, abs/2207.04672.

Ray Smith. 2007. An overview of the Tesseract OCR engine. In *Ninth International Conference on Document Analysis and Recognition (ICDAR 2007)*, volume 2, pages 629–633. IEEE.

Garrett Tanzer et al. 2024. A benchmark for learning to translate a new language from one grammar book. In *The Twelfth International Conference on Learning Representations*.

ProMut: The evolution of NMT didactic tools

Pilar Sánchez-Gijón
Universitat Autònoma de Barcelona
pilar.sanchez.gijon@uab.cat

Gema Ramírez-Sánchez
Prompsit Language Engineering
gramirez@prompsit.com

Abstract

Neural Machine Translation intensifies educational challenges in translation technologies. The MultiTraiNMT project, focused on the creation of open access materials for teaching and learning about machine translation, developed MutNMT, an open-source, didactic platform for training and evaluating NMT systems. Building upon it, the LT-LiDER project introduces the ProMut platform, which implements three main novel features: migration of the core NMT framework from JoeyNMT to MarianNMT, close integration with OPUS datasets, engines and connectors and the addition of a researcher profile for larger datasets and extended training processes and evaluation.

1 Introduction

The integration of language and translation technologies into the education of future professionals has consistently posed significant challenges since these technologies first emerged. The advent of machine translation—especially with the rise of neural machine translation (NMT) systems—has added further layers of complexity, impacting both the training of students and the skill development of educators. These challenges continue to be highly relevant today.

Machine translation has become a cornerstone in the translation industry, driven by ongoing advancements that introduce new functionalities and refine existing systems. Consequently, having access to up-to-date, well-maintained tools is crucial. Such tools must not only clarify the workflows and tasks involved in incorporating neural machine translation into professional practice but also encourage meaningful interactions that enhance users' understanding of these systems.

2 Background

Within the broader context of rapid NMT adoption, the Machine Translation Training for Multilingual Citizens project[1] was conceived to provide the resources needed for both trainers and students to effectively learn about and operate NMT systems. A central achievement of this project was the development of MutNMT, a platform enabling the management and creation of NMT engines. MutNMT also integrated features for evaluating translation quality, enhancing its applicability as both a training and research tool. As open-source software, MutNMT is freely accessible on GitHub[2] alongside comprehensive documentation. Additionally, it is hosted on the servers of the Autonomous University of Barcelona (UAB), where it supports a community of over 700 registered users.

MutNMT allows users to upload data corpora for training engines in any language combination. Based on the Joey NMT framework (Kreutzer et al., 2019), it was developed specifically for pedagogical purposes, with limitations on the volume of training data and the complexity of the training process. Once an engine is trained, it can be used directly within the platform for translation tasks. Users can also leverage various metrics to evaluate translation quality or to compare results with other MT systems. Building on this foundation, the LT-LiDER project[3] expanded the focus to include the development of digital literacy competencies among professionals, trainers, and trainees in translation and multilingual communication. One of its outputs is ProMut, a didactic tool aimed at enabling advanced engagement with and management of NMT systems. ProMut offers functionalities for creating engines and evaluating translation quality, while also broadening the system's capabilities and contexts of use. By deepening technical understanding and diversifying application scenarios, ProMut stands as a robust resource for education and training in translation technologies.

[1] http://multitrain.eu
[2] https://github.com/Prompsit/mutnmt
[3] http://lt-lider.eu

Proceedings of Machine Translation Summit XX Volume 2, pages 91–92, June 23-27, 2025

3 From MutNMT to ProMut

MutNMT is currently an application focused on teaching users of translation technologies the essentials about data management, training, usage and evaluation of machine translation systems. The online application implements different profiles with different rights regarding the ability to train a new engine within the tool. Beginners are not allowed to do it, but they can interact with the rest of the functionality of the tool (see and upload datasets, see engine's training info, translate, inspect, evaluate). Training, though, is only allowed to Expert and Admin profiles and is limited to the following parameters:

- 1-hour of training time slots with the possibility to stop or continue training for 1 more hour successively.
- A maximum of 500k sentence pairs in the training set, 5k for validation and test.
- Training parameters with default values.
- Use of engines only inside the application by lack of integration with external tools.

In order to open up the use of MutNMT to a wider range of usages related with MT research, the LT-LiDER project generously expands the aforementioned limits through ProMut:

- ProMut includes a new profile, the Researcher profile, for which the limits in training time and data sizes are extended along with more flexibility in choosing training parameters.
- Corpus management allows the upload of large corpora and connection to the OPUS (Tiedemann, 2012) parallel data repository.
- ProMut implements the ability to download pre-trained engines from OPUS-MT-train[4] and the possibility to fine-tune these or others already trained within the application.
- To this end, a replacement of the core engine from JoeyNMT to MarianNMT (Junczys-Dowmunt et al., 2018) was implemented to enable compatibility with OPUS-MT models and, at the same time, enable compatibility with OPUS-CAT,[5] allowing to connect ProMut engines to a variety of computer-assisted translation (CAT) tools.
- In evaluation, COMET (Rei et al., 2022) has been added as a new evaluation metric that complements the previous n-gram and character-based metrics.
- ProMut also provides updates to previously-available functionalities (e.g. evaluation and training detailed plots and histograms) as well as technical and user documentation.

ProMut, currently in internal testing by the LT-Lider partners, will be available by May 2025 along with the code under a free/open-source licence.

Acknowledgments

This project has been funded with support from the European Commission. We thank Paula Guerrero Castelló for the contributions, ideas, and comments to the current MutNMT and ProMut frameworks.

References

Marcin Junczys-Dowmunt, Roman Grundkiewicz, Tomasz Dwojak, Hieu Hoang, Kenneth Heafield, Tom Neckermann, Frank Seide, Ulrich Germann, Alham Fikri Aji, Nikolay Bogoychev, André F. T. Martins, and Alexandra Birch. 2018. Marian: Fast neural machine translation in C++. In *Proceedings of ACL 2018, System Demonstrations*, Melbourne, Australia.

Julia Kreutzer, Jasmijn Bastings, and Stefan Riezler. 2019. Joey NMT: A minimalist NMT toolkit for novices. In *Proceedings of the 2019 Conference on Empirical Methods in Natural Language Processing and the 9th International Joint Conference on Natural Language Processing (EMNLP-IJCNLP): System Demonstrations*, pages 109–114, Hong Kong, China. Association for Computational Linguistics.

Ricardo Rei, José G. C. de Souza, Duarte Alves, Chrysoula Zerva, Ana C Farinha, Taisiya Glushkova, Alon Lavie, Luisa Coheur, and André F. T. Martins. 2022. COMET-22: Unbabel-IST 2022 submission for the metrics shared task. In *Proceedings of the Seventh Conference on Machine Translation (WMT)*, pages 578–585, Abu Dhabi, United Arab Emirates (Hybrid). Association for Computational Linguistics.

Jörg Tiedemann. 2012. Parallel data, tools and interfaces in opus. In *Proceedings of the Eight International Conference on Language Resources and Evaluation (LREC'12)*, Istanbul, Turkey. European Language Resources Association (ELRA).

[4]https://github.com/Helsinki-NLP/Opus-MT-train

[5]https://github.com/Helsinki-NLP/OPUS-CAT

The BridgeAI Project

Helena Moniz[1], António Novais[2], Joana Lamego[3], Nuno André[2]
University of Lisbon[1] / Unbabel[2] / Champalimaud Foundation[3]
[1]helena.moniz@campus.ul.pt
[2]{antonio.novais,nuno.andre}@unbabel.com
[3]joana.lamego@research.fchampalimaud.org

Abstract

This paper presents an updated overview of the "BridgeAI" project, a pioneering science-for-policy initiative funded by the Portuguese Foundation for Science and Technology (FCT). Now in its second year, BridgeAI continues to build upon its original goals, working towards a strategy to align Artificial Intelligence (AI) research, policy, and practical application. The project provides Portugal with an evidence-based framework to implement the EU AI Act (AIA), ensuring responsible AI innovation through multidisciplinary collaboration. BridgeAI connects academia, industry, public administration, and civil society to create actionable insights and regulatory recommendations. This paper details the project's latest advancements, key recommendations, and future directions. Although not exclusively focused on MT, the project pertains to NLP in general and ultimately to each of us as citizens.

1 Introduction

AI is reshaping industries, governance, and society at large. While it offers tremendous opportunities for economic growth and efficiency (Floridi et al., 2018), it also poses ethical, social, and environmental challenges (Novelli et al., 2023). The AIA aims to regulate AI systems to ensure safety, accountability, and human-centered design. However, implementing these regulations effectively requires collaboration between policy makers, researchers, and industry leaders (Morley et al., 2019).

Historically, the outcomes from science–policy interfaces have not proved to be straightforward and do not usually lead to the establishment of effective collaborations (Jagannathan et al., 2023). The process by which knowledge is transferred from scientists to decision-makers is usually considered ineffective, due to a lack of understanding.

BridgeAI emerged as a response to this need, positioning Portugal as a leader in responsible AI. The 12-month project bridges the gap between AI regulation and real-world application, fostering a collective effort to create trustworthy AI products that prioritize societal well-being (Jagannathan et al., 2023). BridgeAI aims to respond to these challenges by moving towards a context-based approach that facilitates the creation of actionable knowledge at the intersection of science and practical, ethical, social, legal, and political domains. Furthermore, we aim to enhance the informed and effective implementation of the AIA in Portugal and empower stakeholders to transition from passive compliance with regulations to active participation in the responsible design of AI internationally (Floridi et al., 2018). In its second civil year, BridgeAI has focused on producing concrete recommendations for AI regulation in Portugal.

2 BridgeAI Approach and Implementation

BridgeAI employs a multidisciplinary, evidence-based approach to AI regulation. The project is structured around five key working groups (WGs):

WG0 | AI technological case studies: Foundational and transversal WG that created the case studies of AI products from the Center for responsible AI, serving as the basis for other WGs.

WG1 | Risk Assessment tools in AI products: Develop a practical AI risk assessment tool for public and private entities, based on tools already available to assess responsible AI principles (Morley et al., 2019).

WG2 | AI Ethics in Regulatory Processes: Define how we should address AI ethical concerns in the regulatory processes and how to provide ethical training at several levels.

WG3 | AI Act interface with other regulations, norms, audits and implementation metrics: Determine the key implementation initiatives that should arise to ensure the AI Act is effectively implemented and that all are conciliated (e.g., certification, standards, audits and control).

WG4 | Advanced training and literacy: Define strategic measures for Portugal to increase levels of AI literacy and propose training programs to be developed.

WG5 | AI ethics and regulatory efforts outside the EU: Point out best practices in AI regulation and ethics being developed outside the EU and understand how Portugal can learn from these.

3 Key Partners and People

BridgeAI counts with the following partners: ANACOM, British Embassy Lisbon, Champalimaud Foundation, INESC-ID, Instituto do Conhecimento, Instituto de Telecomunicações, JLM&A, Plano Nacional de Leitura, SGS, The Alan Turing Institute, Unbabel, Universidade Católica, Universidade de Lisboa, Universidade Nova de Lisboa, and VdA. The project also counts with the participation of individual experts from the United Nations (UN), the UN AI Advisory Board, and civil society.

4 Key Recommendations

BridgeAI has formulated several strategic recommendations (SR) for Portugal's AI regulatory landscape, including:

SR 1 | Create and adapt **instruments to identify and assess potential risks associated with AI** applications, facilitating compliance with the AI Act.

SR 2 | Create **red teams**, specialized teams for adversarial testing, to identify vulnerabilities and risks in AI systems, helping companies design and deploy better AI systems.

SR 3 | Establish an **AI regulatory sandbox**, a controlled environment to test and validate disruptive AI solutions before full-scale deployment.

SR 4 | Launch an **AI literacy** survey to understand what citizens know about AI and create multidisciplinary AI literacy initiatives.

Furthermore, there was a unanimous recommendation: Portugal needs **agility, continuity, and talent**. Agility to build new bridges and innovate responsibly through collaboration. Continuity to deepen impact and strengthen multidisciplinary partnerships. And talent—across universities, companies, and public administration—to lead Portugal toward new opportunities for growth and societal well-being.

5 Next Steps and Future Directions

Moving forward, BridgeAI will finalize and deliver a positional paper with all the project's recommendations to the Portuguese public administration, presenting it to relevant governmental and regulatory bodies to support AI policy implementation. Additionally, the project aims to strengthen engagement with governmental bodies to facilitate the seamless adoption of its recommendations, and expand international collaborations to align Portuguese AI regulations with global standards.

6 Acknowledgements

This project is funded by the Portuguese Science Foundation (FCT), under the science-for-policy programme, thematic area "Antecipar a regulação da Inteligência Artificial" reference 2023.10424.S4P23.

References

Floridi, L., Cowls, J., Beltrametti, M., Chatila, R., Chazerand, P., Dignum, V., Luetge, C., Madelin, R., Pagallo, U., Rossi, F., Schäfer, B., Valcke, P., & Vayena, E. 2018. *AI4People—An Ethical Framework for a Good AI Society: Opportunities, Risks, Principles, and Recommendations*. Minds and Machines, 28(4), 689–707.

Jagannathan, K., Emmanuel, G., Arnott, J., Mach, K. J., Bamzai-Dodson, A., Goodrich, K., Meyer, R., Neff, M., Sjostrom, K. D., Timm, K. M., Turnhout, E., Wong-Parodi, G., Bednarek, A. T., Meadow, A., Dewulf, A., Kirchhoff, C. J., Moss, R. H., Nichols, L., Oldach, E., Lemos, M., Klenk, N. 2023. *A research agenda for the science of actionable knowledge: Drawing from a review of the most misguided to the most enlightened claims in the science-policy interface literature*. Environmental Science & Policy, 144, 174–186.

Morley, J., Floridi, L., Kinsey, L., and Elhalal, A. 2019. *From What to How: An Initial Review of Publicly Available AI Ethics Tools, Methods and Research to Translate Principles into Practices*. Science and Engineering Ethics, 26(4), 2141–2168.

Novelli, C. C., Casolari, F., Rotolo, A., Taddeo, M. & Floridi, L. 2023. *Taking AI risks seriously: a new assessment model for the AI Act*. AI & SOCIETY.

DeMINT: Automated Language Debriefing for English Learners via AI Chatbot Analysis of Meeting Transcripts

Miquel Esplà-Gomis, Felipe Sánchez-Martínez,
Víctor M. Sánchez-Cartagena, Juan Antonio Pérez-Ortiz

Dep. de Llenguatges i Sistemes Informàtics, Universitat d'Alacant
E-03690 Sant Vicent del Raspeig (Spain)

`https://github.com/transducens/demint`
`{mespla,fsanchez,vmsanchez,japerez}@dlsi.ua.es`

Abstract

The objective of the DeMINT project is to develop a conversational tutoring system aimed at enhancing non-native English speakers' language skills through post-meeting analysis of the transcriptions of video conferences in which they have participated. This paper describes the model developed and the results obtained through a human evaluation conducted with learners of English as a second language.

1 Project Overview

DeMINT (Automated Language Debriefing for English Learners via AI Chatbot Analysis of Meeting Transcripts) was developed by the Transducens Research Group at Universitat d'Alacant from January to September 2024. It is funded under the UTTER project,[1] a collaborative Research and Innovation project under Horizon Europe (grant agreement ID: 101070631), via *financial support to third parties*.

Conversational intelligent tutoring systems (ITS) are poised to revolutionize education by providing personalized, interactive, and inclusive one-on-one learning. The objective of this project is to develop an educational chatbot aimed at leveraging large language models (LLMs) to improve speakers' language skills through interactive error-driven conversations. A full-length description of our model is described by Pérez-Ortiz et al. (2024). Although not centered on machine translation (MT), our chatbot relies on components common to many MT-related tasks, such as speech transcription or grammatical error correction. Moreover, a similar ITS could also support translation tasks by helping translators improve text quality.

The architecture of our system is described in Figure 1, which reflects the modules that interact to provide a comprehensive tutoring experience:

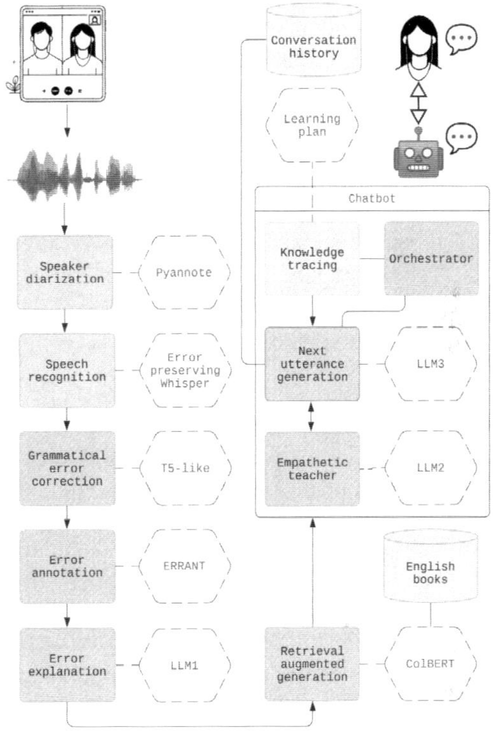

Figure 1: Main components of the DeMINT system.

1. *Diarization*: The pipeline starts by processing the audio recorded during an online meeting with the library `pyannote.audio`,[2] to identify the segments corresponding to each speaker.

2. *Speech Recognition*: Audio fragments are processed by a speech recognition model built by fine-tuning Whisper[3] on a custom dataset of spoken sentences with grammatical errors.[4]

3. *Grammatical Error Correction*: For this task, we employ a T5 model (Raffel et al., 2020) fine-tuned on the JF-LEG dataset.[5]

[1] `https://he-utter.eu`

[2] `https://pyannote.ai/`

[3] `https://openai.com/index/whisper/`

[4] `https://huggingface.co/blog/asr-diarization`

[5] `https://huggingface.co/vennify/`

Proceedings of Machine Translation Summit XX Volume 2, pages 95–96, June 23-27, 2025

4. *Error annotation*: Given the original and the corrected version of each sentence, we use the ERRANT toolkit (Bryant et al., 2017) to annotate the edits necessary to transform one sentence version into the other.

5. *Error explanation*: An LLM is used to generate finer-grained natural-language explanations from the high-level errors annotated with ERRANT via few-shot in-context learning.

6. *Retrieval from Textbooks*: This module uses retrieval-augmented generation (RAG) to get relevant information from English learning textbooks and provide it to the chatbot's *next-dialog-line generator* module.

7. *Empathetic Teacher*: The Llama-3.1-8B[6] model was fine-tuned with real-life, ideally-empathetic teacher-student conversations. This model processes the recent conversation history and provides guidance on how a teacher might respond.

8. *Orchestrator*: The orchestrator is a simple Python program that iterates through the different errors and sentences building the complex prompt that will be used to guide the interaction with the user.

9. *Next-Dialog-Line Generator*: GPT-4 is used to generate the next line of the conversation based on the informative prompt from orchestrator. This step also aims at modeling the learning process of the student; the information is included in the prompt, and is presented in the diagram as *knowledge tracing*.

10. *Chatbot Interface*: The interface is a simple web app built with `gradio`.[7] It shows the chatbot conversation in one column and the transcription, centered on the current sentence, in another. The user types their input, and the machine responds accordingly on the screen.

2 Results of the project

As the results of this project, a prototype of our ITS has been implemented. All the models and the datasets used to build them have been released and are available on the project repository.[8]

`t5-base-grammar-correction`

[6] `https://huggingface.co/meta-llama/Meta-Llama-3.1-8B`

[7] `https://github.com/gradio-app/gradio`

[8] `https://github.com/transducens/demint`

The prototype developed has been evaluated through interactions between the chatbot and L1-Spanish/L2-English students. Seven students with B2/C1 English levels (according to the Common European Framework of Reference for Languages) participated in 15 video-calls. These calls were recorded and processed by our ITS, and students spent about 75 minutes interacting with it. Students were then surveyed on overall user experience and chatbot's effectiveness as an English tutor, using a 1–5 Likert scale. In response to "Did you enjoy interacting with the chatbot?", all gave positive feedback (scores of 4 or 5). Fluency was identified as the main area for improvement, with an average score of 3. Regarding the chatbot's role as a tutor, the main concern was its accuracy in identifying speech errors (average score: 3). Still, most students felt it helped improve aspects of their English, with five out of seven giving a score of 4. When asked about future use of similar tutoring tools in video conferences, all but one rated their interest as 4 or 5, showing overall enthusiasm for such tools.

Acknowledgements

DeMINT was funded under the UTTER project (Horizon Europe, GA: 101070631), via *financial support to third parties*. In addition to the researchers signing this paper, Roman Chernysh, Gabriel Mora-Rodríguez and Lev Berezhnoy were also part of the work team behind this project.

References

Christopher Bryant, Mariano Felice, and Ted Briscoe. 2017. Automatic annotation and evaluation of error types for grammatical error correction. In *Proceedings of the 55th ACL Conference (Volume 1)*, pages 793–805, Vancouver, Canada.

Juan Antonio Pérez-Ortiz, Miquel Esplà-Gomis, Víctor M. Sánchez-Cartagena, Felipe Sánchez-Martínez, Roman Chernysh, Gabriel Mora-Rodríguez, and Lev Berezhnoy. 2024. A conversational intelligent tutoring system for improving English proficiency of non-native speakers via debriefing of online meeting transcriptions. In *Proceedings of the 13th Workshop NLP4CALL*, pages 187–198, Rennes, France.

Colin Raffel, Noam Shazeer, Adam Roberts, Katherine Lee, Sharan Narang, Michael Matena, Yanqi Zhou, Wei Li, and Peter J. Liu. 2020. Exploring the limits of transfer learning with a unified text-to-text transformer. *Journal of Machine Learning Research*, 21(140):1–67.

GAMETRAPP project in progress: Designing a virtual escape room to enhance skills in research abstract post-editing

Cristina Toledo-Báez
Research Institute on Multilingual Language Technologies
University of Málaga
Spain
toledo@uma.es

Luis Carlos Marín-Navarro
Research Institute on Multilingual Language Technologies
University of Málaga
Spain
lmarin@uma.es

Abstract

The "App for post-editing neural machine translation using gamification" (GAMETRAPP) project (TED2021-129789B-I00), funded by the Spanish Ministry of Science and Innovation (2022–2025) and led by the University of Málaga, has been in progress for two and a half years. The project is developing a web application that incorporates a gamified environment, specifically a virtual escape room, to bring post-editing practice closer to scholars. This paper outlines the methodological process followed and provides a brief description of the virtual escape room.

1 Introduction

The breakthrough of artificial intelligence (AI) has significantly impacted the development and advancement of language technologies, including neural machine translation (NMT). This advancement has also led to a greater reliance on post-editing (PE), which has garnered increasing attention from scholars. Previous research has explored the implementation of PE, particularly in academic contexts, focusing on first language (L1) to second or foreign language (L2) translation (Parra Escartín and Goulet, 2020).

Against the backdrop of scientific dissemination in English as L2, the GAMETRAPP project (Toledo-Báez & Noriega-Santiáñez, 2024) is developing a web application that incorporates a gamified environment, specifically a virtual escape room, to enhance the PE of research abstracts translated from Iberian Spanish to American English (L1 to L2). While other applications, such as Kaninjo (Moorkens et al., 2016), have been developed to train users in PE, GAMETRAPP stands out by introducing gamification as an innovative strategy to engage users in the PE learning process.

2 Analyzing NMT and PE to design the gamified environment

The methodological process of the GAMETRAPP project was carried out in four phases, which are outlined as follows: 244 Spanish-language abstracts were selected from Spanish journals ranked in Quartiles 1 and 2 (representing the top 50% of journals) in the *Scientific Journal & Country Ranking 2022*. Of these, only 126 abstracts met the following three criteria: a) published in 2023; b) following the IAMRaC [1] structure; c) authored by scholars affiliated with Spanish universities and/or research centers. Google Translate was selected as the NMT engine because, according to a previous questionnaire conducted to assess the Spanish scholars' needs, it was the most widely used NMT engine.

The 126 abstracts were, on the one hand, translated into English by a professional translator, and, on the other hand, machine-translated with Google Translate and then post-edited into English by a professional post-editor (both of whom had English as their L1). Then, the translated and post-edited abstracts were analyzed, identifying NMT and PE errors and kudos using two metrics. On the one hand, the Multidimensional Quality Metrics was used to detect and classify NMT errors across the following categories: Terminology, Accuracy, Terminology, Accuracy, Linguistic conventions, Style, Locale conventions, Audience appropriateness, and Design and markup. On the other hand, the Post-edit Me! metric (Lefer et al., 2023) was used to detect and classify edits into four categories: value adding/successful edits,

[1] This acronym stands for Introduction, Aims, Methodology, Results, and Conclusion. It is a variant of the IAMRaC structure (i.e., Introduction, Methodology, Results, and Discussion).

Proceedings of Machine Translation Summit XX Volume 2, pages 97–98, June 23-27, 2025

unnecessary edits, incomplete edits, or unsuccessful/error introducing/missing edits.

This dual analysis not only helped identify some of the most frequent NMT errors in machine-translated research abstracts but also revealed specific ES→EN PE patterns. The analysis results provided the foundation for the design of the gamified exercises, as the linguistic material was adapted to create the activities. These activities were organised into three parts: Part 1 focused on detecting NMT errors, Part 2 centered on PE, and Part 3 aimed at identifying successful and unsuccessful edits of PE.

An example of each type of activity is provided below:

Part 1: Identify the error in the following NMT output:

- No hay datos recientes que recojan su adaptación durante la pandemia por la COVID-19.
- There is no recent data that reflect their adaptation during the COVID-19 pandemic.

Part 2: Correct the error in the NMT output:

- La lucha contra la radicalización gana protagonismo.
- The fight against radicalization gains prominence.
- The fight against radicalization __________ prominence.

Correct answer: The fight against radicalization **is gaining** prominence.

Part 3: Indicate whether this post-editing is correct or not:

- Los medios digitales **suelen** entenderse como una herramienta que contribuye a materializar el ideal social.
- Digital media **are** usually understood as a tool that contributes to materializing the social ideal.
- Digital media **is** usually understood as a tool that contributes to materializing the social ideal.

Option 1: Correct
Option 2: **Incorrect**

3 Brief explanation on the gamified environment

The gamified environment, developed using the Articulate tool, is divided into two main sections: a theoretical section and a practical section. The theoretical section introduces the game and covers basic concepts related to NMT, scientific abstracts, and PE. The practical section is divided into 5 worlds: Humanities, Arts, Natural Sciences, Applied Sciences, and Social Sciences. The game is designed as an escape room where users earn a key and a puzzle piece at the end of each world. Throughout the game, players must navigate the five worlds by completing PE activities. Players are ranked based on the time it takes to complete the game. At the end of the game, they complete a brief game experience questionnaire based partially on IJsselsteijn et al. (2013). The first iteration of the GAMETRAPP app and escape room is scheduled for testing with scholars from the University of Málaga between April and May 2025. A second round of usability testing will follow in June/July 2025, after adjustments are made to the app and escape room. The final versions of the GAMETRAPP app and escape room are set to launch in August/September 2025.

Acknowledgments

The GAMETRAPP project (TED2021-129789B-I00/AEI/10.13039/501100011033/Unión Europea NextGenerationEU/PRTR) is funded by the Spanish Ministry for Science and Innovation under the Ecological Transition and Digital Transition Call 2021.

References

IJsselsteijn, W. A., de Kort, Y. A. W., and Poels, K. 2013. The Game Experience Questionnaire. Technische Universiteit Eindhoven.

Lefer, M.-A., Bodart, R., Obrusník, A., and Piette, J. 2023. The Post-Edit Me! project. In *Proceedings of the 24th Annual Conference of the European Association for Machine Translation*, pages 493–494, Tampere, Finland. European Association for Machine Translation. https://aclanthology.org/2023.eamt-1.49/

Moorkens, J., O'Brien, S., and Vreeke, J. 2016. Developing and testing Kanjingo: A mobile app for post-editing. *Revista Tradumàtica,* 14: 58-66. https://doi.org/10.5565/rev/tradumatica.168

Parra Escartín, C., and Goulet M. J. 2020. When the PostEditor is not a Translator: Can machine translation be post-edited by academics to prepare their publications in English? In *Translation Revision and Post-Editing,* pages 89–106. Routledge.

Toledo-Báez, C., and Noriega-Santiáñez, L. 2024. GAMETRAPP project in progress: Designing a gamified environment for post-editing research abstracts. In *Proceedings of the 25th Annual Conference of the European Association for Machine Translation*, pages 18–20, Sheffield, UK. European Association for Machine Translation. https://aclanthology.org/2024.eamt-2.10.pdf

AI4Culture platform: upskilling experts on multilingual / -modal tools

Tom Vanallemeersch and **Sara Szoc** and **Marthe Lamote** and **Frederic Everaert**
CrossLang NV, Franklin Rooseveltlaan 348/8, 9000 Gent, Belgium
firstname.lastname@crosslang.com

Eirini Kaldeli
National Technical University of Athens, Greece
ekaldeli@image.ntua.gr

Abstract

The AI4Culture project, funded by the European Commission (2023-2025), developed a platform (https://ai4culture.eu) to educate cultural heritage (CH) professionals in AI technologies. Acting as an online capacity building hub, the platform describes openly labeled data sets and deployable and reusable tools applying AI technologies in tasks relevant to the CH sector. It also offers tutorials for tools and *recipes* for the combination of tools. In addition, the platform allows users to contribute their own resources. The resources described by project partners involve applications for optical or handwritten character recognition (OCR, HTR), generation and validation of subtitles, machine translation, image analysis, and semantic linking. The partners customized various tools to enhance the usability of interfaces and components. Here, we zoom in on the use case of correcting OCR/HTR output using various means (such as an unstructured manual transcription) to facilitate multilingual accessibility and create structured ground truth (text lines with image coordinates).

1 Introduction

The AI4Culture project, which was funded by the DIGITAL program of the European Commission (EC) and took place from April 2023 until March 2025, developed an online capacity building hub for AI technologies in the sector of cultural heritage (CH). The platform makes CH data and tools involving varying modalities more accessible, understandable, and multilingual, supports heritage preservation, and contributes to making the common European data space for CH[1] more interoperable with AI technologies. The project coordinator is the AILS Laboratory of the National Technical University of Athens (NTUA). Partners in the CH sector include the Europeana Foundation, the European Fashion Heritage Association, the DigitGLAM unit at the University of Leuven, and the Institute for Sound and Vision. The technical partners include CrossLang, Datable, Datoptron, Pangeanic, and Translated, as well as the Machine Translation (MT) Research Unit at Fondazione Bruno Kessler (FBK) and the Digital Safety and Security Center of the Austrian Institute of Technology (AIT).

During the project, the partners focused on four types of technologies: (1) optical or handwritten character recognition (OCR, HTR) of scanned documents and MT of the transcriptions; (2) generation and validation of subtitles; (3) MT of documents and metadata; and (4) enrichment of metadata through image analysis and semantic linking. The partners customized tools to enhance the performance and usability of interfaces and components and organized workshops and a hackathon to involve stakeholders. The latter can also enrich the platform by contributing their own resources.

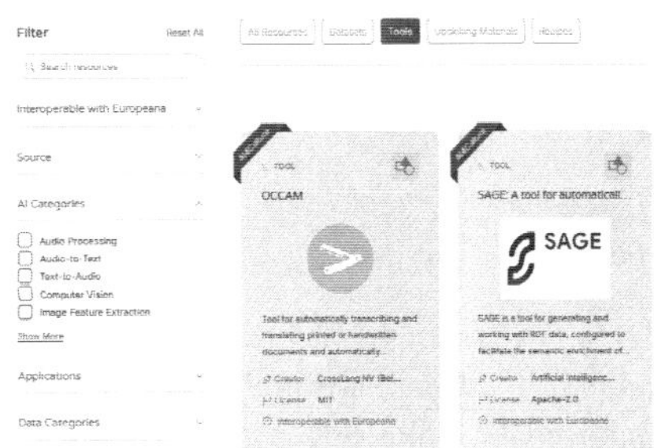

Figure 1: Exploring tools on the AI4Culture platform

2 Platform

The platform https://ai4culture.eu, launched in October 2024 and shown in Figure 1, offers a wide variety of AI-related resources: (1) descriptions of openly labeled data sets for training, testing, and evaluating models; (2) descriptions of de-

[1]https://www.dataspace-culturalheritage.eu/en

Proceedings of Machine Translation Summit XX Volume 2, pages 99–100, June 23-27, 2025

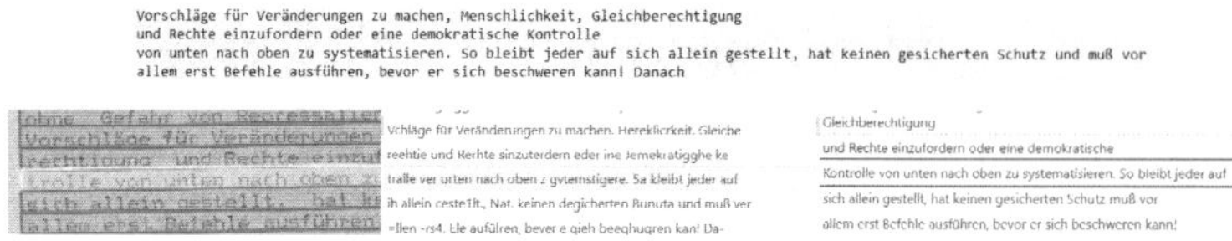

Figure 2: Unstructured manual transcription supporting the correction of OCR output

ployable and reusable tools for applying AI technologies in CH tasks; (3) tutorials (upskilling material) on such tasks; and (4) *recipes* illustrating the combination of tools for complex tasks. Target users include CH professionals and students, data providers, researchers, and AI developers.

The project partners registered descriptions of the tools they customized and other relevant tools. They focused on open source tools and the possibility to run tools locally. The tools provided by the partners can interact with `https://www.europeana.eu` and other CH data space components. The partners created data sets during the project, which they describe on the platform (for instance, PageXML files containing OCR/HTR transcriptions). After registering, platform users can contribute by uploading their own resources, thus raising awareness of their work. The platform allows for looking up resources based on criteria such as the AI technologies used, application types, etc. A resource description links to the repository where the actual resource is stored.

The project hosted a series of capacity building activities to provide professionals with hands-on experience. These include workshops on various technologies, the recordings of which are available on the platform, and a hackathon at the University of Leuven. A series of interviews with technical partners is also available on the platform.

3 Customization

Existing software has been customized in various ways: (1) FBK and Translated set up an open-source automatic subtitling system (Gaido et al., 2024); (2) Pangeanic combined computer-aided translation functionalities with CH-oriented MT engines; (3) NTUA and Datoptron extended their tools for semantic enrichment and validation of metadata and integrated them with the CH data space (Kaldeli et al., 2024); (4) Datable provided an object and color detection tool; (5) CrossLang added an open source HTR tool to its OCCAM transcription and translation environment[2] and functionality for automatic correction of OCR/HTR output and thus improved MT of transcriptions (Vanallemeersch et al., 2024), and (6) AIT interlinked Transcribathon[3] with the OCCAM services.

Regarding OCR/HTR, the two correction approaches reported by Vanallemeersch et al. (2024) (using a lexicon and language models) were extended towards the project end with a method matching output to an existing unstructured manual transcription (i.e. flat text). A final manual validation of the result of the approaches (structured, i.e. text lines with image coordinates) leads to ground truth useful for training new models or fine-tuning existing ones. While the first two approaches show variable performance (especially for low initial output quality), the third one shows clear results, as illustrated in Figure 2, where the (approximate) correspondence between lines in the image and a very long line in the manual transcription is detected. This "recycling" technique allows for reaching a minimally low CER score (character error rate), even for very poor original output quality.

Acknowledgments

AI4Culture is funded by the EC's DIGITAL program (project 101100683).

References

Marco Gaido, Sara Papi, Mauro Cettolo, Roldano Cattoni, Andrea Piergentili, Matteo Negri, and Luisa Bentivogli. 2024. Automatic subtitling and subtitle compression: FBK at the IWSLT 2024 subtitling track. In *Proceedings of IWSLT 2024*, pages 134–144.

Eirini Kaldeli, Alexandros Chortaras, Vassilis Lyberatos, Jason Liartis, Spyridon Kantarelis, and Giorgos Stamou. 2024. Combining automatic annotation with human validation for the semantic enrichment of cultural heritage metadata. In *Proceedings of CHR 2024*, pages 353–368.

Tom Vanallemeersch, Sara Szoc, and Laurens Meeus. 2024. AI4Culture: Towards multilingual access for cultural heritage data. In *Proceedings of EAMT 2024*, pages 59–60.

[2]https://ai4culture.crosslang.dev/ui

[3]https://europeana.transcribathon.eu

HPLT's Second Data Release

Nikolay Arefyev[2], Mikko Aulamo[3], Marta Bañón[4], Laurie Burchell[1], Pinzhen Chen[1], Mariia Fedorova[2], Ona de Gibert[3], Liane Guillou[1], Barry Haddow[1], Jan Hajič[5], Jindřich Helcl[5], Erik Henriksson[6], Andrey Kutuzov[2], Veronika Laippala[6], Bhavitvya Malik[1], Farrokh Mehryary[6], Vladislav Mikhailov[2], Amanda Myntti[6], Dayyán O'Brien[1], Stephan Oepen[2], Sampo Pyysalo[6], Gema Ramírez-Sánchez[4], David Samuel[2], Pavel Stepachev[1], Jörg Tiedemann[3], Dušan Variš[5], Jaume Zaragoza-Bernabeu[4]

[1]University of Edinburgh, [2]University of Oslo, [3]University of Helsinki, [4]Prompsit Language Engineering, [5]Charles University, [6]University of Turku

Contact: `https://hplt-project.org`

Abstract

We describe the progress of the High Performance Language Technologies (HPLT) project, a 3-year EU-funded project that started in September 2022 with two main objectives: derive monotexts and bitexts for multiple languages from web crawls at massive scale and use them to build efficient machine translation models and language models. We focus on the up-to-date results on the release of free text *datasets* derived from web crawls, one of the central objectives of the project. The second release used a revised processing pipeline, and an enlarged set of input crawls. From 4.5 petabytes of web crawls we extracted 7.6T tokens of monolingual text in 193 languages, plus 380 million parallel sentences in 51 language pairs. We also release MultiHPLT, a cross-combination of the parallel data, which produces 1,275 pairs, and the containing documents for all parallel sentences in order to enable research in document-level MT. We report changes in the pipeline, analysis and evaluation results for the second parallel data release based on machine translation systems. All datasets are released under the `CC0` licence.

1 Introduction

The HPLT project runs from 2022 to 2025, and focuses on the processing petabytes of natural language data and large-scale model training. The consortium is made of eight partners: Charles University in Prague (coordinator), University of Edinburgh, University of Helsinki, University of Oslo, University of Turku, Prompsit Language Engineering, and CESNET and Sigma2 HPC centres.

Following the previous release at the end of 2023 (de Gibert et al., 2024), the project has recently completed the release of a new massive multilingual dataset for both monolingual and parallel data along with improved pipelines and tools extensively described in (Burchell et al., 2025).

2 Second Data Release

Datasets The second release includes data processed originally from 4.5 petabytes of the Internet Archive and CommonCrawl to create monolingual and parallel corpora. It is released under the permissive `CC0` licence[1] through our project website[2], OPUS[3][4] and Hugging Face[5]. The updated pipelines and open-source tools to produce this release are on GitHub.[6] The monolingual data extends to 193 languages and contains roughly 7.6 trillion space-separated tokens after deduplication and filtering. The parallel data includes 51 language pairs, with roughly 6.7 billion tokens computed on the English side and 380 million sentence pairs. The bonus multi-parallel dataset, pivoted through English, contains 1,275 language pairs.

Changes in the parallel data pipeline The second release of HPLT data introduces important changes in the pipeline. Parallel data is now derived from the clean and deduplicated documents from the monolingual release instead of the raw data. The text extraction pipeline uses Trafilatura (Barbaresi, 2021), which results in more efficient boilerplate removal. Language identification uses a refined version of OpenLID (Burchell et al., 2023) instead of CLD2. Deduplication and filtering of adult content and non-compliant `robots.txt` web documents happens before executing the parallel data processing. A multilingual Bicleaner AI[7] model replaces the pair-based ones used to annotate parallel sentences for translation likelihood.

[1]We do not own any of the text from which these text data have been extracted. We license the actual packaging of these text data under the `CC0` licence ("no rights reserved").

[2]https://hplt-project.org/datasets/v2.0

[3]opus.nlpl.eu/HPLT.php

[4]https://opus.nlpl.eu/MultiHPLT/corpus/v2/MultiHPLT

[5]https://huggingface.co/datasets/HPLT/HPLT2.0_cleaned

[6]github.com/hplt-project

[7]https://tinyurl.com/3pxkcjf8

Proceedings of Machine Translation Summit XX Volume 2, pages 101–102, June 23-27, 2025

Parallel data stats and analysis The second release of the HPLT parallel data covering 51 language pairs contains 380,710,720 sentence pairs with 6,779,910,082 English words. Our selection of pairs avoided the top 20 highest resourced (according to OPUS) and focused on the next ranked languages, in order to maximise impact. The sizes of the different language pairs show significant variation, with a median of 3,927,371 sentence pairs. This range spans from 273,430 sentence pairs for English– Sinhala to 29,067,875 sentence pairs for English–Finnish, the largest parallel data set.

We get a 36% increase in the number of sentences compared to the first release for the 18 overlapping languages. During filtering, 40% of the parallel sentence pairs are eliminated and an additional 50% is removed due to deduplication. The final corpus shows a 70% decrease in sentence pairs relative to the raw data. This reduction is less significant than in the first release, which we assume is due to starting with cleaner monolingual text.

We inspect the data with the HPLT Analytics tool.[8] We find that small-sized datasets contain larger portions of Wikipedia and religious content while medium/large-sized ones contain high-portions of hotel booking and travel websites. Some popular domains include websites from gaming, software or e-commerce translated into a big number of languages, probably using MT. From the inspection of the most frequent n-grams, we find that they are very similar across all parallel datasets, especially among larger ones, frequently related to hotels and legal notices.

Extrinsic evaluation of the parallel data We train bidirectional MT models on the new released parallel data to extrinsically evaluate the performance of the released datasets. We compare models trained on only HPLT data for both releases and, additionally, models trained with HPLT data in combination with Tatoeba.[9]

We build and release MarianNMT compatible MT models for all bitexts in HPLT v2 using the same tooling as the one used in the previous release: OpusCleaner (data selection and cleaning), OpusTrainer (data scheduling and augmenting), and OpusPocus (training process management). These tools are fully described in the public deliverable of the HPLT project focused on pipelines and tools.[10]

[8]https://github.com/hplt-project/data-analytics-tool

[9]https://github.com/Helsinki-NLP/Tatoeba-Challenge

[10]https://tinyurl.com/y6mc3sfk

Automatic metrics are computed on FLORES-200[11] for evaluation. Results computed on 10 out of the overlapping 18 language pairs between the first and the second release show gains in BLEU in favour of HPLT v2 MT models going into English with an average gain of 4.2 BLEU. From English, the average gain is 3.5 in BLEU, with 7 out of the 10 models being better with HPLT v2 data and the remaining 3 being on par between the first and second release. When combining HPLT v2 data and Tatoeba, MT models result in a 7% relative increase in BLEU for both translation directions.

Acknowledgment

This project has received funding from the European Union's Horizon Europe programme (GA No 101070350) and from UK Research and Innovation (UKRI) under the UK government's Horizon Europe funding guarantee (GA No 10052546). It has also been supported by the Czech MEYS project No. CZ.02.01.01/00/23_025/0008691 and Research Infrastructure project LM2023062.

References

Adrien Barbaresi. 2021. Trafilatura: A web scraping library and command-line tool for text discovery and extraction. In *Proceedings of ACL Demo*.

Laurie Burchell, Alexandra Birch, Nikolay Bogoychev, and Kenneth Heafield. 2023. An open dataset and model for language identification. In *Proceedings of ACL)*.

Laurie Burchell, Ona de Gibert, Nikolay Arefyev, Mikko Aulamo, Marta Bañón, Pinzhen Chen, Mariia Fedorova, Liane Guillou, Barry Haddow, Jan Hajič, Jindřich Helcl, Erik Henriksson, Mateusz Klimaszewski, Ville Komulainen, Andrey Kutuzov, Joona Kytöniemi, Veronika Laippala, Petter Mæhlum, Bhavitvya Malik, Farrokh Mehryary, Vladislav Mikhailov, Nikita Moghe, Amanda Myntti, Dayyán O'Brien, Stephan Oepen, Proyag Pal, Jousia Piha, Sampo Pyysalo, Gema Ramírez-Sánchez, David Samuel, Pavel Stepachev, Jörg Tiedemann, Dušan Variš, Tereza Vojtěchová, and Jaume Zaragoza-Bernabeu. 2025. An expanded massive multilingual dataset for high-performance language technologies. *Preprint*, arXiv:2503.10267.

Ona de Gibert, Graeme Nail, Nikolay Arefyev, Marta Bañón, Jelmer van der Linde, Shaoxiong Ji, Jaume Zaragoza-Bernabeu, Mikko Aulamo, Gema Ramírez-Sánchez, Andrey Kutuzov, Sampo Pyysalo, Stephan Oepen, and Jörg Tiedemann. 2024. A new massive multilingual dataset for high-performance language technologies. In *Proceedings of LREC-COLING*.

[11]https://github.com/facebookresearch/flores

MaTOS: Machine Translation for Open Science

Rachel Bawden[2], Maud Bénard[1], Éric de la Clergerie[2], José Cornejo Cárcamo[1], Nicolas Dahan[2,4], Manon Delorme[3], Mathilde Huguin[3], Natalie Kübler[1], Paul Lerner[4], Alexandra Mestivier[1], Joachim Minder[3], Jean-François Nominé[3], Ziqian Peng[2,4], Laurent Romary[2], Panagiotis Tsolakis[2], Lichao Zhu[1], François Yvon[4]

[1] ALTAE, Université Paris Cité, Paris, France
[2] Inria, Paris, France
[3] INIST, CNRS, Nancy, France
[4] ISIR, CNRS and Sorbonne Université, Paris, France

Correspondence: yvon@isir.upmc.fr

Abstract

This paper is a short presentation of MaTOS (Machine Translation for Open Science), a project focusing on the automatic translation of scholarly documents. Its main aims are (a) to develop resources (term lists and corpora) for high-quality machine translation, (b) to study methods for translating complete, structured documents in a cohesive and consistent manner, (c) to propose novel metrics to evaluate machine translation in technical domains. Publications and resources are available on the project web site: `https://anr-matos.fr`.

Motivations

MaTOS, Machine Translation for Open Science, is a four-year project (2022-2026) aiming to develop new methods for the full machine translation (MT) of scholarly documents, as well as automatic metrics for evaluating the quality of the translations produced. Our main target application is the translation of scholarly articles between French and English, for which linguistic resources can be exploited to obtain high-quality translations. These translation can both be used to speed up publication in a foreign language, but also to improve the discoverability of scientific information, and facilitate its dissemination to the general public. However, efforts to improve the MT of entire documents are hampered by the inability of existing automatic MT metrics to detect and evaluate translation issues that span multiple sentences. Such issues are not rare and happen due to inadequate modeling of discourse phenomena.

MaTOS is part of a growing trend in research and technology to automate the processing of scholarly articles, providing new tools to discover and process an increasing volume of publications. MT is one the most important technologies in this regard, as it holds the promise of facilitating the global discussion about the current state of scientific knowledge beyond the scientific community, where these discussions take place mostly in English. Using MT, other critical applications of scholarly text mining can also be made available in multiple languages, e.g. bibliometric analysis and the automatic detection of plagiarism and articles reporting falsified conclusions. MaTOS will contribute to this general trend by (a) developing new open resources for specialized MT, (b) improving the description of textual consistency markers for scholarly articles, through the study of terminological variation, (c) studying new multilingual processing methods to handle long documents, and (d) proposing dedicated automatic metrics for these tasks.

Challenges

New neural machine translation (NMT) architectures can handle extended contexts, corresponding to paragraphs or even longer parts of documents. However, notwithstanding the limitations of existing computational architectures, efforts to improve MT for complete documents are hindered on the one hand by a general lack of resources, and on the other by the inability of existing automatic metrics to detect system weaknesses and identify the best ways to remedy them.

MaTOS tackles these two difficulties head-on, paying particular attention to the issue of translating complex terms and their variation within documents. The translation of specialized terms, which is critical for academic texts in particular, remains difficult, due to the specific linguistic structures in which the terms appear (e.g., complex nominal phrases), the lack of a stabilized reference translation for emerging terms and the lack of modeling of their variation within texts and corpora.

Participants

MaTOS is a multidisciplinary project, bringing together teams with diverse scientific backgrounds: the ALMAnaCH project-team at Inria, Paris[1] and the MLIA team at ISIR[2] bring expertise in natural language processing and are mostly involved in the technological workpackages, developing methods and tools to automatically identify terms and their variants, to perform translation at the document level and to automatically evaluate whole document translation. ALTAE[3] (Université Paris-Cité), will focus on the development of resources (annotated corpora and term lists) and conduct fine-grained studies of the terminological variation within and across scholarly documents. INIST-CNRS,[4] will also contribute to resource development, in line with their primary missions related to the dissemination of scientific and technological information.

Results

After two years, the project has produced a set of reports documenting the state of the art, focusing notably on (a) human assessments of translation quality (Bénard et al., 2024), (b) automatic evaluation of translation at the document level (Dahan et al., 2024) and (c) computational architectures for document translation (Peng et al., 2024).

Various resources have also been collected, prepared and formatted. These include terminologies for two domains ("Natural Language Processing" and "Earth and Planet Sciences"), as well as monolingual and bilingual corpora, in particular long documents and their translations for the same domains. They can be downloaded from our website.

Regarding natural language processing, efforts have focused on three aspects: (a) the development of tools to identify terms and their variants in corpora (these will be used to document in detail the spectrum of acceptable terminological variations and to thoroughly evaluate the quality of terminology translation at the document level), (b) the study of methods for the automatical suggestion of neologisms for the translation of emerging terms (Lerner and Yvon, 2025), and (c) the development of specialized MT systems able to translate long documents, based on both encoder-decoder architectures and large multilingual language models. Preliminary results are in (Peng et al., 2025).

Regarding evaluation, two pilot studies involving the post-editing of automatically translated abstracts have been carried out with the involvement of specialized translators and members of the academic community, in anticipation of a larger-scale study (Bawden et al., 2024).

[1] `https://almanach.inria.fr`
[2] `https://www.isir.upmc.fr/equipes/mlia`
[3] `https://clillac-arp.u-paris.fr/`
[4] `https://www.inist.fr/`

Acknowledgments

This research was funded by the French Agence Nationale de la Recherche (ANR) under the project MaTOS - "ANR-22-CE23-0033-03". R. Bawden's participation is also partly funded by her chair in the PRAIRIE institute funded by the ANR as part of the "Investissements d'avenir" programme under the reference ANR-19-P3IA-0001.

References

Rachel Bawden, Ziqian Peng, Maud Bénard, Eric Villemonte de La Clergerie, Raphaël Esamotunu, Mathilde Huguin, Natalie Kübler, Alexandra Mestivier, Mona Michelot, Laurent Romary, Lichao Zhu, and François Yvon. 2024. Translate your Own: a Post-Editing Experiment in the NLP domain. In *Proceedings of the 25th Annual Conference of the European Association for Machine Translation (Volume 1)*, page 431–443, Sheffield, United Kingdom.

Maud Bénard, Natalie Kübler, Alexandra Mestivier, Joachim Minder, and Lichao Zhu. 2024. Étude des Protocoles d'Évaluation Humaine pour la Traduction de Documents. Technical Report Delivrable D4.1.1, Projet ANR MaTOS.

Nicolas Dahan, Rachel Bawden, and François Yvon. 2024. Survey of Automatic Metrics for Evaluating Machine Translation at the Document Level. Technical Report Deliverable D4.5.1, Projet ANR MaTOS.

Paul Lerner and François Yvon. 2025. Towards the machine translation of scientific neologisms. In *Proceedings of the 31st International Conference on Computational Linguistics*, pages 947–963, Abu Dhabi, UAE.

Ziqian Peng, Rachel Bawden, and François Yvon. 2024. Handling Very Long Contexts in Neural Machine Translation: a Survey. Technical Report Delivrable D3.2.1, Projet ANR MaTOS.

Ziqian Peng, Rachel Bawden, and François Yvon. 2025. Investigating length issues in document-level machine translation. In *Proceedings of Machine Translation Summit XX, Vol. 1: Research Track*, Geneva, Switzerland.

Prompt-based Explainable Quality Estimation for English-Malayalam

Archchana Sindhujan, Diptesh Kanojia, Constantin Orăsan

Institute for People-Centred AI and Centre for Translation Studies,
University of Surrey, United Kingdom
{a.sindhujan, d.kanojia, c.orasan}@surrey.ac.uk

Abstract

This project aimed to curate data for the English-Malayalam language pair for the tasks of Quality Estimation (QE) and Automatic Post-Editing (APE) of Machine Translation. Whilst the primary aim of the project was to create a dataset for a low-resource language pair, we plan to use this dataset to investigate different zero-shot and few-shot prompting strategies, including chain-of-thought, towards a unified explainable QE-APE framework.

1 Introduction

This project is a one-year-long initiative funded by the European Association for Machine Translation (EAMT)[1]. The primary focus of our project was to create novel Quality Estimation (QE) and Automatic Post-editing (APE) datasets for the English (En) - Malayalam (Ml) language pair. QE refers to the task of automatically predicting the quality of machine-translated output without reference translations, while APE aims to automatically correct errors in machine translations. The Malayalam language is a low-resource language with over 38 million speakers across the world. Despite its presence with 86,553 Wikipedia articles[2] on the web, there was no available data for evaluating the quality of translation from English to Malayalam. For English to low-resource Indic language pairs, QE data exists for English to {Hindi, Marathi, and Gujarati} where target languages belong to the Indo-Aryan language family. However, from the Dravidian language family, QE data is only available for English-Tamil and English-Telugu (Blain et al., 2023). Our project addresses this gap by introducing a novel English-Malayalam QE dataset, expanding QE research within the Dravidian language family. The dataset comprises three direct assessment (DA) scores assigned by human annotators, along with human post-edited translations for the APE task. The manual post-editing process further facilitates the creation of word-level QE data[3], enriching its usability for fine-grained evaluation. Additionally, the project aimed at a comprehensive evaluation of multiple large language models (LLMs) for QE of low-resource language pairs.

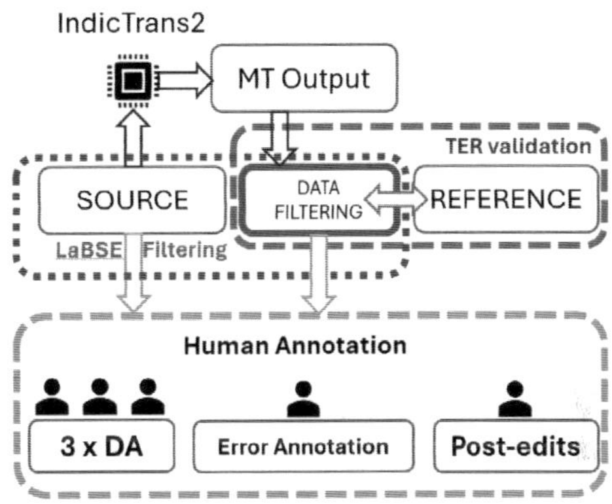

Figure 1: Our data curation workflow for QE-APE

2 Project Progress & Impact

Figure 1 depicts our workflow as described below. Our workflow consisted of- filtering high-quality parallel data, machine translation, TER-based validation, and human annotation for QE & APE.

2.1 Data Curation

We perform initial data curation leveraging data filtration techniques and iterative feedback to guidelines for annotation. For an initial comparison with existing references, we obtain a parallel corpus

[1]This is an individual project carried out at the University of Surrey

[2]en.wikipedia.org/wiki/Malayalam_Wikipedia

[3]github.com/WMT-QE-Task

Proceedings of Machine Translation Summit XX Volume 2, pages 105–106, June 23-27, 2025

for En-Ml translations via the Anuvaad parallel corpus[4], which provides domain-specific parallel data. We selected data instances from the finance, legal, and news domains to curate an initial larger set of instances. We filter out high-quality parallel data leveraging Language-agnostic BERT Sentence Embedding (LaBSE) scores with a high threshold (0.8) for contextual accuracy.

Post data filtration, we performed the translation using IndicTrans2 (Gala et al., 2023) model[5], the first fully open-source Transformer-based multilingual NMT model that supports translations across 22 Indic languages. The model adopts script unification wherever feasible to leverage transfer learning by lexical sharing between languages, which minimizes subword vocabulary fragmentation and enables the use of a smaller subword vocabulary.

To assess the translation quality, we compute the Translation Edit Rate (TER) by comparing the outputs of IndicTrans2 with the corresponding references from Anuvaad. TER acts as a reliable early indicator of translation quality and helps us manage DA score distribution. To validate this translation quality, a random sample of 25 translations was manually reviewed by a native Malayalam speaker fluent in English, providing early insights on common errors. For the final stage, we select 8,000 segments, ensuring a balanced TER distribution. Our approach ensures that the curated dataset is well-distributed in terms of DA, suitable for segment-level computational modelling.

2.2 Annotation and Human Post-edits

After data curation, we shared segments with source and MT output, for DA score annotation with the annotation agency *TechLiebe*. First, a sample of 500 data instances was shared. At this step, we determine any deviations from the annotation guidelines and provide early feedback, then iteratively over weekly meetings. Each segment was evaluated and assigned a DA score by *three native speakers of Malayalam*, who are also fluent in English. Additionally, annotators were asked to provide a brief description of the identified errors. These *error descriptions* will act as 'weak error explanations', and will support the implementation of an explainable QE approach. After reviewing the 500 annotated samples and updating our annotation guidelines addressing the identified issues, we initiated the DA annotation in two batches, each containing 3750 segments. In weekly meetings, validation of random samples from the annotated data was performed. Any discrepancies observed were conveyed to all three annotators. Updated annotations were then re-evaluated in subsequent meetings to ensure alignment and consistency.

We started the post-editing process in parallel to the DA score annotation process with the help of an evaluator who was not involved in the DA annotation. The objective of post-editing is to make minimal edits to the translated output to convey the meaning of the source sentences. Initially, we shared a sample of 500 instances, validated the edits, and refined the post-editing guidelines before proceeding with two larger batches of 3750 segments each. By enhancing both translation evaluation and correction, this dataset aims to improve the performance of QE and APE of En-Ml.

2.3 Conclusion and Future Work

The annotation process progressed as planned, but validation and iterative corrections during weekly reviews required more time than expected. Prioritizing quality over speed ensured accuracy and consistency. Despite these challenges, our rigorous approach has guaranteed a high-quality English-Malayalam QE and APE dataset, with the majority of annotations completed and public release planned soon.

In future, we would like to perform synthetic reasoning generation based on error descriptions provided by human annotators collected with our dataset, leveraging LLMs to identify the penalization of DA score more accurately, further leading to improved QE and APE.

References

Frederic Blain, Chrysoula Zerva, Ricardo Rei, Nuno M. Guerreiro, Diptesh Kanojia, José G. C. de Souza, Beatriz Silva, Tânia Vaz, Yan Jingxuan, Fatemeh Azadi, Constantin Orasan, and André Martins. 2023. Findings of the WMT 2023 shared task on quality estimation. pages 629–653, Singapore.

Jay Gala, Pranjal A Chitale, Raghavan AK, Varun Gumma, Sumanth Doddapaneni, Aswanth Kumar, Janki Nawale, Anupama Sujatha, Ratish Puduppully, Vivek Raghavan, et al. 2023. IndicTrans2: Towards high-quality and accessible Machine Translation models for all 22 Scheduled Indian Languages. *arXiv preprint arXiv:2305.16307*.

[4]github.com/project-anuvaad/anuvaad-parallel-corpus
[5]github.com/AI4Bharat/IndicTrans2

MTxGames: Machine Translation Post-Editing in Video Game Translation – Findings on User Experience and Preliminary Results on Productivity

Judith Brenner
University of Eastern Finland

jbrenner@uef.fi

Abstract

MTxGames is a doctoral research project examining three different translation modes with varying degrees of machine translation post-editing when translating video game texts. For realistic experimental conditions, data elicitation took place at the workplaces of professional game translators. In a mixed-methods approach, quantitative data was elicited through keylogging, eye-tracking, error annotation, and questionnaires as well as qualitative data through interviews. Aspects to be analyzed are translation productivity, cognitive effort, translation quality, and translators' user experience.

1 Introduction

Reports from the video game localization industry suggest that machine translation post-editing (MTPE) is increasing in demand, with game translation buyers hoping to reduce translation time and/or costs. However, there is hardly any research that could provide evidence to base this practice on. Therefore, the MTxGames project aims to shed light on the MTPE process of professional game translators when translating video games. Translators performed three different translation tasks over the course of one day: translation from scratch, static post-editing (PE), and flexible PE. Data gathered during this study allow for analyzing translation productivity, translation quality, cognitive effort, and user experience. At the current stage of analysis, preliminary results on productivity and final results on user experience are available.

The research questions and design of this study were informed by MTPE studies on informative text types as well as from creative fields such as literary translation and from multimodal fields such as subtitling. While increases in productivity have been reported, they do not necessarily happen for all translators and show high variability (Terribile, 2024). In creative fields such as literary translation, productivity can even be decreased (Guerberof-Arenas and Toral, 2022). With contradictory results on productivity between studies with informative texts and with literary texts, the question remains how productivity is affected when translating video games by post-editing MT output. Video games are complex entities and translating them combines aspects of software localization, technical translation, creative translation, and multimodal translation (Bernal-Merino, 2015). According to several manifestos published by associations representing game translators, among other types of creative translators, translators oppose the use of MT and the MTPE practice (e.g., Deryagin et al., 2021). To include translators' perspectives, the experience of the translator as user of MT is of interest in this study. A recent study on MT user experience (Briva-Iglesias, 2024) showed higher user experience when MT was incorporated into the translation production process in another form than doing static PE. Also, Hansen and Houlmont (2022) suggest using MT as additional resource to a translation memory (TM), instead of for MTPE, to not constrain creativity when translating games. Therefore, this study compares translation from scratch with two different types of MTPE.

2 The Study

The study was conducted in collaboration with the game localization service provider Native Prime. Native Prime recruited and compensated the study participants (14 freelance game translators and 1 in-house game localization project manager), provided the game texts, access to the MT system (ModernMT), the TM and the terminology database (TB) from the original game localization project, and set up the project in the translation environment system (memoQ TMS 11.2).

Data were generated at participants' home offices between December 2024 and January 2025. Tasks were carried out on a laptop and a display provided by the researcher. Else, participants used their own equipment (keyboard, mouse, etc.). This setup ensured participants worked in their usual environment instead of in a laboratory and at the same time protected their privacy and data security as no software was installed on participants' PCs.

An eye-tracker (Tobii Pro X3-120 plus EPU) logged the time taken for the translation tasks, keystrokes, mouse actions, and gaze data, and captured screen recordings. Moreover, translations after the three tasks were saved for a subsequent error analysis. Participants replied to a pre-task questionnaire on demographic data and previous experience with MT and PE. After each task, they filled out a short user experience questionnaire (Laugwitz et al., 2008) with 26 opposing adjective pairs. Finally, a short interview discussed the overall experience with all three tasks.

Participants translated 3 texts (ca. 830 words each) that were compiled by selecting similar strings from the same game. These 3 texts were translated from English into French, Italian, German, or Spanish under 3 different conditions: 1) translation from scratch with a TM and a TB available as resources; 2) static PE of the text pre-translated by ModernMT, with TM and TB available; 3) flexible PE, a combination of translation from scratch and static PE, where the target segments were empty, but ModernMT suggestions were available as a resource, additionally to TM and TB. Conditions and texts were rotated among participants to account for learning and fatigue effects. Furthermore, participants were divided into two groups, generic MT and domain-adapted MT. For generic MT, ModernMT was used as is. For domain-adapted MT, a TM with around 74,000 words of the game under translation was added to ModernMT.

3 Results

Results show a poor user experience with static PE, especially when combined with generic MT, a neutral experience with flexible PE that leans toward positive when combined with domain-adapted MT, and a markedly positive experience with translation from scratch (Brenner and Othlinghaus-Wulhorst, forthcoming). Regarding productivity, results are preliminary. For 5 participants translation from scratch seems to be the fastest, for another 5 flexible PE, and for 2 the fastest seems to be static PE.

Acknowledgments

This research was funded by the Finnish Kone Foundation (2023–2025, project number 202202303) and the European Association for Machine Translation (EAMT), Sponsorship of Activities, Students' Edition 2023 and supported by Native Prime and 15 study participants.

References

Miguel Á Bernal-Merino. 2015. Translation and localisation in video games: making entertainment software global. Routledge, London; New York. https://doi.org/10.4324/9781315752334

Judith Brenner, Julia Othlinghaus-Wulhorst. Forthcoming. 'Effects of Domain-adapted Machine Translation on the Machine Translation User Experience of Video Game Translators'. Accepted by the 2nd Workshop on Creative-text Translation and Technology. Geneva, Switzerland.

Vicent Briva-Iglesias. 2024. Fostering human-centered, augmented machine translation: Analysing interactive post-editing. Ph.D. thesis, Dublin City University, Dublin, Ireland.

Max Deryagin, Miroslav Pošta, and Daniel Landes. 2021. Machine Translation Manifesto. Audiovisual Translators Europe.

Ana Guerberof-Arenas and Antonio Toral. 2022. Creativity in translation: Machine translation as a constraint for literary texts. *Translation Spaces* 11 (2), 184–212. https://doi.org/10.1075/ts.21025.gue

Damien Hansen and Pierre-Yves Houlmont. 2022. A Snapshot into the Possibility of Video Game Machine Translation. In Proceedings of the 15th Biennial Conference of the Association for Machine Translation in the Americas (Volume 2: Users and Providers Track and Government Track), pages 257–269, Orlando, USA. Association for Machine Translation in the Americas.

Bettina Laugwitz, Martin Schrepp, and Theo Held. 2008. Construction and evaluation of a user experience questionnaire. In Andreas Holzinger, editor, *USAB 2008, Lecture Notes in Computer Science, Vol. 5298*, pages 63–76, Graz, Austria. https://doi.org/10.1007/978-3-540-89350-9_6

Silvia Terribile. 2024. Is post-editing really faster than human translation? *Translation Spaces* 13 (2), 171–199. https://doi.org/10.1075/ts.22044.ter

Machine translation as support for epistemic capacities: Findings from the DECA project

Maarit Koponen[1], **Nina Havumetsä**[1], **Juha Lång**[1], **Mary Nurminen**[2]
[1]University of Eastern Finland, [2]Tampere University,
[1]`firstname.lastname@uef.fi`, [2]`firstname.lastname@tuni.fi`

Abstract

The DECA project consortium investigates epistemic capacities, defined as an individual's access to reliable knowledge, their ability to participate in knowledge production, and society's capacity to make informed, sustainable policy decisions. As a tool both for accessing information across language barriers and for producing multilingual information, machine translation also plays a potential role in supporting these epistemic capacities. In this paper, we present an overview of DECA's research on two perspectives: 1) how migrants use machine translation to access information, and 2) how journalists use machine translation in their work.

1 Introduction

The ability to access relevant, reliable knowledge and information is an essential part of epistemic capacity (Werkheiser, 2016). From the perspective of individuals, equal availability and accessibility of information can be seen as a fundamental epistemic right (Nieminen, 2024). While modern societies are increasingly multilingual, information produced by societal institutions like public administration and media is generally limited to dominant local languages and to a lesser extent some lingua franca (e.g. English). Information is therefore not equally accessible and intelligible to all members of society.

Questions of epistemic capacities and epistemic rights are at the core of the research carried out by the project consortium Democratic epistemic capacity in the age of algorithms (DECA) formed by University of Helsinki (consortium coordinator), University of Eastern Finland, Tampere University, Aalto University and the Finnish Youth Research Society. It is funded by the Strategic Research Council established within the Research Council of Finland (2022–2025). Different work packages of this multidisciplinary consortium[1] address various aspects of epistemic rights and capabilities from the perspective of institutions, infrastructures and individuals.

This paper focuses on WP3 *Linguistic barriers, algorithms and epistemic capabilities*, which investigates linguistic accessibility and the role of machine translation (MT) in realising epistemic rights and capacities. The work conducted by the research team at the University of Eastern Finland in collaboration with the Finnish Youth Research Society has two main lines of research. The first line focuses on the use of MT by migrants as support for finding and accessing information. The second investigates how journalists use MT as part of their work. The next sections outline the current status of the work conducted in these lines of research, as well as directions for future work.

2 MT for linguistic accessibility

MT is an important tool for migrants, particularly vulnerable migrants like refugees and asylum seekers (Vieira, 2024a). DECA has aimed to investigate in more detail how migrants who do not speak Finnish use MT to find, access and use information about Finnish society. We have focused on people who have arrived in Finland from Ukraine or Russia since 2022.

Data collection started in spring 2024 with focus group discussions (n=35) mapping the participants' information needs, information sources and linguistic barriers they encounter. Participants were then invited for individual interviews (n=29) complemented with simulated information search experiments. The experiment consisted of tasks where the participants were asked to find information related to aspects of life in Finland (e.g. library services,

[1]See `https://www.decatutkimus.fi/research`

Proceedings of Machine Translation Summit XX Volume 2, pages 109–110, June 23-27, 2025

public transport). The purpose of the task was to observe their strategies for searching information and their use or MT. Screen recordings and think-aloud were recorded for analysis.

A preliminary analysis shows that most participants attempted to find information in their first language (Ukrainian or Russian), which provided relatively little information. The most effective use of MT was first translating the search phrases into Finnish to find relevant pages and then using MT to read these pages. However, this strategy was used by only a minority of the participants, mainly young adults who showed good information skills. A more detailed analysis of the interviews and tasks is currently ongoing.

3 MT in journalism

Journalism plays a vital role in providing relevant societal information (Watson, 2018; Nieminen, 2024). While previous work has developed MT tools for use in journalism (e.g. van der Kreeft et al., 2022), the perspective of journalists using MT remains relatively unexplored. DECA has therefore aimed to investigate more closely the ways in which journalists in Finland use MT in their work.

The first stage of research starting in 2023 focused on journalists at the Finnish national broadcasting company Yle producing news in English, Russian and Ukrainian. We conducted interviews (n=7) exploring how the journalists see their role in promoting the epistemic capacities of different language groups and how they use MT as part of their work (Havumetsä and Nurminen, 2025). Findings from the interviews show that MT use varies in the different departments. The Ukrainian news are mainly produced by translating Finnish news, and the work relies on an MT tool provided by Yle. In the other departments, MT use is less common, and the attitudes of journalists toward MT vary. Benefits identified by the journalists include making their work faster and allowing them to access more diverse sources in different languages. On the other hand, they expressed some doubts related to the quality of MT and ethical aspects.

In 2024, the work has been extended to MT use by journalists producing news in Finnish. We conducted interviews (n=10) and a survey (n=69) focusing on the use of MT, which was circulated to journalists working at Finnish media houses. Analysis of the data is currently ongoing.

4 Future work

As next stage of the work, we aim to further investigate the use of MT in Finnish public institutions, particularly immigration and integration services. A survey inspired by prior work carried out in the UK (Vieira, 2024b) and discussions with stakeholders in the field is being planned for 2025. Additionally, we are producing materials aimed at increasing MT literacy among different user groups, such as journalists, public administration or teachers, to be published in 2025.

Acknowledgments

This work is part of the DECA project funded by the Strategic Research Council established within the Research Council of Finland, funding agreements 352577 (University of Eastern Finland) and 352557 (consortium coordinator University of Helsinki).

References

Nina Havumetsä and Mary Nurminen. 2025. (Kone)kääntäminen Ylessä ja muunkielisten episteemiset oikeudet. *Mikael: Finnish Journal of Translation and Interpreting Studies*, 18(1):7–22.

Hannu Nieminen. 2024. Why We Need Epistemic Rights. In Minna Aslama Horowitz, Hannu Nieminen, Katja Lehtisaari, and Alessandro D'Arma, editors, *Epistemic Rights in the Era of Digital Disruption*, pages 11–28. Springer International Publishing, Cham.

Peggy van der Kreeft, Alexandra Birch, Sevi Sariisik, Felipe Sánchez-Martínez, and Wilker Aziz. 2022. GoURMET – Machine Translation for Low-Resourced Languages. In *Proceedings of the 23rd Annual Conference of the European Association for Machine Translation*, pages 339–340, Ghent, Belgium. European Association for Machine Translation.

Lucas Nunes Vieira. 2024a. Machine translation and migration. In Brigid Maher, Loredana Polezzi, and Rita Wilson, editors, *The Routledge Handbook of Translation and Migration*, pages 221–234. Routledge, London.

Lucas Nunes Vieira. 2024b. Uses of AI Translation in UK Public Service Contexts: A Preliminary Report. Technical report, Chartered Institute of Linguists CIOL.

Lani Watson. 2018. Systematic Epistemic Rights Violations in the Media: A Brexit Case Study. *Social Epistemology*, 32(2):88–102.

Ian Werkheiser. 2016. Community Epistemic Capacity. *Social Epistemology*, 30(1):25–44.

Reverso Define: An AI-Powered Contextual Dictionary for Professionals

Quentin Pleplé
Reverso

Théo Hoffenberg
Reverso

Abstract

We present Reverso Define, an innovative English dictionary designed to support translation professionals with AI-powered, context-aware definitions. Built using a hybrid approach combining Large Language Models (LLMs) and expert linguists, it offers precise definitions with special attention to multi-word expressions and domain-specific terminology. The system provides comprehensive coverage of technical domains relevant to professional translators while maintaining daily updates to address emerging terminology needs. It also provides indicative translations in 26 languages. This paper provides insights into its design and creation process, illustrating various use cases and examples.

1 Introduction

Professional translators and post-editors working with machine translation (MT) systems or LLMs face significant challenges in determining precise contextual meanings, particularly for domain-specific terms and multiword expressions. Traditional dictionaries often fall short due to limited coverage, complex definitions, and poor handling of expressions that are typically buried within word entries. Domain-specific terminology frequently lacks clear field indicators in conventional resources, forcing professionals to consult multiple specialized sources, company-specific term databases, and ultimately rely on search engines without editorial guidance.

Reverso Define tackles these limitations through an AI-driven approach that reimagines dictionary organization. The system elevates multi-word expressions to standalone entries, provides clear, non-circular definitions optimized for non-native English speakers, and integrates domain indicators for technical terminology. This design directly addresses the needs of translation professionals who require quick access to precise, contextual meanings to maintain efficient workflows.

Figure 1: Reverso Define on the mobile app

2 System Description

2.1 Technical Architecture

The core of Reverso Define is built on a hybrid approach combining LLMs with expert linguistic curation. This methodology enables systematic application of editorial decisions across the entire dictionary while maintaining high-quality standards through human expertise. When we implement linguistic guidelines, the AI pipeline applies these constraints systematically rather than requiring manual revision of each entry.

The system employs a sophisticated pipeline where LLMs generate initial definitions and structure, followed by expert linguist review and refinement. This iterative process ensures consistency while allowing for nuanced handling of complex linguistic cases. The dictionary currently contains over 450,000 meanings across 250,000 unique words, expressions, and compounds, with continuous expansion.

Our technical implementation leverages Retrieval-Augmented Generation (RAG) to ground

Proceedings of Machine Translation Summit XX Volume 2, pages 111–112, June 23-27, 2025

LLM outputs in authoritative sources, particularly crucial for domain-specific terminology. Automated quality checks verify aspects such as definition clarity and non-circularity, while linguistic experts provide final validation and refinement of entries.

2.2 Comparison with Traditional Resources

Reverso Define addresses several key limitations of traditional dictionaries that impact translation professionals. Unlike Oxford, Merriam-Webster, and Collins dictionaries, our system treats expressions as first-class entries rather than burying them within main entries. For example, "influence peddling" is directly accessible as its own entry, eliminating the need to search for both "influence" and "peddle."

Traditional dictionaries often use complex, circular definitions challenging for non-native speakers. Our system prioritizes clarity and simplicity, with concise definitions crafted specifically for professional use. Domain indicators in conventional resources tend to be limited and inconsistent, whereas Reverso Define implements comprehensive tagging across legal, medical, technical, and financial fields.

While specialized terminology resources exist, they typically lack integration with translation workflows. Reverso Define integrates directly into the post-editing process through extensions and applications, reducing context switching. Additionally, our system implements continuous updates rather than edition-based cycles, ensuring that new terminology is available without delay.

3 Use Cases and Evaluation

3.1 Post-Editing Support

In machine translation post-editing workflows, speed and accuracy in terminology verification are crucial. Preliminary feedback shows that Reverso Define's domain indicators and expression-level entries allow faster disambiguation of technical terms compared to traditional reference workflows. For instance, when encountering "consideration" in a legal text, a post-editor can immediately access its domain-specific definition ("something of value given in exchange for goods or services") rather than sifting through multiple general meanings.

The system's non-circular definitions prove particularly valuable when working with machine translation output in technical domains. By providing clear, concise explanations using simple terms, it helps post-editors quickly verify whether the MT system has correctly handled specialized terminology.

3.2 Translation Workflow Integration

The desktop application and the browser extension integrate seamlessly into workflows, allowing immediate definition access through double-click functionality on any text. This integration maintains workflow momentum while providing precise terminology support. User feedback indicates that this integration reduces lookup time compared to traditional dictionary consultation.

4 Availability and Future Development

Reverso Define is available across web, mobile, and desktop platforms. The web version is free to use, while desktop and browser extensions follow a freemium model with basic features available at no cost and advanced features requiring subscription. Enterprise licensing options are available for CAT tool integration, with pricing based on user volume and integration requirements. A public API for direct CAT tool integration is currently in development.

The system provides definitions in English with indicative translations in 26 languages, including French (France/Canada), Spanish, Catalan, Italian, Portuguese (European/Brazilian), Romanian, German, Danish, Dutch, Swedish, Yiddish, Russian, Ukrainian, Polish, Greek, Arabic, Hebrew, Bengali, Persian, Hindi, Japanese, Korean, Thai, Turkish, Vietnamese and Chinese.

Future development plans focus on an even larger coverage of specialty domains and less common idioms, more languages supported for definitions, and a constant review of accuracy of definitions, examples, and translations.

5 Conclusion

Reverso Define represents a significant advance in dictionary technology for translation professionals, combining AI capabilities with linguistic expertise to provide precise and contextual definitions. Its focus on expression-level entries and domain-specific terminology, coupled with seamless workflow integration, makes it a valuable companion tool for professional translation workflows. Continuous updates of the system ensure that it remains a current resource for the translation community. `https://dictionary.reverso.net`

Reverso Documents, The New Generation Document Translation Platform

Théo Hoffenberg and Elodie Segrestan
Reverso, Paris, France
theo@reverso.com

Abstract

Reverso Documents is a widely-adopted translation and post-editing platform that combines advanced machine translation with extensive document format support and layout preservation capabilities. The system features AI-based rephrasing, bilingual dictionaries, and translation memory integration, enabling both professional translators and general users to work efficiently with complex documents. Used by millions globally, it provides API access for workflow integration and batch processing. The upcoming 2025 release will introduce LLM-based translation such as customizable settings with additional context, audio processing and anonymization features. This paper describes the platform's functionality, technical evolution, pricing structure, and competitive advantages in the market.

1 Introduction

Reverso Documents emerged from the European project Flavius (2017-2020, EU Horizon 2020 program, grant agreement No. 779360) as a solution to the growing need for **accessible yet powerful document translation tools**. The system uniquely positions itself between professional translation tools and consumer-grade solutions, offering advanced features while maintaining ease of use. The platform is commercially available and actively maintained by Reverso.

2 System Overview

Reverso Documents supports a wide range of **document formats**, including PDF, Docx, Xlsx, HTML, and XML, while preserving the original **layout**. The system enables sentence-level **editing** in a side-by-side interface, maintaining translation memories for post-editing tracking.

The core functionalities include:

- Documents translation supporting 10+ formats (PDF, Docx, ...) with **editable output and a preserved layout**
- **Advanced machine translation** capabilities integrated since 2020, with continuous quality improvements and 25+ languages
- **Online collaborative revision** platform, enabling users to:
  - review the translation directly on the platform, with **side-by-side** segments
  - invite colleagues to review at no extra cost
  - save changes in **translation memory** and apply it to future projects, ensuring terminology consistency
  - import translation memory from another tools, or export translation memory created on the platform
  - use AI-based **rephrasing** system while reviewing, generating full-sentence alternatives
  - access integrated bilingual **dictionaries** directly from the revision platform, for precise word and expression-level work

These features work in concert to provide a comprehensive translation workflow that balances automation with human control, distinguishing it from basic MT services and traditional CAT tools.

3 Technical Evolution

The system's technological advancement has followed a carefully planned trajectory:

- 2020: Integration of **NMT** technologies, marking a significant milestone in translation quality

- 2023: Implementation of AI-based **rephraser**, enhancing the system's ability to suggest alternative translations
- 2025 (Q3 planned release): Introduction of **LLM-based translation** features with customizable translation setting, enhanced named entity identification, audio files processing, content anonymization features and post-editing time reduction. The post-editing time reduction will be accomplished through a combination of improved translation quality from LLM models fine-tuned on specific domains and intelligent contextual suggestions that learn from user edits.

4 Applications and User Base

Reverso Documents serves a diverse and extensive user base that includes **professional translators** seeking efficiency and quality, **students** developing skills with professional-grade tools, **professionals across various domains** needing accurate translations of business documents such as contracts or presentations, and **academic researchers** requiring precise translations of technical content. The system's versatility is enhanced by its **API**, which enables seamless integration into existing workflows and supports batch translation processing. This flexibility makes it equally suitable for individual translators and enterprise-scale operations.

5 Pricing and Licensing Options

Reverso Documents offers a tiered pricing structure to accommodate different user needs:

- **Free trial**: Up to 2,500 words for document translation
- **Premium**: Up to 50,000 words per year, files up to 30Mo, PDF up to 100 pages each + Premium on all Reverso suite
- **Pro**: Premium + Up to 200,000 words per year, files up to 120Mo, PDF up to 250 pages each
- **Enterprise** plans: Tailor-made plan and additional features such as SSO
- **Academic** licenses: 75% discount for educational institutions
- **One-time credits**: Document translation credits for a specific project

All plans include the core translation technology, while **advanced features** like OCR for scanned PDF or API access are reserved for paid plans.

6 Competitive Advantages

In comparison to other translation platforms, Reverso Documents offers several distinct advantages:

- Superior **layout** preservation
- More **user-friendly** interface than professional CAT tools
- Better integration of AI-based **rephrasing** than competitors
- More **affordable pricing** than enterprise-focused solutions
- Emphasis on **data privacy and security**, with no use of users' data to train our models and option to delete documents at any time

7 Future Developments

The roadmap for Reverso Documents includes several significant enhancements to its capabilities:

- Multimedia file processing support, offering new possibilities for content translation including audio transcription and translation
- Enhanced proofreading capabilities providing users with more tools for ensuring translation accuracy
- Advanced rephrasing system offering more nuanced alternatives based on context and domain
- **LLM-based features** including enhanced named entity identification, content anonymization features and post-editing time reduction

8 Conclusion

Reverso Documents represents a significant step forward in **making high-quality, secure machine translation accessible to a broader audience**. Its structured approach and user control features differentiate it from direct LLM use, while its continuous evolution ensures it remains at the forefront of translation technology. The platform's success in serving millions of users while maintaining high standards of translation quality demonstrates the effectiveness of its design philosophy and implementation.

https://documents.reverso.net

eSTÓR: Curating Irish Datasets for Machine Translation

Abigail Walsh[1], Órla Ní Loinsigh[1], Jane Adkins[1], Ornait O'Connell[1], Mark Andrade[1], Teresa Clifford[1], Federico Gaspari[1], Jane Dunne[1], Brian Davis[1]
[1]ADAPT Centre, Dublin City University
firstname.lastname@adaptcentre.ie

Abstract

Minority languages such as Irish are massively under-resourced, particularly in terms of high-quality domain-relevant data, limiting the capabilities of machine translation (MT) engines, even those integrating large language models (LLMs). The eSTÓR project, described in this paper, focuses on the collection and curation of high-quality Irish text data for diverse domains.

1 Introduction

Despite the growing ubiquity of digital technologies, the Irish language lacks robust language technology that serves Irish speakers adequately in the digital sphere, with Irish language classified as in the "weak or no support" category of European languages (Lynn, 2022). This digital disconnect poses a significant threat to the vitality and sustainability of the Irish language resulting in the very real threat of *digital extinction* in the medium to long term.

The Digital Plan for Irish 2023-2027 (Ní Chasaide et al., 2022) is a detailed guide regarding areas in Irish language technology that require development. The eSTÓR (*Sonraí Teanga Óstáilte i gcomhair Ríomhphróiseála* "Hosted Language Data for Digital Processing") project is funded by the Irish government (Department of Tourism, Culture, Arts, Gaeltacht, Sport and Media) from 2021 to 2025, to address the lack of high-quality data described in the Digital Plan, by providing a digital platform (`https://estor.ie/`) for **sharing bilingual and monolingual Irish text data**. In addition to data collection, the project aims to **further research and technological innovation**, **promote language accessibility**, and **educate members of the public and government bodies** on the value of Irish language data. Additionally, the project collaborates with the European Commission to share language data with the online machine translation system, eTranslation (Commission) in order to enhance the performance and accuracy of their EN<>GA engine.

2 Data Curation and Back-translation Experiments

Text data shared to the eSTÓR platform originates mainly from individuals or organisations in the public or government bodies of Ireland, often through direct contact. To date, 188 parallel language resources, totalling 185,343 Translation Units have been uploaded and processed on the eSTÓR platform, and 201,719 words of monolingual data. While sourcing the data from trusted language producers encourages reuse of existing high-quality data sources, and spreads awareness of the importance of data sharing, this resource-intensive approach is difficult to scale in order to meet the increasing demands for large data collections. Additionally, the text types collected from these sources offer limited variety of style, tone, and topic, resulting in unbalanced coverage in NLP models.

To address these issues, the eSTÓR project has begun experimenting with alternative methods of data collection and production. Web crawling is a popular method of sourcing large quantities of language data that can be largely automated, but the quality is difficult to ensure. Employing a blend of manual inspection and automatic filtering, the eSTÓR project has experimented with selecting high-quality articles from Irish Wikipedia Vicipéid (`https://ga.wikipedia.org/`), and using the eTranslation Irish-to-English General model to perform back-translation to generate synthetic parallel datasets covering diverse topics. This dataset can then be employed as test data to investigate coverage of existing Irish MT models.

Proceedings of Machine Translation Summit XX Volume 2, pages 115–116, June 23-27, 2025

3 Data Cleaning

Much of the importance of the eSTÓR project lies in the data cleaning work, which requires meticulous attention to detail and a robust knowledge of Irish and English language to ensure correctly-aligned, relevant, and high-quality clean data. The impact of this essential work in the development of powerful NLP tools and applications is still underplayed in the larger NLP community (Sambasivan et al., 2021), and precise details of the task can often be glossed over or omitted in reporting. There are many components to process the data in its raw form, although at a minimum the following steps are undertaken:

Initial Input Assessment: Typically files uploaded to eSTÓR are aligned (e.g. translation memories, spreadsheets, aligned plain-text), unaligned editable (e.g. word processing types, unaligned plain-text), or unaligned uneditable (e.g. PDF generated by software). Raster formats are typically not accepted due to the additional challenge of running Optical Character Recognition, although scans of hard-copy data are currently being processed as part of collaborative digitisation work.

Text Extraction and Normalisation: While text file types are processed using hand-written text extraction tools, library support is used for extracting text from binary file types (e.g. PDFs). Normalisation of text encoding maintains consistency throughout the data, and helps prevent incorrectly encoded characters or Unicode-equivalence errors.

Language Identification: Text is sampled at regular intervals throughout the dataset to perform language identification and ensure that the file contains the correct language. A standardised Irish language model was trained for this task, using the langdetect[1] Python port of the original tool (Nakatani, 2010).

Sentence Splitting: It is often necessary to reconstruct sentence boundary information in order to produce the sentence-aligned output. This task can be as trivial as splitting on sentence-final punctuation (e.g. '.', '?'), but becomes more challenging when processing text containing e.g. abbreviations (e.g. 'etc.', 'Dr.'). As abbreviations in Irish differ from English (e.g. *uimhir* 'number' is abbreviated as 'uimh.'), it was necessary to define bespoke rules to process most of these cases automatically.

Document and Sentence Alignment: While unmatched Irish text files can be published as monolingual data, any files uploaded in English must be aligned with an Irish file to be considered of use. Sentence alignment ensures that the text on each line of each aligned file pair corresponds with the text on that same line in the other language, employing the Hunalign (Varga et al., 2005) tool.

Verification: The final step is to assess aligned document pairs to ensure that the data has been correctly processed according to specified criteria (e.g. numerals appearing on one side should appear on the other). The text is checked through a series of automatic checks, and potential bad alignments are flagged for manual review.

4 Conclusion

We present the eSTÓR project, an effort in curating and cleaning high-quality Irish text data for the development of language technology, including improved MT engines. The project has many components, but this paper focuses on the data cleaning and selection tasks, which constitutes a vital step in the development of any NLP applications.

References

European Commission. eTranslation - The European Commission's Machine Translation System. https://commission.europa.eu/resources-partners/etranslation_en.

Teresa Lynn. 2022. Report on the Irish language. https://european-language-equality.eu/deliverables/. Technical Report D1.20, European Language Equality Project.

Shuyo Nakatani. 2010. Language detection library for java.

Ailbhe Ní Chasaide, Neasa Ní Chiarán, Elaine Uí Dhonnchadha, Teresa Lynn, and John Judge. 2022. Digital Plan for the Irish Language Speech and Language Technologies 2023-2027. Available at https://assets.gov.ie/241755/e82c256a-6f47-4ddb-8ce6-ff81df208bb1.pdf.

Nithya Sambasivan, Shivani Kapania, Hannah Highfill, Diana Akrong, Praveen Kumar Paritosh, and Lora Mois Aroyo. 2021. "Everyone wants to do the model work, not the data work": Data Cascades in High-Stakes AI. In *"Proceedings of the 2021 CHI Conference on Human Factors in Computing Systems"*, pages 1–15.

Dániel Varga, László Németh, Péter Halácsy, András Kornai, Viktor Trón, and Viktor Nagy. 2005. Parallel corpora for medium density languages. *Proceedings of the International Conference Recent Advances in Natural Language Processing (RANLP-2005)*, pages 590–596.

[1]https://pypi.org/project/langdetect/

Author Index

The MTSummit organizers gratefully acknowledge the support from the following sponsors.

Platinum

BIG LANGUAGE SOLUTIONS

STAR

WIPO WORLD INTELLECTUAL PROPERTY ORGANIZATION

Gold

SYSTRAN by CHAPSVISION

Silver

Reverso

translated.

Unbabel

Bronze

AppTek AI

CROSSLANG

TRANSPERFECT

ZOO

Supporters

Media

With the support of: